THE MIDDLE DISTANCE

THE MIDDLE DISTANCE

A Comparative History of American

Imaginative Literature: 1919–1932

by John McCormick

The Free Press $\boxed{Fp}$ New York

PS
157
M3

To Jig, Logan, and other bears

Awake, chaos: we have napped.
—E. E. CUMMINGS

Acknowledgments

I am most grateful to the John Simon Guggenheim Memorial Foundation and to the Rutgers University Research Council for making available to me those necessities, time and money. I am indebted to Quentin Anderson for his painstaking reading of the manuscript and to my students, present and former, with whom many of the postulates in this book were developed. In particular, I am indebted to Charles Aycock, Lawrence Blonquist, Mrs. Ann Kaplan, and Mrs. Mary Rannells for invaluable assistance.

Chapter 11, "A Postscript on Method," originally appeared in slightly different form in *Comparative Literature Studies* (V, no. 2, June, 1968). Permission to reprint is owing to that journal, as it is to the following publishers for use of excerpts from their books: from "Three," copyright © 1965 by Carolyn Kizer. From *Knock Upon Silence* by Carolyn Kizer. Reprinted by permission of Doubleday & Company, Inc. To Harcourt, Brace & World, Inc., New York, for permission to reprint excerpts from T. S. Eliot's verse in *The Waste Land, Ash-Wednesday,* and *Four Quartets,* all contained in *The Complete Poems and Plays: 1909–1950* copyright © 1962; and to the same publisher for permission to reprint excerpts from E. E. Cummings, *Poems, 1923–1954,* copyright © 1954. The epigraph "Awake, chaos, we have napped" is also from Cummings' *Poems.* To Alfred A. Knopf/Random House, Inc., New York, for permission to reprint excerpts from *The Collected Poems* of *Wallace Stevens,* copyright © 1955; to the Macmillan Company, New York, for permission to quote in full from *The Complete Poems of Marianne Moore,* copyright © 1967, the poem "In the Days of Prismatic Color." Miss Moore's sentence "Omissions are not accidents," is reproduced by permission of The Viking Press, Inc., New York. To Charles Scribner's Sons, New York, my thanks for permission to quote excerpts from Ernest Hemingway, *A Farewell to Arms, The Sun Also Rises,* and *In Our Time.* The excerpt from Octavio Paz, "The Word as Foundation," is reproduced from *The Times Literary Supplement* (November 14, 1968) by permission. And my sincere thanks to Mr. H. F. Broch de Rothermann and to Mrs. Anne-Marie Meier-Graefe Broch for their gracious permission to quote from the unpublished writings of the late Hermann Broch in the Beinecke Library, Yale University.

J. McC.

Preface

In the Postscript on Method to this book, I have remarked that perhaps all the literary historian can do is to give aesthetic proportion to the
past. It is pertinent further to remark at the outset that "aesthetic proportion" in the period covered by this volume, 1919 to 1932, means to me the
necessity of passing over certain writers who are traditionally included in
histories and including many European writers in order to establish a just
frame of reference. Or as Miss Marianne Moore wrote with admirable
economy about verse not included in her *Complete Poems*, "Omissions are
not accidents." One of my omissions, not accidental, is any consideration
of literature of the theater. Such literature as was written, Eugene O'Neill's
foremost, seems to me qualitatively different from poetry or prose fiction and best left to critics and historians of the theater. I have omitted
playwrights, that is, just as I would omit the authors of film scripts or
radio broadcasts. However excellent, such literature seems off the central
point.

The slice-of-chronology method enforced by the fact that this is one
volume in a series may appear as a disadvantage in the case of a complex
and voluminous writer such as William Faulkner. To offset that disadvantage, I have tried to write out of my awareness of the entire corpus
of the work, while the slice-of-chronology method may offer advantages
that are lost in other chronological schemes.

Textual problems are minor in the period; where they arise, as with
Fitzgerald, I have duly noted them. In the case of verse, I have quoted the
most recently revised version. Unless otherwise noted, translations are
mine.

J. McC.

Foreword

This is the second volume in a projected series of seven which will deal with the history of our literature from its beginnings to the 1960's. The first, by Warner Berthoff, *The Ferment of Realism, 1884–1919*, was published in 1965. In the foreword to that book I noted that literary history had been called in question as an activity proper to the student of literature. Our imaginative divorce from the community around us, noticeable then, has become still more marked as we enter the 1970's. But the effect is simply to intensify the need to reckon with the cultural and historical circumstances in which our literature arose. Now that the impulse to rediscover or re-create our humanity has become so strong, we are more sharply reminded that men make books and books image men. Modernist literature often encouraged an atemporal and acommunal view of the world. Now that people wander the streets looking for apocalypse, the modernist impulse has been actualized in human behavior. This behavior had a genesis in time, and partly in literature itself, as this book helps to show.

Professor McCormick's account of his period focuses not on the legend of the gaiety and abandonment of the 1920's, but on the First World War and its revelation of the abyss, and on the extraordinary feats of the artists who won imaginative order from a world in which the abyss was never out of sight. It was a wider, graver world than the legend of Greenwich Village assumes, and it was clearly transnational—most clearly so in our poets, who in this volume are given the primacy which a cumulative judgment has assigned them.

I ought once more to observe that Professor McCormick's work is his own, unconstrained by any agreement among the seven contributors to this series save their common view of the usefulness of a historical record of our literature.

Quentin Anderson
General Editor

Contents

THE MIDDLE DISTANCE

1

Lost
and
Found

"You are all a lost generation." Attributed to Gertrude Stein, Ernest Hemingway's ambiguous epigraph to *The Sun Also Rises* has attained a fame bordering on notoriety. It may remind us of other gnomic catchwords that history has preserved, such as "We who are about to die salute you" or "Do you want to live forever?" We have to doubt that gladiators in the Roman arena were so lucidly correct in their last minutes of life, while we may be certain that the Marines at Belleau Wood indeed wanted to live forever, like the rest of us. However gnomic, Gertrude Stein's words and the conjunction in 1922 of the wicked old virgin from Baltimore and the talented, ambitious Hemingway in Paris offer us one of those confrontations so right, so correct, that one is tempted to think it must have been apocryphal. In Gertrude Stein, egoist, heavy-lidded and self-indulgent naif, former student of William James, self-publicist, individualist, fosterer of a tiny talent, we find a representative of the pre-war world, by no means typical, yet containing within herself various components that the world would never see again. Lesbianism made her expatriation advisable; a comfortable inheritance made it possible. In her art collecting and gourmandizing she evokes the last of the nineteenth-century big spenders; in her involuted and solipsistic writing she evokes a Jewish Emily Dickinson with only a fraction of the poet's capacity. Her fortune, together with her nostalgia for middle-class rituals, roots her firmly in the late nineteenth and early twentieth centuries, as does her view of writing as playful and non-intellectual to the point of silliness.

Hemingway, in contrast, like so many young men of the period, wanted, or pretended to want, a clean break with the pre-war world. The First World War had left a mark on him, a mark of which he was proud and which he tended to exaggerate. The war gave him, however, a subject—violence—and suggested to him an aesthetic for dealing with violence. Unlike Gertrude Stein's, his expatriation was more apparent than real, and not terribly important to his work. Each was nostalgic for America, but in different ways. Gertrude Stein's nostalgia was for a tree-shaded upper-middle-class residential area with plenty of Negro help in the kitchen in the Middle Atlantic or New England area, *circa* 1905. Hemingway's was for a timeless pre-industrial upper Midwest and for a timeless, never-existent guilelessness. His seriousness was at odds with her playfulness; if the two shared an enormous egotism, they were at fundamental odds through differences in age and basic differences about what in life and literature was important. If she could claim that she and Sherwood Anderson between them "formed" Hemingway, he could claim vehemently that she had no part in his formation.[1] Both were capable of playing cat and mouse with each other and with the public. What, then, did that tag, "lost generation," which has performed such heavy labor in recent literary history, mean to either Gertrude Stein or Ernest Hemingway? To review its possible meanings is to embark upon a study of that curious, wonderful, and exasperating decade that subsequent decades have constructed into a transcendent metaphor, the twenties.

Before seeking secondary, tertiary, or symbolic meanings for the "lost generation," we would do well to think of Hemingway's own account of the phrase in *A Moveable Feast*, written long after the event and published after his death in 1962. Hemingway's recollection is that the owner of a garage in Paris had said, "You are all a *génération perdue*" to his mechanic, who had botched his work on the ignition system of Gertrude Stein's Ford, and that she in turn used the phrase on Hemingway and men of his age who had been in the war because they lacked respect and drank too much. Hemingway's flow of recollection then moves,

---

[1] Gertrude Stein, *The Autobiography of Alice B. Toklas* (New York: Harcourt, Brace and Co., 1933), p. 265. And see Ernest Hemingway, *A Moveable Feast* (New York: Charles Scribner's Sons, 1964), pp. 13–31.

rather like that of a militaristic Proust, to identification with the told-off mechanic, who might have been wounded in the war and transported in one of the ambulances that he, Hemingway, had driven; to the statue of Marshall Ney near the Closerie des Lilas; to loyalty to Gertrude Stein for her loyalty to the dying Apollinaire, "But the hell with her lost-generation talk and all the dirty, easy labels."[2] Like *The Autobiography of Alice B. Toklas, A Moveable Feast* does both more and less than its author intends. Each is an amusing, splendidly written, sly self-portrait, done with loving care to establish the exact planes and shadings in the visage that the author wants the public to accept as definitive; each is therefore not so much unreliable as it is constructed on a varying scale of veracity. Hemingway's account of the *génération perdue*, when scrutinized skeptically, still holds a large measure of truth if only because he had worked over that area of truth in his novel, *The Sun Also Rises*. There, as I shall presently suggest, Hemingway established the idea of a "generation" as it had not been established before in American writing, and only rarely in European writing. Only for two movements in German literature and one in Spanish was the idea of "generation" held so self-consciously by a significant group of writers: the *Sturm und Drang* movement in early German romanticism; the group attached to Stefan George before the First World War; and the Generation of 1898 in Spain. The generation that Hemingway had in mind was of course the generation born near the turn of the century, but his special reverence was reserved for those who had seen not just military service in the war but maiming combat. In much of his fiction, to say nothing of his reportage and autobiographical sketches, Hemingway indicated a mystical attachment to purification through violence and attendant suffering. At the same time, he awarded lesser marks to contemporaries of the war generation. Virtue rubbed off on them, even though they had not been so fortunate as to suffer combat, because they too were aligned against the older, pre-war group—soft and relatively carefree types like Gertrude Stein and Sherwood Anderson. "Lost," then, meant not *perdue*, in the garage keeper's meaning of incompetent, or lacking in a sense of duty to the job (*oficio* in Spanish), but a change in sensibility brought about by the trauma of war or of conviction about the pre-war past. It meant the revelation in life, and above all in art, of areas of existence, moral attitudes, and views of society that the deprived older generation could not understand or accept. "Lost" implied a heroic abandonment of certainties that would be

[2] *A Moveable Feast*, pp. 29–31.

rewarded by large horizons, as against the slack, indulgent bohemian posings of the earlier generation. "Lost," in Hemingway's sense, really meant "found"; in retrospect, we may say that no generation was less lost and more found, for there was brilliance, talent, hard work, and achievement in abundance then.

Lost implied loss, but here matters become opaque. The theme of loss—of childhood, of innocence, of a green and golden time—is as old as mythology, yet in no literature was it been so continually present as in American literature. Reasons for its prominence in the past, whether Calvinism, romanticism, the frontier, the disappearance of the Red Indians, or the savaging of the countryside, cannot detain us here. Suffice to say that after World War I, the theme of loss took a new and interesting turn. Loss meant not only the things Hemingway treated with relation to the war, it also meant loss of country in a most peculiar sense. It is a commonplace of literary history that a few very good American writers and artists and a large number of ordinary ones, to say nothing of hangers-on, casual travelers and intellectual voyeurs, left the United States for varying periods of time to take up residence in Europe, most of them in Paris. "Expatriation" is the term usually reserved for that group, but expatriation is itself ambiguous and very far from being the portmanteau word it usually is made to be in literary history.[3] With respect to the American "expatriates," it is essential to distinguish among those whose work projects a sense of unwilled banishment, willed banishment, and those who resided abroad merely because their dollars bought more drink and rent than they would have done at home.

Ezra Pound and T. S. Eliot, in varying ways, are writers whose expatriation derived from a conviction that their country could not provide what they needed for literary nourishment, in the tradition of Hawthorne's and Henry James' complaints about the poverty of the American landscape. Pound expressed his views through indignation and comic anger, while Eliot, finding in himself loyalty to the French and English traditions, worked his way through, in *Four Quartets*, to a Vergilian quality of loss and sorrow. Both Eliot and Pound functioned within a historical framework, however, that attempted to place the war in long perspective. Younger writers like Hemingway and Glenway

[3] The substantive derives from the transitive verb meaning "to banish." The reflexive, self-banishment, in the Oxford English Dictionary, is secondary. It is also relevant that the word became common during the dominant years of romanticism in England.

Wescott took the war as their point of departure. Loss for them, in many of the stories in Hemingway's *In Our Time* and in all of Wescott's fiction of the twenties—*The Apple of the Eye* (1924), *Like A Lover* (1926), *The Grandmothers* (1927), and *Goodbye, Wisconsin* (1928)—is loss of the good, green America of youth, loss of innocence. And with that loss goes the inescapable suggestion that residence abroad, expatriation, was inevitable for them, determined by their time of birth, their sensibility, and their role as writers. Their views of the past are not historical, no matter how often, as in the case of Wescott, the past is invoked, because always the past is alive in the present, alive in the sensibility of the narrator or character. No matter how long their expatriation, all four writers remain American at root. Eliot's and Pound's banishment was willed and self-imposed; Hemingway's and Wescott's, in a literary sense, was not. All share, in varying degrees (Eliot, of course, far less than the others), a romantic impatience with the given, their country of birth, and a romantic disposition to confuse physical motion with interior, spiritual movement.

For the others, with a few exceptions—Kay Boyle, possibly Djuna Barnes—"abroad," Paris in particular, was a village or an American suburb, with Gertrude Stein as Mayor and with Robert McAlmon and Harry and Caresse Crosby as Deputy Sheriffs by virtue of their having capital to publish their friends' work. A village through which various travellers moved: Scott Fitzgerald and his wife, Sinclair Lewis, John Dos Passos, Alfred Kreymbourg, William Carlos Williams, Malcolm Cowley —the list is as long as it is familiar. Expatriation as an idea does not apply. Abroad was fashionable, useful; drink was available there, and the illusion of freedom if not license. But the impact of Europe was far more subtle than the misapplied notion of expatriation.

If Gertrude Stein was serious, or *also* serious, in saying, "You are all a lost generation," where might her seriousness lie? It lay, I suspect, in her apprehension of the inability of naturalism, particularly in its American form, to cope with the post-war world. Or in other terms, it lay in her apprehension of bravado in a man like Hemingway, who may have been biting off more than he could intellectually chew. Gertrude Stein, the former clever student of William James and the hawk-eyed, long-time resident of Paris, was in a good position to assess the differences between rational America and irrational Europe. Proof may be found in her own work, in the continuing vacillation between naturalism and verbal foolishness; in her tastes in painting; and in her place as salon mistress and lion hunter. In still other terms, Paris in the early 1920's was the scene of a rich, explosive confrontation between two basically different modes of thought and art: the American, essentially rational, mode and the European, essentially irrational, mode. After the confrontation, neither was to be quite the same again, but before we can examine the aftermath, we need to look back in time to various European and American antecedents of the post-war confrontation.

Irrational Europe, rational America. Let me construct some necessarily large generalizations to support this hypothesis. European society since the early medieval period may be seen as a series of barriers for keeping the monsters at bay. The monsters were variously identified as Satan, famine, disease, oriental invasion, and very powerful, the dispossessed, war and anarchy. For a few decades during the Renaissance and again during the eighteenth century, men seemed to have constructed a permanent barrier against the monsters, and in those periods the dominant philosophical and literary mode was in truth rational. First the Reformation, then Deism, took care of God; advances in the natural sciences apparently were taking care of nature; a return to Greek and Roman models seemed to be taking care of aesthetics. The French Revolution, however, put an end to all that. The most shattering impact of the revolution was not upon the divine right of kings, the clergy, or any of the political or economic institutions challenged, but upon European loyalty to the processes of the human mind, upon the long-held belief that man was the master of himself and of his world. In art, romanticism, before the revolution a recessive movement, became dominant after 1789, so dominant that it is still very much with us. Romanticism was not one movement, but rather a complex of movements, a devious set of related philosphies that flowed like water into a new reservoir to fill up all the gaps and low-lying places created by the revolution. So powerful a rush of water sets up counter-eddies, but invariably, thus far, the counter-eddies have not generated sufficient force to counteract the main flow. The central reason for the power of romanticism is that instead of keeping the monsters at bay, it invited them into the household, not only into the sitting room of philosophy, but on up to the bedroom of poetry and fiction. The romantic complex was efficient in its recognition of madness, in the cachet it gave to unreason, its frequent celebrations of anti-intellectualism, its terrifying blessings upon nationalism and war. Berkeley and Hume were the unwitting precursors of romanticism in their epistemological skepticism, European idealism fought a long, doomed, rear-guard action against epistemology until the current triumphs of Husserl, Heidegger, and company, who wander out of the romantic German forests with despairing, non-logical syllogisms for our neo-romantic delectation.

If one basic aspect of the romantic complex—perhaps *the* basic aspect—is its coming to terms with the forces of unreason, then our habit of seeing an unyielding opposition between realism and romanticism in nineteenth-century European literature is mistaken. What historians have done is to say, accurately, that such an opposition does exist between classical and romantic, as exemplified in the differences between Pope and Novalis, or Chodlerlos de Laclos and Emily Brontë. Trouble arises when the historian equates the classical with the realistic, mistaking the part for the whole, in opposition to the villain, romantic.[4] There is indeed a realistic, as opposed to a romantic, sensibility. Balzac is not identical with Scott, nor Flaubert with Monk Lewis. But for nineteenth-century fiction, the words "realistic" and "romantic" are useful for defining differences in craft: diction, rhythm, length of sentence, sets of mind of a given writer; they do not define differences in philosophy. Since Balzac—indeed, since Cervantes—realist and romanticist alike have been engaged in coming to terms with monsters. The great European realists, from Balzac to Proust and including writers such as Stendhal, Flaubert, Dostoevsky, Dickens, George Eliot, Verga, Galdós, and Thomas Mann, did not differ philosphically from the romantics, while in each we find episodes, characters, attitudes, and apprehensions made possible only by the romantic revolution.[5] The romantic complex opened doors never again to be closed; the road from *Sturm und Drang* to Nietzsche to Freud is straight, if not narrow.

In European poetry, the evidence is even more incontrovertible than it is for prose, while criticism, for once, is in substantial agreement about that evidence.[6] Although this road is neither straight nor narrow, it is clear. It moves from Poe in America to Baudelaire's amusing half-comprehension of Poe to Mallarmé (via Banville and Hegel) to Valéry;

[4] The so-called neo-humanists, P. E. More and Irving Babbitt, were particularly guilty of that fallacy.

[5] Donald Fanger's term, "romantic realism," deserves widespread adoption. See his excellent study, *Dostoevsky and Romantic Realism*, 1965.

[6] For example, there is no quarrel among C. M. Bowra, *The Heritage of Symbolism* (1934); Marcel Raymond, *From Baudelaire to Surrealism* (1947); and R. P. Blackmur, *Anni Mirabiles: 1921–1925* (1956): English, French, and American respectively.

and from Corbière and Verlaine to Laforgue; (it returns to America in Pound, Eliot, Hart Crane, and Wallace Stevens; it takes us to Darío in Hispanic America, and to Antonio and Manuel Machado, Jorge Guillén, and García Lorca in Spain; to Montale, to George, Hofmansthal, Rilke and Benn. It takes us, that is to say, by way of French symbolism, that great taproot of modern poetry, directly into and through the modern movement. However we define that movement, whether as anti-romantic or neo-romantic, we cannot fail to recognize its break with the rational, classical past, its explicit acknowledgment of unreason, and its quasi-religious cast. The familiar point need not be labored here.

In America, however, a similar intellectual history did not necessarily produce the same conclusion. Nor, until the nineteenth century, was the history of Europe and the history of America all that similar. In seventeenth- and eighteenth-century America, theological discourse of one sort or another dominated in bulk and often in quality. Laymen's work was mainly practical, written to entice settlers from Europe, to convince an electorate, to investigate urgent issues of the day. Addressing men in a new land having unfamiliar flora, fauna, and dangers, needing accuracy for simple survival, writers developed an attitude toward nature and objects in nature that was different from anything in Europe. An American vocabulary grew up, a distinctly American apprehension of nature, and most important, a disposition to provide an answer to every manner of question. A fair number of people emigrated to America in order to solve a theological and political conundrum; their posterity were encouraged by the long movement westward, by the Revolution of 1776, by the economic and social organization of American life to be impatient of any sort of question that seemed to have no ready answer. The monsters, European style, were not admitted to exist, or if so, they were given theological names.

That the monsters were there, however, is obvious, and true American literature might be thought of as having been invented to cope with them. It is not an accident that memorable American writing began with the first impact of romanticism. The first settlements were a product of the Reformation, not of the European Renaissance; thus Renaissance modes made negligible impact. Neo-classicism was quite unsuited to American needs, for American society had not sufficiently coagulated; it was not sufficiently rich, aristocratic, or leisured to permit neo-classical modes to flourish. But romanticism was a liberation for American writers. Bryant and Cooper found ways to name their monsters—industrialism, civilization, the destruction of the native Indians—and loose forms suited to their needs. Gothic fiction, in Europe a slight offshoot of the romantic complex, became a central American form. Charles Brockden Brown's novels gave both the romantic *frisson* and the American pragmatic explanation for the *frisson*—mesmerism (in *Wieland*) and sleepwalking (*Edgar Huntly*)—just as Hawthorne was to do later in *The Blithedale Romance*. The great bulk of Hawthorne's fiction is pervaded by his taste for the gothic, as is Poe's, and to a lesser degree, Melville's. A gothic strain is present in Mark Twain's work, recessive in *Huckleberry Finn* but dominant in the later short fiction. It is there in Stephen Crane's work and overpoweringly present in William Faulkner's.[7] The gothic genre attained such vitality in America because it offered a technique for dealing with violence, with extremes of experience. In the course of its American history, the gothic mode became transformed from its European origins as a blunt device for producing shock to a double-edged weapon for psychological investigation, as in the case of Melville's "The Encantadas," and with its other edge, for anticipating some of the subtler effects of expressionism and surrealism, as in Faulkner's *As I Lay Dying*. But it fully retained its romantic outline.

If the gothic gave a primitive and irrational direction to romanticism, American style, German metaphysics, both in the raw and filtered through Coleridge, Carlyle, and Frederick Henry Hedge, provided the other extreme. The central figure here, of course, is Emerson. No one responded to Kant, Herder, the Schlegels, and the rest of the Germans more vividly than Emerson did, and no one had a more seminal influence upon American nineteenth-century thought. Brought up in the Calvinist tradition, Emerson found conventional theology inadequate for his needs. Attracted to German transcendental explanations of nature, art, and the place of the artist, he was at the same time repelled by the logic of the romantic theory of genius. Endowed as a writer with the American eye for hard fact, his contribution was to tame some of the wildness of the European romantic fury and to give a more or less satisfying ethical overtone to his version of the transcendental philosophy. Readers who are put off by his piousness are nevertheless delighted by his eye for things

---

[7] An examination of the continuing vitality of the gothic in contemporary works as various as those of Nathanael West, William Styron, Truman Capote, Flannery O'Connor, Norman Mailer, Ralph Ellison, Thomas Pynchon, and John Barth lies outside the scope of this book.

and his ability to render precision of observation. Both his piousness and his precision are peculiarly American, and are useful to us in distinguishing between the European early abandonment of reason and the late American loyalty to reason.

In that connection, we have only to reflect that the "standard" American poets of the nineteenth century, the good gray bearded men who were most widely read and respected, were contemporaries of the French symbolists. Leconte de Lisle and James Russell Lowell were born in the same year, 1819. Whittier and Longfellow were born in 1807; Théodore de Banville in 1823. Sidney Lanier and Mallarmé were born in 1842; Corbière was born in 1845. Long-lived, the good gray Americans' careers spanned those of the younger symbolists and their successors: Baudelaire, 1821–1867; Laforgue, 1860–1887. The vital statistics of the un-good, un-gray poets—Emily Dickinson, 1830–1886, and Walt Whitman, 1819–1892—who seemed to their contemporaries to have nothing to do with anything, are also relevant. This is not to recapitulate the obvious—that modern French influence upon American verse is a recent affair—but to emphasize again the difference between European unreason and the American version of reason. It is relevant that American poetry before Pound was generally of a piece with English late romantic and Victorian work. At its commonplace average, it is gentle if not genteel, idealistic, orderly, reasonably accomplished, and moribund. Among the splendid exceptions, Melville's poetry went unread; Whitman had to publish his own work; Emily Dickinson's best poems were smoothed out by stupid editing.

Unreason, for nineteenth-century America, was acknowledged and tamed in the form of Emersonian transcendentalism. Unreason, its teeth undrawn in the form of Melville's *Moby Dick* or *Pierre*, went unread. Furious romanticism did not suit the official ethos. Facts, candied over by Protestant bourgeois icing, were what mattered. The representative poem was Longfellow's "Excelsior," not Melville's "The Maldive Shark." In 1866, Henry James abandoned America, leaving William Dean Howells as the foremost native writer of fiction. Excellent though some of Howells' work was, it was insufficiently commanding to establish his position as a vital model. Howells' girl-next-door realism, together with the popular vogue for costume romance, turned a new generation in desperation to what they thought was European naturalism. Stephen Crane, Jack London, Hamlin Garland, and Frank Norris, in varying degrees of effectiveness and intellectual awareness, looked to European naturalism, above all to Zola's version of it in *Le Roman expérimental*, of their model.[8]

At this point, we encounter an intriguing paradox. Why was it that although the accomplishments of the programmatic American naturalists were aesthetically slight, naturalism became, at least until 1945, the dominant American mode of fiction? History provides the solution. European programmatic naturalism, with its specious treatment of causality, its emphasis upon documentation, satisfied a familiar American hunger for uncomplicated fact. What seemed new, the naturalist's *nostalgie de la boue*, their turning to sex, drink, madness, prostitution, dirty politics—to "real" life—coincided in America with the post-Civil War disillusion, the impulse to examine the national conscience, to expose corruption and so to reform excesses of all sorts. Unprogrammatic naturalism in the form of documentation and transcendental insistence upon fact, together with American discomfort with metaphysical speculation, made European naturalism very welcome indeed. Not least was the chracteristic of naturalism which caused it to turn back upon itself into romanticism: its tendency to go to extremes of experience, to glorify disaster, to revel in trouble. Frank Norris's recipe for American fiction, "No teacup tragedies," in "The Responsibilities of the Novelist" is as much a romantic document as are Wordsworth's prefaces. That basic romantic habit of turning all fact into symbol is fully present in Zola's descriptions of the earth in *La Terre*, just as it is in Norris's treatment of the railroad in *The Octopus*. The intellectual failure of naturalism that allowed such writers to have their romantic cake and eat it, too, lay in their appeal to what they believed to be scientific method, together with post-Darwinian deterministic pessimism. If all the writer need do is to place his characters in the grasp of indifferent nature, then observation takes the place of reflection, observation blessed in the name of holy science. Both intellectual and formal problems were solved, once and for all. Formal naturalism, then, suited America for a long time. It echoed habits of mind that can be traced to the seventeenth century; it made available to writers material that cried out, in a sociological sense, for treatment; it still satisfied a romantic American longing for heroes and

---

[8] Not exclusively to Zola, of course. Garland, a true provincial, reflects the native influences of Whitman and Henry George. London's work is an addled mixture of Darwin, Nietzsche, Spencer, and Marx. Crane read widely beyond Zola, so much so that problems of influence in his work are subtle indeed. Of the four, Norris was most nakedly indebted to Zola. See his essay, "The Responsibilities of the Novelist."

heroic action; it made available to literature American mores and the rich American language; and most important, it satisfied another basic American need for process, for fact, for at least the illusion of the pragmatic.[9]

Whether Gertrude Stein's words on the "lost generation" were a joke or not, whether she actually had those historical considerations in mind when she talked to Hemingway, they help us to account for the resonance the phrase has taken on subsequently in other men's minds. The Europe of the anti-hero in fiction, of poetic experiment in the wake of symbolism, of metaphysical despair after World War I was hardly a world that American experience had prepared Hemingway and the rest to grasp fully at first confrontation. Their loss was in part a loss of familiar assumptions about the world and about art; their triumphs, when they occurred, were triumphs either of nostalgia or of negotiation with the new, post-war world.

[9] In terms of cultural history, the extraordinary American passion for sociology and psychology would seem to have its roots in these same facts.

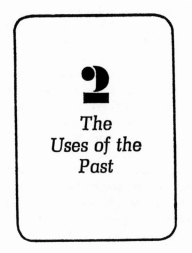

2

The
Uses of the
Past

In a period of four years and three months, from August, 1914, to November, 1918, ten million men were killed in combat or died of wounds or diseases incurred during the war. No monster more terrifying had arisen before in the West. All writers responded, directly or indirectly, to the war merely because they were alive. In Europe, the agony of the war caused their views of the past, all the uses of tradition, to explode in their faces. Paul Valéry defined the process more elegantly when he wrote, after 1914, "We later civilizations, we too now know that we are mortal."[1] And again in 1919, in an arresting Shakespearian metaphor:

> Now, on a courtyard of Elsinore of immense scale which runs from Basel to Cologne, bordering on the sands of Nieuport and on the marches of the Somme; which runs from the chalk fields of Champagne to the granite of Alsace,—the European Hamlet surveys millions of ghosts.

Those ghosts are the ghosts of European civilization; this "intellectual Hamlet" takes up not Yorick's skull, but the skulls of Leibnitz, Kant, Hegel, and Marx. The meditation concludes:

> "Adieu, ghosts. The world no longer needs you. Nor me. The world, which baptizes its deadly aims with the name of progress, seeks to unite the

[1] Paul Valéry, "La Crise de l'esprit," *Athenaeum* (London: April 11 and May 2, 1919). Also in *Nouvelle Revue Française*, August 1, 1919, and in *Variété*, Paris, 1924.

benefits of life to the advantages of death. A certain confusion still reigns, but soon it will be cleared away; we shall finally see the appearance of the miracle of an animal society, a perfect and final ant-heap."[2]

Jacques Rivière, as a German prisoner-of-war, used the metaphor of "deliquescence" to register his apprehension of what was occurring: "the frightful deliquescence of everything around me. . . ."[3] Ernst Jünger, on the other hand, wrote that there was nothing in the 1920's that had not been apparent to "Poe, Melville, Hölderlin, Tocqueville, Dostoevsky, Burckhardt, Nietzsche, Rimbaud, Conrad . . . Léon Bloy [and] Kierkegaard. . . ." Jünger thus indicated a perhaps guilty effort to affirm continuity with at least one tradition in Europe, the apocalyptic one. Yet he added to his list, significantly, the remark that although "The catastrophe had been foreseen down to its slightest details, . . . the texts were often hieroglyphs, like invisible writing which can only be deciphered over flames."[4]

Whether in philosophical statement, in political action, or in performance in the entire range of the arts, Europeans made clear their awareness of the break with the past and their dominant fears and recessive hopes for the future. In Russia, the Revolution of 1917 produced equal measures of visionary idealism, social experimentation as inept as it was interesting, and finally terror. Germany lay in chaos, then made itself hesitantly ready for the surrender to Hitler, just as Italy had unhesitantly surrendered to Mussolini. The rumblings of discontent in the British, French, and Spanish empires were not so clearly heeded as, with hindsight, one knows they should have been. European writers were swifter to respond to post-war realities than European politicians. As a result, what had looked experimental before the war now was standard. Writers could only, however sadly, align themselves with the present. Anything else was at best an evasion of truth and at worst a betrayal.

In the United States, however, matters were less clearly defined. The affectations of loss by individuals like Ernest Hemingway and others of the self-consciously "lost" generation were valid for neither the society as a whole nor the literature as a whole. The poets came closer to the truth as European writers apprehended it than did writers of prose

[2] Paul Valéry, *Variété* (Paris, 1919), pp. 19–21.
[3] Jacques and Isabelle Rivière, *La Guérison* (Paris, 1936), p. 96.
[4] Ernst Jünger, *Journal: 1914–1943*, trans. anonymous, two vols. (Paris, 1951), I, 10.

fiction. No novel of the period is comparable to T. S. Eliot's *The Waste Land*, or even to Hart Crane's *The Bridge*. But that may only be to repeat the truism that poetry is the purer, and therefore the truer, art. In any event, I wish to take up prose fiction first, reserving poetry for a later chapter. Because of its special relationship to everyday reality (whatever that may be), prose fiction provides literary history with an extraordinarily valuable insight for the interpretation of events of a given period. Its special kind of evidence, because of its emotional base, although phrased in the logic and grammar of what we call reality, is more valid for history than the photograph, the eye-witness report, or the newspaper account.

The prose fiction of 1919 to 1932, together with the other sources available to us, reveals an America whose response to the war was equivocal and diffuse. Such writers as Ernest Hemingway, E. E. Cummings, John Dos Passos, Ernest Boyd, Willa Cather, Edith Wharton, and Lawrence Stallings, among many others, dealt with the war directly to indicate how they personally or a segment of society had been altered by it.[5] But more frequently, the American response was indirect. During the twenties, the country pulled back from its Wilsonian wartime commitments to Europe and to international peace, not because it was warlike, but because the illusion of invulnerability to the ills of Europe was fostered by a prosperous and ever-increasing industrialism and by a politics of retreat from exterior commitment. The slogans of the Presidents of the period—Harding, Coolidge, and Hoover—sound like Dada, notably Calvin Coolidge's pronouncement that "The business of America is business." At a time when politicians capitalized upon the public disposition to ignore the world beyond the United States, many writers and critics arrived at a position hardly distinguishable from that of the political isolationists. An influential group of writers and critics whose views had been shaped before the war, men such as Van Wyck Brooks, Paul Rosenfeld, and Waldo Frank, seemed to turn their backs upon politics. In no period of American history had writers paid so little attention to politics, domestic or foreign. Even so dominant an event as the Russian Revolution was not evaluated in any depth by intellectuals

---

[5] I assume here that the category "war fiction" is only pseudo-critical and even false, since it defines nothing more than superficial content. The great majority of "war" novels were technically uninteresting, relying for their effect upon the most weary kind of nineteenth-century naturalism. War, vast and disorderly, is a difficult subject for fiction, which by definition seeks order and insight.

until the 1930's, that is, until the implications of the event became an immediate American problem.[6]

The equivocal political and social history of the twenties provided prose fiction with a context, a frame of reference, a marked degree of imaginative freedom that was reinforced by a striking development of the historical dimension. The period honored technical experiment so much that it was often confused with great merit. At the same time, the twenties placed a premium upon content, upon originality, and tended to confuse content with formal experiment.

Writers of fiction may for convenience be grouped according to their retrospective or prospective qualities, with the war always present as a sign of the historical process. The retrospective writers are those whose techniques and mental sets were determined by the past; they were not necessarily traditional in Eliot's sense, but they were dominated, consciously or not, by tradition. This generalization holds true for Europe, too, although the European outline may differ from the American. Retrospection was first and most obviously a matter of generation, second and more significantly a matter of sensibility. The prospective might be seen as rebellion and a disposition to experiment in technique, but only secondly as a matter of generation. Sherwood Anderson (born 1876), according to this description, is retrospective by generation and accomplishment despite his ardent will to rebellion and experimentation; so is André Gide in France. F. Scott Fitzgerald (born 1896) is both retrospective and prospective, while Jean Cocteau (born 1889), a lesser writer, is entirely prospective. The work of Anderson and Fitzgerald may be regarded as exemplary; in it one sees the vivid illustration of certain dilemmas and perplexities posed to writers by history, by a rapidly changing society, and by the evolution of the art of fiction.

Sherwood Anderson's high reputation in the twenties was made possible by the war, even though he took no direct part in it, and if we are to credit the evidence of his work, letters, memoirs, or biographers, the war made no impact upon him whatsoever. His references to it are few and bombastic.[7] Although Anderson wrote only one work that may

[6] John Reed's *Ten Days That Shook the World* (1919), which is at best inspired reportage, was more widely read in the thirties than in the twenties.

[7] For example, a letter to Waldo Frank dated "Before November, 1918." in *Letters of Sherwood Anderson*, ed., Howard M. Jones and Walter B. Rideout (Boston, 1953), pp. 24–25: "In the catastrophe that has come upon the world all of the more subtle and delicately adjusted impulses and aspirations of peoples have been lost sight of. It is good to see you willing to try to swim ahead in this uncertain sea."

endure, *Winesburg, Ohio* (1919), and the slightest handful of memorable sketches thereafter, both his contemporaries and later critics were remarkably kind to him. Reasons for that kindness lie deeply embedded in the American mind and spirit at the end of the war, as well as in the rather panhandling personality of Anderson, who begged for and in a sense enforced generosity to himself. With characteristic shrewdness, Anderson contrived to appear to Van Wyck Brooks and Paul Rosenfeld at the end of the war as a middle-aged Lochinvar come out of the West, a genuine American to reinforce their hope for a distinctively American future. Behind their response to Anderson lay the failure in 1917 of their pacifist review, *The Seven Arts*, together with a conviction (shared by a large segment of the population) that the war had put a full stop to a major phase of history, had in fact "settled history"[8] and created a climate in which one could re-examine the American past quite independently of European antecedents. Brooks' attempt, in particular, was related to a movement in American universities to establish American literature as a subject in itself and independent of English studies. Worthy and even necessary though the movement may have been, it tended to result in literary chauvinism, and the inflation of minor writers past and present. In its initial energy and its excesses, the movement was closely related to the political climate of the day.

Like a hypochondriac checking his pulse and taking his temperature in fearful pleasure, Brooks went to the American past to discover the "usable" and to define certain qualities as peculiarly American. In three early essays, "America's Coming of Age" (1915), "Letters and Leadership" (1918), and "The Literary Life in America" (1921), Brooks examined American writing and found it wanting, just as he found the careers of American writers fragmentary and disappointing for lack of commitment to a tradition, to "the sense that one is *working in a great line.*"[9] He went on in two biographies, *The Ordeal of Mark Twain* (1920) and *The Pilgrimage of Henry James* (1925), to contrast apparently contradictory careers: that of Twain, who stayed at home and suffered from provincialism, and that of James, who went abroad and suffered from being out of touch with home. In his long, productive career, Brooks was never to reach a satisfactory answer to his question, possibly because his question was irrelevant. When he seemed to have found an answer in his later history

[8] Harry Levin, *Refractions* (New York, Oxford University Press, 1966), p. 286.
[9] Van Wyck Brooks. "The Literary Life in America," *Emerson and Others* (New York, 1927), p. 238. Brooks' italics.

of American writing, *Makers and Finders*, that answer remained unconvincing to readers who were unsatisfied with the question that Brooks continued to ask about the relationship between nationality and literary art. If the question was not irrelevant, it seemed so from the urgency with which it was asked. Brooks seemed to demand, here and now, that American writers "use" their country, their experience, and their language to fulfill a literary destiny. Brooks' compulsion led him into certain misadventures, the most egregious being his reception of Sherwood Anderson.

Brooks' and Waldo Frank's prospectus for *The Seven Arts* asserted that America had reached "that national self-consciousness which is the beginning of greatness." However dubious the assertion, it expressed a frame of mind that at once evokes the shades of Emerson and Whitman, a disposition which we encounter repeatedly between the world wars and which goes far to explain that eastern group's welcome to Anderson, the self-proclaimed chanter of "Mid-America." Anderson, a pure product of the American Midwest, recalls William Carlos Williams' statement, "The pure products of America go crazy." Brought up in poverty, self-educated insofar as he ever was educated, Anderson drifted into copy-writing for advertising agencies, into paint manufacture, then back to copy-writing, a craft at which he was ominously efficient. He began to write fiction in about 1911; by 1912, at age thirty-six, he had left his two children, the wife whom he later divorced, and his career as "The Roof-Fix Man" for Chicago, where he encountered the literary life of the so-called Chicago Renaissance. There he wrote some of the stories for *Winesburg, Ohio*, took up painting, and became easy prey to the provincial attitudinizing that characterized so many of the Chicago group. He emerged as a bohemian of the boondocks and remained such until his death, if not always in appearance, then in intellectual outlook.

Brooks and his companions knew Anderson through Waldo Frank, with whom Anderson had begun to correspond in 1916. Frank had asked Anderson to contribute to *The Seven Arts*, and when he received the story "The Untold Lie," Frank wrote an article entitled "Emerging Greatness" for the first issue, thus originating a view of Anderson that has been maintained ever since. Frank, Rosenfeld, and to a lesser degree Brooks himself, saw Anderson as the embodiment of their call for native American genius, for a voice having not the slightest European accent to it, an answer, in brief, to a loud, long American appeal from the eastern seaboard to the midwestern prairie. The difference between what Waldo

Frank and his friends saw in Anderson and what Anderson really was is a fair guide to the ambiguity in Anderson's posthumous reputation. A devious man always, Anderson posed as a midwestern original and was so received. In fact, he was the opposite; his strength as a writer lay in his representativeness not his originality. Until very recently, every midwestern factory of any size and every small town has had an Anderson in it: the local self-proclaimed intellectual who drank and whored with the boys, yet who dabbled in the arts and read books on the side. Like Anderson, many such men left the factory and the small town for Chicago or New York, only to bog down in the city or to return to the known and safe place. Anderson had more talent than most and through his deviousness created his own good fortune.

While posing as a shy countryman to his new-found friends, he was in truth a successful advertising salesman and copy-writer who announced what a "smooth son of a bitch" he was as a salesman. In his raw pleas to Brooks and Rosenfeld for mental sustenance, he was not so much envying them their culture and education as setting himself up as the untutored genius. One who reads Anderson's correspondence of the 1916–1924 period receives an uncomfortable impression of duality which Anderson did not intend. Neither his new friendships nor his European tour of 1921 changed him from the intellectual *flaneur* he in essence was. Nevertheless, during the twenties Anderson wrote a great deal of work that was well received in the United States and in Europe.[10]

In 1921 Anderson received the signal honor of *The Dial*'s first annual award of $2,000; by the mid-twenties, Virginia Woolf reported that Anderson and Sinclair Lewis were the two American novelists most widely read and discussed in Britain.[11] The splendid Italian novelist and critic Cesare Pavese, writing in 1931, remarked Anderson's "poetic" style, his anti-industrialism in theme, and praised him as a "primitive." Pavese regarded *Dark Laughter* as Anderson's most important novel, while he praised Anderson for giving form to the "chaos" of American

[10] *Windy McPherson's Son* had appeared in 1916 and *Marching Men* in 1917. The unfortunate Carl Sandburg-like *Mid-American Chants* appeared in 1918. Thereafter: *Winesburg, Ohio* (1919), *Poor White* (1921), *The Triumph of the Egg* (1921), *Many Marriages* (1923), *Horses and Men* (1923), *A Story Teller's Story* (1924), *Dark Laughter* (1925), *The Modern Writer* (1925), *Tar: A Midwest Childhood* (1926), *Sherwood Anderson's Notebook* (1926), *A New Testament* (1927), *Hello Towns* (1929), *Perhaps Women* (1931), *Beyond Desire* (1932), and *Death in the Woods* (1933).

[11] Virginia Woolf, "American Fiction," *Saturday Review of Literature*, II, no. 1 (Aug. 1, 1925) 1.

life.[12] Anderson knew most American and some European writers of the twenties, and he corresponded with many of them. He met Gertrude Stein and James Joyce in Paris and William Faulkner in New Orleans. The character Dawson Fairchild in Faulkner's *Mosquitoes* (1927) is unquestionably modelled on Anderson, while Faulkner dedicated *Sartoris* (1929) to him.[13] Paul Rosenfeld summarized a common American view when he wrote,

[12] Cesare Pavese, "Sherwood Anderson," *La Revue des lettres modernes*, X, nos. 78–80 (1963), 37–50. Pavese's judgment of *Dark Laughter* must strike the English-language reader as mysterious. It is an example of what so often has happened to American works of secondary relevance abroad: witness the Russian vogue for Upton Sinclair, the German vogue for Thomas Wolfe, or the Scandinavian vogue for John Steinbeck.

[13] Further witness to Anderson's contemporary reputation is Faulkner's "Sherwood Anderson, an Appreciation," *Atlantic Monthly*, CXCI (June, 1953), 27–29. Faulkner wrote of Dawson Fairchild in *Mosquitoes:* in the voice of Julius, the "semitic" man:

"His writing seems fumbling, not because life is unclear to him, but because of his innate humorless belief that, though it bewilder him at times, life at bottom is sound and admirable and fine; and because hovering over this American scene into which he has been thrust, the ghosts of the Emersons and Lowells and other exemplifiers of Education with a capital E who, 'seated on chairs in handsomely carpeted parlors' are surrounded by an atmosphere of half calf and security, dominated American letters in its most healthy American phase 'without heat or vulgarity,' simper yet in a sort of ubiquitous watchfulness. A sort of puerile bravado in flouting while he fears. . . ."

"But," his sister said, "for a man like Dawson there is no better American tradition than theirs—if he but knew it. They may have sat among their objects, transcribing their Greek and Latin and holding correspondences across the Atlantic, but they still found time to put out of their New England ports with the Word of God in one hand and a belaying pin in the other and all sails drawing aloft; and whatever they fell foul of was American. And it was American. And is yet."

"Yes," her brother agreed again. "But he lacks what they had at command among their shelves of discrete [sic] books and their dearth of heat and vulgarity— a standard of literature that is international. No, not a standard, exactly: a belief, a conviction that his talent need not be restricted to delineating things which his conscious mind assures him are American reactions."

"Freedom?" suggested Mark Frost hollowly.

"No. No one needs freedom. We cannot bear it. He need only let himself go, let himself forget all this fetich [sic] of culture and education which his upbringing and the ghosts of those whom circumstance permitted to reside longer at college than himself, and whom despite himself he regards with awe, assure him that he lacks. For by getting himself and his own bewilderment and inhibitions out of

... if mid-America lies as densely as it does about these stories it is also because as a whole their prose is one of those happy media which not only with their peculiar accent but with their flavor and entire quality mysteriously represent special regions and entire lands. Anderson's prose is as American as that of Mark Twain, from which indubitably it was descended; an embodiment of the Western earth like Whitman's verse, Sullivan's architecture, the painting of Homer Martin [sic] or of Marin.[14]

Since many of his critics were impressed by Anderson's style, it is appropriate to look at a representative example from his best work. 'The Untold Lie" is one of the narratives of *Winesburg, Ohio;* it concerns two farm hands, one middle-aged, one young. Ray Pearson, the older, had been trapped in marriage by sexual carelessness and has lived to regret both his wife and his ragged children. The young man, Hal Winters, finds himself in a similar trap. He asks Pearson what to do about it, but Pearson cannot bring himself to answer. Later in the day the story concludes:

The beauty of the country about Winesburg was too much for Ray on that fall evening. That was all there was to it. He could not stand it. Of a sudden he forgot all about being a quiet old farmhand and throwing off the torn overcoat began to run across the field. As he ran he shouted a protest against his life, against all life, against everything that makes life ugly. "There was no promise made," he cried into the empty spaces that lay about him. "I didn't promise my Minnie anything and Hal hasn't made any promise to Nell. I know he hasn't. She went into the woods with him because she wanted to go. What he wanted she wanted. Why should I pay? Why should Hal pay? Why should anyone pay? I don't want Hal to become old and worn out. I'll tell him. I won't let it go on. I'll catch Hal before he gets to town and I'll tell him."

Pearson then runs across the fields, finds Winters, but also finds that Winters has made up his own mind: he will do the "right" thing, because he really wants to settle down with Nell "and have kids." Pearson tells himself that it is for the best, because "Whatever I told him would have been a lie."

---

the way by describing, in a manner that even translation cannot injure (as Balzac did) American life as American life is, it will become eternal and timeless despite him.["] *Mosquitoes* (New York, 1927), pp. 242–243.

[14] Paul Rosenfeld, Introduction, *The Sherwood Anderson Reader* (Boston, 1947), p. xviii. "Homer Martin" presumably is Winslow Homer.

Whatever the style is, it is not "poetic," or what criticism seems to intend by that term, vague and evasive when applied to prose. The sentences have verbs, as Anderson's sentences do not have when he *is* being "poetic." The diction is simple and, in some turns of phrase, colloquial: "That was all there was to it"; "Of a sudden." The character's thoughts, presented not in interior monologue but in direct discourse, convey an appropriate awkwardness, as in "There was no promise made." Most characteristic are the Andersonian cosmic questions addressed to the wind, a device which Anderson used repeatedly to establish the groping (one of his favorite words), puzzled, naïve, honest nature of his usual narrator or central character. The sentence rhythms are right, and the entire story is of exactly the proper length for the vignette that Anderson set out to present. As in all the vignettes of *Winesburg, Ohio* and in his other fiction of merit, an aesthetically fine economy of means is at work. That style, however, is only in the most superficial sense "indubitably . . . descended" from Mark Twain's. It relates to Twain's only in its manipulation of the colloquial, a point that applies to virtually every American writer since Twain, for a large part of Twain's accomplishment was to make the colloquial available to writers.

Anderson had none of Twain's ability to write convincing dialogue. Anderson's characters speak with one voice only, that of Sherwood Anderson. Twain was firmly within the great English tradition of realism, while Anderson was in another location altogether. That fact alone removes him from Twain's stylistic tradition. When, as in the first few chapters of *Poor White* and in parts of *Dark Laughter*, Anderson frankly imitated *Huckleberry Finn*, he produced only transparent pastiche. But what we read in the above excerpt, in all the sketches that make up *Winesburg, Ohio*, and in all of Anderson's best work except the story "Death in the Woods", is a familiar phenomenon: the revelation of insight through "beauty" at a moment of crisis in the character's existence. Such revelation belongs to the tradition of neither realism nor naturalism, but to symbolism, in Anderson's case as that movement gave impulse to the aestheticism of English *fin de siècle* work. Anderson's novelty lay in his appropriating to ordinary and sub-ordinary Americans a sensibility conventionally attributed to gorgeous young aesthetes or to Stephen Daedalus-like intellectuals. But the gestures of Anderson's passionate young woman stripping off her clothes and running out onto the street in the rain ("Adventure"), of his race track swipe who sees in the barroom mirror not his own face but a girl's, and of the same swipe becoming entangled in a horse's skeleton in the moonlight as he is pursued by Negroes intending rape ("The Man Who Became a Woman") are the gestures of Oscar Wilde, or more ludicrously, of Lautréaumont rather than of Mark Twain. Anderson took from Twain a character and a tone. His boys and men are first Sherwood Anderson, and second Huck Finn. The tone, however, is violated by the persistent brooding, the search for the pastoral past, and the foggy, half-baked philosophizing that characterizes Anderson's indifferent average in fiction.

Readers have been teased by the problem of whether *Winesburg, Ohio* is a novel, a collection of short stories, sketches, or whatever. That problem is interesting, for it places in relief Anderson's salient strengths and crippling weaknesses. Most of the matter in the collection was written as independent short stories, tales, vignettes, or sketches. Anderson then found an apparent solution in his title and his device of creating a linking personage, George Willard. Willard is the prototype of the Andersonian hero: questioning, unhappy, wounded, uncomprehending, but through it all burning for escape from small town life and longing for "freedom." He enters briefly into or bounces off the narratives of the other characters, and his own narrative and theme of freedom introduce and conclude the book. The other device, as mentioned, is the title. By implication, the work concerns not individuals, but the community of Winesburg. As in Edgar Lee Masters' book of verse, *Spoon River Anthology* (1915), the subject becomes the community itself. Ideally, both Masters and Anderson attempted to transcend the parts, and by transcending them, to create an intangible but unified whole that would be greater than the sum of its parts. Anderson said that he had found a new, "looser form" for the novel and justified that form in his belief that "Life is a loose flowing thing."[15] Anderson had displayed something of his impulse to portray the mass, the vaguely apprehended communal entity, as against individual emotion in his second novel, *Marching Men*, and he was to continue to do so in his lean, later years of flagging imagination when he wrote his devious *Memoirs*, *Hello Towns*, and *Puzzled America*.

Anderson's intuition of form in *Winesburg, Ohio* has been compared by his least critical biographer to Balzac's in *The Human Comedy*.[16] There is no relationship. A more fruitful and chronologically timely

[15] *Sherwood Anderson's Memoirs* (New York, 1942), p. 289.
[16] James Schevill, *Sherwood Anderson: His Life and Work* (University of Denver Press, 1951), pp. 98–99.

comparison might be made with Jules Romains' theory of *unanimisme*. As early as 1908, Romains (born 1885) had written a book of verse entitled *La Vie unanime*. From then until 1932, when he began *Les Hommes de bonne volonté*, he developed his theory that men in groups participate in collective, as opposed to individual, thought and enter into instinctive community with the "unanimity"; that the writer can express that intuition of unanimity and, by so doing, aid the individual to integrate himself into the collectivity. Romains' intermittently superb *roman-fleuve* was a prolonged (1932–1946) if not entirely convincing demonstration of his hypothesis. Anderson's collectivity in *Winesburg, Ohio* differed not only in scope but also in impulse. Romains wrote in opposition to what he saw as the extreme spiritual isolation of the individual, which he believed the work of Freud and Proust, in particular, had encouraged. And one may see the *roman-fleuve*, in the hands of Romains and Roger Martin du Gard after the Great War, as an attempt to put the world together again after its recent shattering.

Although it is possible that Anderson knew Romains' organizing principle of *unanimisme* through Waldo Frank, who wrote novels in that vein,[17] it is unlikely that Romains influenced Anderson directly any more than Balzac did. It is rather a matter of parallel sensibilities more or less at work. Anderson, however, differed in impulse from Romains in one important aspect: far from establishing any manner of participation, his characters, like D. H. Lawrence's, are all the more isolated from the community by their perceptions and intuitions. Where Romains implies the basic health and decency of the community, Anderson and Lawrence establish its illness and brutality. Their characters' search for freedom is not freedom in communal integration. They want sexual freedom, and beyond sex, romantic escape in a geographical sense, otherwise undefined in personal, social, or philosophical terms. Indeed, no contrast could be more eloquent than that between Jules Romains and Sherwood Anderson. Romains, of solid bourgeois stock, attended the Lycée Condorcet in Paris, then became a student of philosophy and biology in the Ecole Normale Supérieure. He brought to writing a disciplined, logical mind which, while irrelevant to ultimate aesthetic success, nevertheless helps us to see the limitations that such a man as Anderson tried ineffectually to overcome. Romains and the large majority of other French writers were formed by their society and by a formal, disciplined education. Anderson was not only self-made but also self-invented.

[17] *Rahab* (1922) and *City Block* (1922).

Winesburg, Ohio is not a novel, but rather what Anderson called it before his publisher changed the title, *The Book of the Grotesque*, or what we might call a book of grotesques. On the evidence of his work, Anderson was apparently incapable of writing a novel, in spite of his several works approximating the genre. His talent was not for sustained narrative but for fictionalized meditation and for the creation of highly charged, momentary states of emotion. The characters of *Winesburg, Ohio* qualify as "grotesques" because their emotional time is not solar, but lunar or sidereal; each contains Anderson's notion of a "truth," usually of a sexual nature, about humanity as he conceives it: that some men are homosexual; that some men prefer to sleep with women but do not; that some women prefer to sleep with men but do not; that mores in Winesburg are stupefying, and the like. In his free use of symbolism, Anderson extended the confining bounds of naturalism, but his curious declarative quality frequently made his symbolism easy, then forced, so weakening its power. One example is the second paragraph of the much-admired story "Hands," the theme of which is Wing Biddlebaum's necessity for human companionship, misinterpreted by the town as homosexuality:

> Wing Biddlebaum, forever frightened and beset by a ghostly band of doubts, did not think of himself as in any way a part of the life of the town where he had lived for twenty years. Among all the people of Winesburg but one had come close to him. With George Willard, son of Tom Willard, the proprietor of the new Willard House, he had formed something like a friendship. George Willard was the reporter on the *Winesburg Eagle* and sometimes in the evenings he walked out along the highway to Wing Biddlebaum's house. Now as the old man walked up and down on the veranda, his hands moving nervously about, he was hoping that George Willard would come and spend the evening with him.

Even when the sentence is varied in structure from the declarative, it retains a declarative quality which in turn creates the tone of naïveté of which Anderson was so fond. It also establishes a sense of authenticity, and Anderson's final appeal and justification is to authenticity.

In part because of the sexual matter in *Winesburg, Ohio*, then more obviously with the publication of *Many Marriages* (1923) and *Dark Laughter* (1925), Anderson was labelled a Freudian by his contemporaries, a label that has stuck. Anderson himself said he never read Freud, although again one must bear in mind that his own word was rarely trustworthy. He obviously had heard and probably spoke the Freudian jargon of his day; we know that in 1916 he attended a lecture by Trigant Burrows, one of the first American psychoanalysts.[18] But given his undisciplined, and in the worst sense romantic, mind, it is hard to disbelieve Anderson's own word in this instance. Irving Howe is surely correct in locating D. H. Lawrence as the major influence rather than Freud.[19] Anderson read *Women in Love* in 1921, and when he later read *Lady Chatterley's Lover*, he told friends that it was the novel that he had wanted to write. *Many Marriages* and *Dark Laughter* read like parodies of Lawrence at his worst, with their themes of "freedom" again, freedom from wives, children, work, and release into "life," conceived in *Dark Laughter* as a sinking into the arms of hot-blooded black women in the musty South. But again, it is not a case of direct influence, but of parallel sensibilities. In many respects, Anderson is the American Lawrence. Years before reading Lawrence, he had established the brooding, essayistic, declarative tone, together with the impulse toward transcendental freedom to be achieved through fidelity to the senses and emotions, a fidelity possible only by the rejection of industrialism and the affirmation of something very like Lawrence's fatuous doctrine of "blood." Anderson did discover authority in Lawrence for certain of his insights about sex, but to consider him only as a disciple is to do him injustice. Both men, incidentally, arrived at a system that possessed authoritarian overtones, Anderson in *Marching Men* (although "system" is a misnomer) and Lawrence in *Kangaroo* and *The Plumed Serpent*. Neither, properly speaking, was a novelist; both wrote a handful of superb short stories, sketches, and episodes in novels *manqués*. If Lawrence lacked Anderson's attractive freshness and directness, his prose often possessed a nobility that we cannot find in Anderson. Lawrence's was the finer and subtler mind, yet his characters are closely akin to Anderson's. They, too, are "grotesques."

Anderson's best work, *Winesburg, Ohio*, a few of the later stories in *Horses and Men*, and the story "Death in the Woods" may remind us, in their frank use of symbolism and treatment of children and child-like people, of his French contemporary, Henri Fournier (Alain-Fournier), and of his remarkable novel, *Le Grand Meaulnes* (1913). Although the two writers are notably similar in their apprehensions and objectives, their work resists final comparison. The reasons take us again outside the work

---

[18] Irving Howe, *Sherwood Anderson* (New York, 1951), p. 179.
[19] Howe, pp. 179–196.

to tradition and intellectual background. Like Anderson, Henri Fournier was a provincial, from the Bordeaux region, but like Jules Romains he was also a product of a good Parisian lycée and of a profound personal study of the French literary tradition from the seventeenth century to the twentieth. Not least, he was formed by his intimate intellectual friendship with the fine critic, his boyhood friend, Jacques Rivière. His early impulses were very like Anderson's: to write lyrically and without discipline. His novel is indeed lyrical, but it is disciplined; this we know from the fine and continual control of diction and rhythm in the completed work. Anderson, on the contrary, had for literary mentors not a Jacques Rivière, but people like Ben Hecht and Floyd Dell in his Chicago years, and then Waldo Frank, none of whom was exactly a master of fiction or literary criticism. The nearest thing to a Rivière America had to offer was H. L. Mencken, Van Wyck Brooks, or Edmund Wilson, and because of his own limitations and narcissistic preoccupations, Anderson was not open to comment from so good a critic as Wilson. To a degree, the tradition of Mark Twain served Anderson well, although when he tried frankly to borrow Twain's accent, he came to grief; a voice like Twain's is not on loan. At a farther remove, one may apprehend the influence of Walt Whitman as vulgarized by Carl Sandburg. Whitman could be useful to a poet like Hart Crane, but his influence upon prose merely encouraged the vein of tired, tag-end American and British romanticism on which Anderson had been brought up.

Like many other American writers before and since, Anderson was forced back upon himself exclusively, and his work displays the occasional strengths and frequent weaknesses of that self. His deviousness is witness to a lack of integrity, not in any social or moral sense, but integrity to word and fiction. He brooded not about art but about "being an artist," and he wasted energy trying to encompass themes that were foreign to his talent. His limitations kept him provincial and retrospective, never more so than when he tried to be "modern." Needing ideas, he was born to a time and a society in which the ideas served up to him could not serve him. To paraphrase Eliot on James, one must say that he had a mind so coarse that no idea could violate it. When Paul Rosenberg and Van Wyck Brooks greeted him as the savior, as the authentic American of the new era, they did him a disservice. He was at first delighted, then uneasy, then despairing at the impossibility of maintaining the role thrust upon him. A sentimental, retrospective interpretation of the American past could only distort a view of the American post-war present.

Despite their differences in age and achievement, Sherwood Anderson and F. Scott Fitzgerald (1896–1940) have more in common than first might be apparent. They shared a view of the American midwest and of the historical past which they inserted in their fiction for a virtually metaphysical purpose. Both placed the theme of material success versus failure at the center to their work, and both thought of themselves as uniquely representing their time and generation. Their contemporaries agreed so completely that it has become difficult for history to disentangle the men from their works. Even more than in the case of Anderson, accounts of Fitzgerald's wife, daughter, income, expenses, drinking habits, and various other intimacies that are none of our business have obscured our reading of his fiction as fiction. Criticism has been kind to Fitzgerald, as to Anderson, although with greater justification. After having fallen into neglect following the publication of *Tender Is the Night* in 1934, Fitzgerald was taken up again after 1945 and presented as a giant of the modern movement. While it remains undeniable that Fitzgerald caught and pinned down a segment of American social history after World War I, literary history must question the magnitude of his post-World War II reputation as a writer, if not as an Emersonian representative man.

Like Anderson a relentlessly autobiographical writer, Fitzgerald forces us to note certain biographical facts: his midwestern birth and middle-class childhood in St. Paul, Minnesota; a New Jersey Roman Catholic preparatory school; then Princeton, World War I, early marriage, money and reputation from the publication of *This Side of Paradise* (1920); a daughter, intermittent residence in France, his wife's mental illness; his own physical decline and early death. From such materials Fitzgerald drew his single, pervading theme: the Flaubertian theme of the sentimental education with its allied depiction of the character's failure to grasp the disparity between youthful illusion and the world's mauling of that illusion in maturity. It is a useable theme for the moralist and satirist that Fitzgerald was. Historically considered, it is the great theme that the romantics made available to fiction, and one which many writers found useful after World War I. That Fitzgerald was aware of its full possibilities is clear from the fact that the theme lies at the center of all his fiction; he was able to realize it fully only in *The*

Great Gatsby (1925) and to approach it again in *Tender Is the Night* (1934).[20] Fitzgerald gave the theme of the sentimental education a particular American coloration, to become "the thesis that Beauty is a concealed form of Money."[21] It is characteristic of Fitzgerald that he apprehended his theme only fitfully and intuitively; it was not the product of disciplined study. His conventionally good education introduced him only to individuals and social groups, not to ideas. He left Princeton unscathed by formal education, but with a mass of dimly perceived literary ideas and the friendship of such men as Edmund Wilson and John Peale Bishop, who were to help him discard the trash with which he had burdened an unpowerful mind. He was not an intellectual, but he was a born writer who possessed an integrity to the word that Anderson never approached.

Those fragments of the past which we call periods are such because they have their individual argot, their pose, their peculiar manner and turn of individuality. Fitzgerald's initial success can be accounted for only by his having caught and defined certain gestures of pre- and post-World War I society. *This Side of Paradise* broke upon the America of 1920 rather as *The Sorrows of Young Werther* broke upon the Germany of 1774. Fitzgerald and Goethe not only wrote what they observed in others and felt in themselves, but in so doing they seemed to define the ambience of the world for its inhabitants. *Werther*, of course, remains a charming minor work; *This Side of Paradise* remains of interest only as a social document and as a measure of the distance Fitzgerald travelled in the brief five years to the publication of *The Great Gatsby*. Our awareness of that distance is all the greater if we note the grab bag of literary influences at work upon Fitzgerald in his undergraduate years and apparent to the point of pastiche in his first novel. The work is not so much novel as prettified autobiography, a portmanteau into which Fitzgerald stuffed various bits and pieces of verse, monologue, dialogue, and purple patches which had occupied him for the six years or so before 1920. Amory Blaine is Scott Fitzgerald with a patina, and the record of Amory Blaine's

---

[20] Many critics, notably Arthur Mizener, have said that *The Last Tycoon* (1941) would have surpassed Fitzgerald's other work had he been granted life to finish it. It remains a fragment which I do not pretend to deal with, nor can I agree with Mizener's generous appraisal (in *The Sense of Life in the Modern Novel* [Boston, 1964], p. 204).

[21] Miles Burrows, "Scroo! Scroo! Scroo!" *New Statesman* (January 7, 1966), 18.

experience is precisely Fitzgerald's; whatever form the work has derives from his life.

This Side of Paradise provided a mirror image to Fitzgerald's contemporaries of their own mental furnishings. Whatever had gone into their literary education was present, with a twist or a turn, in his. The list is predictable but nevertheless banal for a writer who seemed revolutionary. There were Keats, Browning, Tennyson, Swinburne, Poe, Verlaine, Rupert Brooke, Oscar Wilde, H. G. Wells, G. K. Chesterton, Booth Tarkington, and possibly a touch of James Joyce, the only surprising name of the lot. Amory Blaine's boyhood dialogue is lifted directly from Booth Tarkington's *Penrod;* at Princeton, Amory and his friends write verse that is two parts Keats, one part Swinburne, and one part Tennyson, while Amory quotes Swinburne and Poe throughout. The pseudo-decadent atmosphere of Book I derives straight from Wilde's *The Picture of Dorian Gray*, while the undergraduate blasé posturings and affectations of "beauty" reflect an indiscriminate awareness of English *fin de siècle* fashions in verse and life. H. G. Wells was much on Fitzgerald's mind. In 1917 he wrote that *The New Machiavelli* was "the greatest English novel of the century," and he was acquainted with Wells' theory of the novel as set forth in *Boon* and in the ensuing controversy with Henry James. Wells' defense of amplitude and discursiveness seems to have given Fitzgerald encouragement for his conscious formlessness in *This Side of Paradise*. One cannot agree that Joyce's *A Portrait of the Artist as a Young Man* was a model for Fitzgerald.[22] In temperament, intellectual equipment, and sensibility, Fitzgerald was profoundly different from Joyce. There is a Joycean echo, however, near the end of the novel when Amory, riding a bus, indulges in stream-of-consciousness, which further intrudes upon what passes for narrative in the novel.

The elements of pastiche in *This Side of Paradise* mar a sprightly, energetic surface, but they do not form a major weakness; its weakness lies in the fact that the novel is not really written. At this point in his career, Fitzgerald was unable to invent imaginative material, and when he departed from lived experience, he violated his own canon of truth, a canon that we dimly apprehend in a welter of contradictory impressions. Although he could register manners brilliantly, his talent was never for naturalism, nor even for realism, but for moral fantasy made firm by a

---

[22] Sergio Perosa, *The Art of F. Scott Fitzgerald*, tr. Charles Matz and Sergio Perosa (Ann Arbor, 1965), pp. 22–25 and note 16.

tone of voice and mind—in brief, by style. When in his first novel he lapsed into conventional realism, he violated his particular gift. Fitzgerald could construct fantasy upon observed experience, but he could not invent and dress his invention in the clothing of reality. He had not, for example, seen combat in the war or left the United States during his brief period in uniform, yet he tried to make of Amory a war-embittered type by casual reference to combat. At the conclusion of the novel, Amory is hitchhiking to Princeton from New York:

> Frost and the promise of winter thrilled him now, made him think of a wild battle between St. Regis and Groton, ages ago, seven years ago—and of an autumn day in France twelve months before when he had lain in tall grass, his platoon flattened down close around him, waiting to tap the shoulders of a Lewis gunner. He saw the two pictures together with somewhat the same primitive exaltation—two games he had played, differing in quality of acerbity, linked in a way that differed them from Rosalind or the subject of labyrinths which were, after all, the business of life.

In spite of the banality of the comparison, the passage almost succeeds by the grace of the prose. But finally it rings false; Fitzgerald was not yet able to project secondary material into a useable literary idea.

Fitzgerald's gift for fantasy had two poles, positive and negative. The positive pole enabled him to work outward from knowledge and intuition of character to the creation of credible individuals. This imaginative activity is not psychological, however; if we put Fitzgerald to the psychological test, we mis-read him. At its best, positive fantasy produced a Jay Gatsby. At its negative worst, fantasy lapsed into mere grotesquerie, as when the devil appears to Amory Blaine in the course of a spree in New York, his young virginity imperilled.[23] The episode, at once Poesque and redolent of *The Yellow Book*, intrudes most violently upon the subsidiary themes of loss of religious faith and Amory's search for a satisfactory substitute. Fitzgerald's fantasy, only loosely in hand in his first novel, was to become a fine instrument later on. But before we move forward, we should observe one further prominent characteristic of *This Side of Paradise* that is also related to his fantasy: his un-American lack of ease with external nature. Fitzgerald is like Henry James in being a distinctly indoor writer. Whenever narrative forces him out into the open, fantasy again takes the place of typical American realism or

[23] The episode is borrowed from Compton Mackenzie's *Sinister Street* (1913–1914), as were several other episodes and characters.

naturalism. Nature is a setting, sweet if not sickly, an occasion for drama reflecting the states of mind of his characters, but never a force to be mastered or a challenge to be overcome. Thousands of stars glimmer in his skies, water sparkles in his lakes, waves break in his oceans, but the apprehension is fantastic, not naturalistic. In this sense, Fitzgerald's imagination was un-American and even refreshing. It set him apart from Anderson, Faulkner, Hemingway, and most of his American contemporaries.

Because he was a moralist, Fitzgerald wrote novels of ideas of a sort. Part of his power as a writer derived from his incapacity for abstract thought. Lacking intellectual tidiness, he was forced to grope his way through narrative, through the fictional comings and goings of his characters, to an essence which he himself grasped imperfectly and fleetingly. In *This Side of Paradise*, that subterranean idea has to do with the adolescent's necessity for pose, for role-playing in order to arm himself against the onslaughts of an uncomprehending world. The closest Fitzgerald came to expressing his idea occurs at the conclusion, when Amory Blaine, shorn of illusion and finished with poses, "stretched out his arms to the crystalline, radiant sky. 'I know myself,' he cried, 'but that is all'." The gesture, reminiscent of D. H. Lawrence's conclusion to *Sons and Lovers* and of many novels of the period, takes the place of thought and sets a grandiloquent full stop to the novel. It is conventional in a novel that was received as unconventional, familiar to the point of cliché.

1922, the year in which *The Beautiful and Damned* and *Tales of the Jazz Age* appeared, was also the year in which Joyce's *Ulysses* was published in Paris, the year of Eliot's *The Waste Land*, of Rilke's *Duino Elegies* and *Sonnets to Orpheus*, and of collections by Hardy, Housman, Yeats, and Valéry. It was the year of D. H. Lawrence's *Aaron's Rod*, Katherine Mansfield's *The Garden Party*, and Virginia Woolf's *Jacob's Room*. *Sodome et Gomorrhe*, the fourth large section of *A la Recherche du temps perdu*, appeared, and in November, Marcel Proust died. Henry de Montherlant, Fitzgerald's exact contemporary, published his first novel, *Le Songe*. The richness of that year reminds us that Fitzgerald was not working in a vacuum, even though it may appear unfair to place the apprentice in the company of his eminent contemporaries.

Tales of the Jazz Age, like the earlier *Flappers and Philosophers* (1920) and the collections of short fiction still to come, need not detain us.

Fitzgerald wrote the majority of his more than sixty short stories in haste to earn money; perhaps half a dozen are of lasting if minor merit. The stories tell us a good deal about Fitzgerald's personal development but disappointingly little about those shifts and slidings of the sensibility that make up an artist's true career. For that we must go to the novels, for which Fitzgerald reserved his full strength.

Fitzgerald had begun *This Side of Paradise* as an undergraduate *jeu*, then had revised it at the insistence of friends and publisher. *The Beautiful and Damned*, on the contrary, was his first full effort as a professional novelist. The effort was perhaps too full, for the novel is deeply flawed by Fitzgerald's continuing compulsion to put in everything. The novel falls into layers, but the layering process was only partially intended and intermittently controlled. There is first a layer of objective plot, posing the question of whether Anthony Patch will inherit his grandfather's forty million dollars. Simple and silly, the plot contrasts with a second layer of satire and burlesque. Set in the years 1912–1920, the novel is at once a serious commentary upon the activities of actually or potentially wealthy wastrels and a satire upon social climbing and American salesmanship. Fitzgerald's gift for satire too easily blends into burlesque and structural anarchy; he invents characters and situations that are used, then sent into novelistic limbo. Gloria's parents, for example, are observed, used, then abandoned. A third layer, which again violates unity and coherence, is autobiographical. Anthony's courtship of Gloria, the couple's odd and sometimes charming combination of sophistication and moral rigor, the difficulties of their marriage, are material straight from Fitzgerald's life. We know this not necessarily from biography, but centrally from tone and from the opaqueness that attends the writer who projects himself as the central character. A fourth layer is a mixture of autobiography and unsatisfactory invention: episodes of Army camp life, Anthony's affair with Dorothy, and Dorothy's appearance in New York after the war.

The identity of the fifth and final layer of Fitzgerald's multi-layered novel is suggested by a passage, early on, in which Anthony Patch, courting Gloria and rebuffed by her, to pass the time reads Flaubert's *L'Education sentimental*. The allusion to Flaubert's novel jars, for Anthony has been presented as a chic, rather stupid young man whose Harvard education has influenced his manners but not his mind. The allusion is sufficient, however, to indicate that Fitzgerald very ambitiously was attempting a counterpart to Flaubert's study of French society, and more particularly of Frédéric Moreau in the person of Anthony Patch. The characters occupy equivalent positions in society; both have sufficient money to affect a certain style of life, but both are constantly oppressed by affectation; both float on the surface of the richer lives about them; both are uxorious; both are crippled by a "sentimental," which is to say false, education for the circumstances of their lives; and both suffer an alarming personal decline as a result of the disparity between their expectations and reality. *L'Education sentimental* is as good as it is because of Flaubert's rigid fulfillment of his intention, his objectivity, knowledge, and intellectual grasp of what he was about. Frédéric Moreau remains Frédéric Moreau and does not turn into Gustave Flaubert. Anthony Patch, however, breaks in two, if not in three, as Fitzgerald's narrative unfolds.

The first Anthony is Frédéric Moreau, a spoiled, not very bright young man just down to New York from Harvard, living on an adequate inheritance from his mother and putting in time as pleasantly as possible until his grandfather's death, which will make him rich. In that guise, Anthony is a fairly convincing social and political observer and exemplar of a way of life that Fitzgerald found fascinating. In his second role, as lover then husband of the willful Gloria, Anthony is Fitzgerald himself. The third Anthony seems compounded of O. Henry and Theodore Dreiser: Anthony as alcoholic and anti-Semite, a burden to his wife, his friends, and himself; weak, brutish, and without hope in his suit to win his inheritance. The final scene is straight from O. Henry. Anthony and Gloria, suddenly triumphant in gaining the inheritance, sail in the *Berengaria* for their long-delayed European tour. It is unworthy and distasteful, despite Fitzgerald's assurance that both characters have been permanently crippled by their humiliations. The moralist has turned moralistic.

Gloria is a more successful character than Anthony, although she is too much a product of adjectives and adverbs. She is intended to be that gay, beautiful, carefree, selfish, tough-soft creature who emerged just before the war into American life to be crowned with the title "flapper" just after the war. She is a part of Fitzgerald's contribution to social history, but as a literary character she is sentimental, for she remains essentially rhetorical. Like Anthony, Gloria is shoddy, and Fitzgerald wants us to think so; yet one comes away with the uneasy feeling that his central characters are even more shoddy than their creator knows. Not only in *The Beautiful and Damned*, but in virtually all his fiction, one may have the sense of having opened a door and witnessed a scene never intended for public eyes.

One consequence of the layering process is that too great a burden is placed upon style, and the style also becomes fragmented and inconsistent. We find the same striving after aphorism and epigram as in Fitzgerald's first novel, together with peculiar shifts from winsome charm to conceit to clotted, graceless, naturalistic description. At its average, the style is complex, pseudo-poetic, and self-conscious:

> In the foyer of the theatre they waited a few moments to see the first-night crowd come in. There were opera-cloaks stitched of myriad, many-colored silks and furs; there were jewels dripping from arms and throats and ear-tips of white and rose; there were innumerable broad shimmers down the middles of innumerable silk hats; there were shoes of gold and bronze and red and shining black; there were the high-piled, tight-packed coiffures of many women and the slick, watered hair of well-kept men—most of all there was the ebbing, flowing, chattering chuckling, foaming, slow-rolling wave effect of this cheerful sea of people as tonight it poured its glittering torrent into the artificial lake of laughter. . . .

Fitzgerald never entirely got over his fondness for gratuitous set pieces, although he did learn the art of orchestrating them in such a manner that they did not appear so self-conscious.

One is at a loss to account for what happened to Fitzgerald between the writing of *The Beautiful and Damned* and *The Great Gatsby;* to account in any real sense, that is, for the difference in so brief a time between the clever amateur and the near-master. In retrospect, it is clear that the earlier novel served to indicate to Fitzgerald what he could not do, and perhaps to guide him to what he could do. He could write neither *L'Education sentimental* in twentieth-century terms nor a counterpart to *A Portrait of the Artist as a Young Man.* Biography does not give us the answer, nor can it ever do so. Source study turns up the fact that Fitzgerald read Anatole France, Stephen Crane, Edith Wharton, Joseph Conrad, and a bit of Henry James in the interval between the two novels,[24] and it may be comforting to believe that he learned the use of a narrator and the strict control present in *The Great Gatsby* from such models as Conrad, James, and Wharton. Yet one must doubt that such models were of immediate use to Fitzgerald. He seemed not to possess the kind of mind that was open to primary influence, while he

[24] Perosa, *The Art of F. Scott Fitzgerald*, pp. 76–78.

himself complained that he needed to learn everything in writing by trial and error. If there was an influence at work upon *The Great Gatsby*, I suspect that it was again the influence of Flaubert, specifically *Madame Bovary*, an influence at once pervasive and peripheral, as opposed to the more obvious and provable parallel between Anthony Patch and Frédéric Moreau.[25] Both of Fitzgerald's earlier novels had suffered from the vice of contemporaneity, the attempt to catch and record the fashionable moment. Fitzgerald had seized upon the present and had tried to isolate it from the immediate past and from history.

In *The Great Gatsby*, by contrast, Fitzgerald returned, however unwittingly, to that richest of veins for the American novelist, to history itself, to the continuities and disparities between possibility and reality as conceived by the historical imagination. Much of *The Great Gatsby*'s staying power has to do with the fact that in this novel Fitzgerald took his place alongside Hawthorne, Melville, and James as a writer who realized the marvelous possibilities of the historical dimension in fiction. As in certain of the novels of his contemporaries—Hemingway, Dos Passos, and Faulkner—Fitzgerald perceived the past as a resonant and moving force upon the present, a force that liberated him from the curse of contemporaneity while it also made possible a degree of control over his materials that was lacking in his earlier work. History does not intrude disproportionately, however, as it does through rhetoric in Sherwood Anderson's work, or in some of Faulkner's through both rhetoric and obsession. Complex yet brief, *The Great Gatsby* is unique in American fiction for its lovely justness of proportion. Unlike other American writers who strove for proportion, Willa Cather for one, Fitzgerald here was not bloodless or dry. His novel is fully realized, not only in terms of history but also in terms of manners. It is a brilliant rendering of what is and is not possible in the society he set out to depict.

It is worth noting some of Fitzgerald's techniques in *The Great Gatsby*. It may be said that whoever uses a narrator in fiction courts disaster. One thinks of the chaos of Dostoevsky's *The Possessed*, which succeeds, when it does, in spite of the narrator. One's teeth may be set on edge by

[25] William Troy has suggested a relationship between Emma Bovary and Dick Diver in *Tender Is the Night*. While there is a ration of validity in the suggestion, I believe that the parallel between Emma Bovary and Jay Gatsby is more obvious. See "Scott Fitzgerald—The Authority of Failure" in *F. Scott Fitzgerald: The Man and His Work*, ed. Alfred Kazin (New York, 1962), p. 191.

Conrad's Marlowe and his wretched pipe; one may become annoyed by Nabokov's Humbert Humbert and his mannered verbal fireworks. More fictional narrators fail than succeed; although the use of a narrator solves the writer's problems of immediacy and continuity, the device also creates problems of strategy and credibility. Too often the narrator is likely to resemble Proust's, out in the bushes peering through the window at the shenanigans of Mademoiselle Vinteuil and her lesbian playmate. Fitzgerald's narrator, Nick Carraway, succeeds unequivocally for a variety of reasons. The principal reason is that he is not a mere structural device; he is rather a fully imagined character who not only relates the narrative but also interestingly debates the matter while telling it, and through his debates, judges it. He provides the "moral center" that James insisted upon but did not always fully realize. It is through Carraway's responses that we respond, both to the other major characters and to the central propositions of Fitzgerald's novel. Carraway is not only a device for transmitting narrative and effecting moral judgment. He is also fully engaged in the action of the novel. His affair with the treacherous Jordan Baker, for example, is one agent of his engagement, serving to prepare us for his interesting defense of Jay Gatsby and for his ultimate contempt for Tom and Daisy Buchanan. If Conrad's Marlowe stays in the mind as a man in need of a pipe cleaner and still another match, Carraway remains in the mind as a man of wit, charm, and intelligence rather than as a mechanical narrator.

The success or failure of *The Great Gatsby* depends upon our response to Jay Gatsby, and here Fitzgerald wrought better than he knew. He expressed dissatisfaction with the character and tended to agree with contemporary reviewers who were bothered by the figure of Gatsby. To be sure, the difference between Gatsby and the rest of the cast, in both conception and execution, is considerable. Tom Buchanan, with his "shining arrogant eyes," his wealth, and his "body capable of enormous leverage—a cruel body," is precisely right, precisely stupid and clever enough to bear fully Fitzgerald's vision of a certain kind of power and brutality in American life. Daisy Buchanan is a vindication of Fitzgerald's earlier partial failures to portray the beautiful, selfish, willful girl-woman flapper of the period. Her dizziness is charming, and her final corruption is convincing. It is convincing because she is the agent of Gatsby's downfall, just as she had been the agent of his rise. Through Daisy's association with Gatsby, she moves far beyond flapperdom to that great, good, mysterious place of fictional heroines and heroes who achieve immortality not through psychological or sociological fidelity or mechanical relationship to plot, but through their embodiment of fictional truth.

Jay Gatsby succeeds as a character (where Dick Diver fails) because he is the projection of an intuition of life rather than a "true" character; he is a "fantastic," but he emphatically is not an Andersonian grotesque. Presented ambiguously as a liar, poseur, gangster, and bootlegger, Gatsby nevertheless emerges not only as sympathetic, but as authentically heroic and authentically tragic.[26] He is a male Bovary whose romantic dream—his *Bovarysme*—is not simply personal and escapist, but representative, historical, and largely American. Fitzgerald succeeds in his Flaubertian parallel by giving us not one Emma but two. Myrtle Wilson, Buchanan's horrible mistress, is a brilliant satirical preparation for our reaction to Gatsby, just as her death under the wheels of the car that Daisy Buchanan is driving is a preparation for Gatsby's murder. Gatsby emerges, like a creature of myth, from the shores of Lake Superior; he drifts into obsession, into possession of the energy required to assemble the money and material things—the house, cars, shirts, and shoes—to aspire to the possession of Daisy. That he thinks of Daisy in terms of material goods is pathetic and amusing, but not tragic. What makes Gatsby tragic is revealed, in part, in the climactic confrontation between Gatsby and Buchanan, when Gatsby, forcing Daisy to tell Tom that she does not love him, says, "Just tell him the truth—that you never loved him—and it's all wiped out forever."[27] It is here that Fitzgerald subtly injects the historical note. Gatsby really believes that the past can be wiped out, that it does not matter, that a man can create himself anew by the exercise of his own will and energy.

Fitzgerald's instinctive fastening upon this quality in American life in his portrait of Gatsby is impressive for both its truth and its exemplification of how an artist may think with his viscera rather than with his brains. At least from the time of the predominance of industrialism, the comparative openness and restlessness of American society had encouraged men to indulge in the human desire to be re-born, to wipe out the mistakes of the past and to give oneself the second chance that we all so ardently want. The industrial and business folklore of the post-World

---

[26] A question arises whether the word "tragic" can be used of prose fiction. I believe that it can, although another book would be required to establish the evidence. Usage has given the word at least connotative validity, however.

[27] Faulkner causes one of his characters to say, "The past isn't dead. It ain't even past."

War I period held that a man could lift himself by his own bootstraps. The implication behind this idea was not only that appearance is more important than reality, but that appearance in fact *is* reality. In *The Great Gatsby*, Fitzgerald invented a rich situation balancing, on one side, the world of wealth, roots in family, and corresponding manners and mores, and on the other, the effort of Gatsby to compete with that rooted (and corrupt) world with his pink suit and his five months at Oxford. But the folklore of appearance gives Gatsby the energy to try to fulfill his vision, to secure, by whatever means, the money and things that he is encouraged to think will deliver Daisy into his arms.

That basic situation—the appearance versus the reality of American life—was responsible for most of Sinclair Lewis' work during the same period. What makes Fitzgerald's novel so superior to Lewis' work is the historical dimension, which has been there all along but which Fitzgerald does not insist upon until his beautifully written conclusion. First, we are shown Nick Carraway's Wordsworthian rejection of the wicked, citified east and his return to the "good" midwest: by implication a turning from contemporary moral shoddiness to an earlier, pastoral point in history when men were close to Nature and therefore virtuous. Then Fitzgerald gives us, through Nick's eyes, a remarkable, brief insight into Gatsby's plight, an insight made possible only by history:

> Most of the big shore places were closed now and there were hardly any lights except the shadowy, moving glow of a ferryboat across the Sound. And as the moon rose higher the inessential houses began to melt away until gradually I became aware of the old island here that flowered once for Dutch sailors' eyes—a fresh, green breast of the new world. Its vanished trees, the trees that had made way for Gatsby's house, had once pandered in whispers to the last and greatest of all human dreams; for a transitory enchanted moment man must have held his breath in the presence of this continent, compelled into an aesthetic contemplation he neither understood nor desired, face to face for the last time in history with something commensurate to his capacity for wonder.

Gatsby's desire for Daisy thus transcends mere lust for sexual and material indulgence. He becomes, through his belief in the "orgastic future," however futile, a historical hero in his very denial of history, and his adventure is saved from tawdriness by his implied identity with the Dutch sailors "face to face for the last time in history with something commensurate to [man's] capacity for wonder." A certain irony lies in the fact that what Brooks and Rosenfeld thought they had found in Sherwood Anderson was fully present a short time later in Fitzgerald's conception of Gatsby.

Thus Fitzgerald moved on from his earlier theme of youthful illusion and reality, that easy and conventional novel of *Bildung*, to broach a far more interesting theme, one that is at the same time a natural transformation of *Bildung:* the role of will in human destiny. It is one of the great modern themes, and one that permits us to place Fitzgerald within the perspective of a group of fine European novelists, specifically the Unamuno of *Abel Sánchez*, the Pío Baroja of *El Arbol de la ciencia*, of André Gide's best work, and above all, the fiction of André Malraux. At the same time, Fitzgerald's apprehension of history in *The Great Gatsby* allies him to such contemporary poets as Hart Crane in *The Bridge*, T. S. Eliot in *The Waste Land*, and Ezra Pound in the *Cantos*. It is an honorable company.

Unfortunately, Fitzgerald was not certain that he belonged in such company, nor did the literary climate of the day offer him enough of substance to countermand his self-distrust. It did offer him easy success, quite a lot of money, and reasons to be vulgar and contemporary in the manner that came readily to him. Although there existed in America a specialized philosophical circle, the philosophical sustenance that Fitzgerald needed was not available to him. More accurately, he was not available to it, nor was any other contemporary writer of power and originality. The European had at least the illusion that he lived in a society that encouraged him to use the full reaches of his mind both inventively and philosophically, or that he lived in a society in which he was left alone to go his way. Fitzgerald looked for a schema and found only a one-way trip to Hollywood.

By the time *Tender Is the Night* appeared in 1934, his last novel to appear during his lifetime, Fitzgerald's self-distrust was such that he reverted to his earlier pattern of the tragic situation lacking a tragic cast to portray it. For all the occasional finenesses of that novel, Dick and Nicole Diver, the central figures, are realized only as pathetic and, in a peculiar manner, personal. Again, one must feel that Fitzgerald opened doors without realizing it, that when he thought he was being objective, he was in truth merely writing autobiographically. Still, without *The Great Gatsby*, *Tender Is the Night* would have to rank as Fitzgerald's masterpiece. Following upon *The Great Gatsby*, however, it appears eccentric and thin for lack of the rich social and historical context of the earlier novel. Fitzgerald's self-confidence after 1934 was so shaken that he actually changed the sequence of events in *Tender Is the Night* in response to criticism. In the opinion of many subsequent readers, this further weakened the novel.

Fitzgerald's suspicion of himself and his gifts further resulted in his apparent need to flagellate himself in public and to carry on about his "failure." He wanted to be seen as an innocent, gifted, thirty- to forty-year-old youth, and at the same time as a master of his craft. To an unusual degree the world indulged him, but it broke him in the process. He is peculiarly American in all this, and it is no mystery that both his work and his life have continued to attract more than their share of attention: there seems to be something of all Americans in his contradictory makeup, qualities at once crass and delicate. He was a representative man; he knew it, and his knowledge was more than he could live with. He was forty-four at the time of his death in 1940.

3
The
Useable
Present

With the exception of T. S. Eliot and William Faulkner, no recent American writer's place in literary history is more secure than Ernest Hemingway's. At the same time, the evidence for his eminence is uniquely contradictory and confusing. No other writer has posed such problems. Since the American publication of *In Our Time* in 1925 and continuing without abatement in the years after his death in 1961, commentators have been by turns excessively familiar or uncomfortable, rashly laudatory or insulting, about Hemingway's literary output. He has been seen as a primitive and as a decadent sophisticate; as prototypical American and as displaced, uprooted cosmopolitan; as a realist, a naturalist, a romantic, a classicist, and a symbolist; as a merely clever reporter and as a master of the rank of Stendhal, Flaubert, and Stephen Crane; as nihilist, Ur-existentialist, and humanist. No writer's personal life, not even Byron's (to whom he also has been compared), has been more fully sifted for matter with which to slur his literary reputation. Hemingway, accordingly, is a fascinating and difficult subject for literary history. He is still close to us in time, and still subject to an acrimonious debate in which the literary and the non-literary continue to be confused.

Reasons for the critical fury over Hemingway are not far to seek, and at the center of the tempest is the figure of Hemingway himself, a victim, in a sense, of his considerable public success after the appearance of *A Farewell to Arms* in 1929, when he was thirty. He then began to assume the mask that he was to wear with increasing frequency until his death. In metaphors from boxing and baseball, he contrived to outrage many of his admirers and to delight his enemies. From the beginning of his fame, Hemingway displayed an American discomfort with the public role of writer and intellectual that necessarily was his on the evidence of his published work. As so many of his critics complained, he preferred to pose as a fisherman, big game hunter, boxer, rail bird, heavy drinker, sexual athelete, aficionado of baseball, bullfighting, and warfare rather than as a writer, as what in Europe would be called unblushingly a "man of letters." Although there has been some change on the part of both the public and writers, Americans are still uncomfortable with the idea of the "man of letters," and we must recall that men of letters such as Henry James, T. S. Eliot—and Ernest Hemingway—preferred residence in England, the Continent, or Cuba to their native country. To assume a mask was common in the period, as we know from the example of Pound, Yeats, and Eliot. Hemingway's mask, however, annoyed people with his seeming refusal to be serious, his aggressive anti-intellectualism, and finally, by the time of the writing of *A Moveable Feast*,[1] with his cruelty and uncharacteristic lack of generosity.

No matter how he chose to present himself to reporters and to the many other people who pressed in upon him for their own particular purposes, Hemingway was foremost and finally a deeply serious writer. As in the case of Fitzgerald or any other artist, Hemingway's personal life belongs to his memory, it belongs to him; it is none of our business. His writing belongs to us, however, and when gossip about him in the guise of biography is no longer occasion for public *frisson*, we shall be more fully capable of gratitude to Hemingway for that writing. The poet Delmore Schwartz struck the proper objective and serious note when he wrote that in the perspective of the past, Hemingway was most like Jane Austen, "who was very much interested in a special kind of conduct. . . . She also used conversation for the sake of a kind of rhetoric."[2] The idea of comparing the creator of Mr. Knightley with the creator of

---

[1] Only disease and impending death can explain Hemingway's disturbing portraits in that book of F. Scott Fitzgerald, Gertrude Stein, Ford Madox Ford, and Wyndham Lewis.

[2] Delmore Schwartz, "Ernest Hemingway's Literary Situation," in John K. McCaffery (ed.), *Ernest Hemingway: The Man and His Work* (Cleveland and New York, 1950), p. 117.

Count Mippipopolous may be shocking, yet Schwartz's perception is wonderfully evocative. It opens out Hemingway's work and reveals to us the nature of his seriousness and power, as well as his limitations. This is to agree, with reservations, with the judgment that Hemingway was a kind of classicist in his best work, the work up to but not including *Death in the Afternoon* (1932).[3] Before considering his "classical" attributes in detail, however, one must observe Hemingway's Byronic, romantic effect upon his time, the degree to which he influenced not only literary style but also public and private conduct. Two excellent witnesses, Scott Fitzgerald and Robert Penn Warren, testify to these two aspects of Hemingway's influence. In 1934, Fitzgerald wrote to Hemingway:

> I think it is obvious that my respect for your artistic life is absolutely unqualified, that save for a few of the dead or dying old men you are the only man writing fiction in America that I look up to very much. There are pieces and paragraphs of your work that I read over and over—in fact, I stopped myself doing it for a year and a half because I was afraid that your particular rhythms were going to creep in on mine by process of infiltration.[4]

Warren wrote:

> *A Farewell to Arms*, which appeared ten years after the First World War and on the eve of the collapse of the Great Boom, seemed to sum up and bring to focus an inner meaning of the decade being finished. It worked thus, not because it disclosed the end results that the life of the decade was producing —the discontents and disasters that were beginning to be noticed even by unreflective people—but because it cut back to the beginning of the process, to the moment that had held within itself the explanation of the subsequent process. Those who had grown up in the war, in the shadow of the war, could look back nostalgically, as it were, to the lost moment of innocence of motive and purity of emotion.[5]

Even before *A Farewell to Arms*, however, Hemingway had defined a style of speech and indeed a style of life for a generation, a style that

---

[3] Hemingway's published writing of the period of this history was: *Three Stories and Ten Poems* (Paris), 1923; *In Our Time* (Paris), 1924 [the sketches which were to make up the inter-chapters of the American edition of the next year]; *In Our Time* (New York), 1925; *The Torrents of Spring* and *The Sun Also Rises*, 1926; *Men Without Women*, 1927; *A Farewell to Arms*, 1929; *Death in the Afternoon*, 1932.

[4] Letter of June 1, 1934. Andrew Turnbull (ed.), *The Letters of F. Scott Fitzgerald* (New York, 1963), p. 309.

[5] Robert Penn Warren, Introduction to *A Farewell to Arms*, *Three Novels of Ernest Hemingway* (New York, 1962), pp. iv–v.

continued to dominate the impressionable until World War II. To Warren's comment about the twenties, one must add that for the young of the thirties, the generation of World War II, Hemingway more than any other writer defined war and one's place, or lack of place, in it. Without hesitation, one may attribute the lack of idealism, together with an uncrippling stoicism on the part of combatants in World War II in large part to Hemingway.[6] This fact provided the case for a return to Byron to find so widespread an influence of a writer upon so large a public. If anything, Hemingway's influence was more pervasive than Byron's. Hemingway attained that legendary state, like Marx and Freud, in which people who had not read him were nevertheless influenced by him. In World War II, men who had read him and men who had not learned from him how to live with disaster, and many learned how to die with it. Few writers have taught so direct a lesson.

In any attempt to account for Hemingway's impact, it is at once obvious that the answer has little or nothing to do with his subject matter, his paraphraseable content. Other writers, notably Henry de Montherlant in France, covered the same subject matter. Montherlant wrote of bullfighting, sport, and war before Hemingway, of boyhood, religion, love, and death, but Montherlant's impact, although considerable, has been negligible in comparison to Hemingway's. Hemingway's impact lay in his style. He was the first American since Mark Twain to alter radically the literary language of the country. While he stands in the line of Mark Twain, Hemingway is not simply another direct product of Twain, like Sherwood Anderson. It is essential to observe his conception of style, in theory and in fact.[7]

Hemingway was generous, and generous to himself, in analyses of

[6] This is in no sense to agree with Van Wyck Brooks, Bernard De Voto, or Archibald MacLeish, who at the outbreak of World War II accused Hemingway, John Dos Passos, and other writers of the period of incapacitating the young for war service by their unpatriotic cynicism. The truth, in the event, was exactly the opposite. The accusation is answered in Chapter 9.

[7] Leon Edel has written that Hemingway "belongs to the second shelf of American fiction, not the first," along with Sinclair Lewis, because he gave only the illusion of style. "A Style involves substance as well as form. . . . I would argue that Hemingway has not created a Style: he has rather created the artful illusion of a Style. . . . He has conjured up the *effect* of a Style by a process of evasion, very much as he sets up an aura of emotion—by walking directly away from emotion! . . . He has not written an 'adult' novel." "The Art of Evasion," in *Hemingway: A Collection of Critical Essays*, (ed.) R. P. Weeks (Englewood Cliffs, N. J., 1962), pp. 169–170.

his own style. We need to read with skepticism his accounts of his difficult apprenticeship after World War I, his comparison in *Death in the Afternoon* of a good style (his) to an iceberg, seven-eighths under water; his description of reaching down, through rigorous excision, to the exact sequence of event, emotion, and words. One of the things that put people off Hemingway is his implication that he was the only writer who ever taught himself to write, the only writer who ever went hungry and suffered for his art. As for his famous event-emotion-word sequence, it is unduly behavioristic and over-simplified. A more trustworthy analysis may be found in the fiction itself. One example is the early story "Soldier's Home," from Hemingway's first collection of stories, *In Our Time.* Young Krebs has returned from the war to his Kansas home town to find that no one wants to hear the truth about experience in combat, for the townspeople have heard so many atrocities that truth is tame. Krebs, like the other returned soldiers, obliges with lies:

> Krebs found that to be listened to at all he had to lie, and after he had done this twice he, too, had a reaction against the war and against talking about it. A distaste for everything that had happened to him in the war set in because of the lies he had told. All of the times that had been able to make him feel cool and clear inside himself when he thought of them; the times so long back when he had done the one thing, the only thing for a man to do, easily and naturally, when he might have done something else, now lost their cool, valuable quality and then were lost themselves. . . .
>
> Krebs acquired the nausea in regard to experience that is the result of untruth and exaggeration. . . .

One of Hemingway's best stories, "Soldier's Home," ends with Krebs' pious mother conveying to him that his father thinks it is time for him to "settle down" and get a job. Krebs' blank reaction leads the mother to ask whether he loves her. He answers no, that he doesn't love anyone. She weeps, forces him to pray with her, and forces from him the lie that he does love her. He feels sorry for her, "and she had made him lie." He determines to go to Kansas City to get a job. In the meantime, he goes to the schoolyard to watch his sister play indoor baseball, the little sister whom he indeed loves.

The conception not only of a literary style, but also of a life style, far from a simple one, *pace* Leon Edel, is manifest in this short story. It is also present in considerably more complex form in Hemingway's novels of the twenties. But in Krebs' thoughts, the conception is more simple than the reality. Hemingway seems to confine Krebs, and himself, to "the times that had been able to make him feel cool and clear inside himself . . . the times so long back when he had done the one thing, the only thing for a man to do, easily and naturally, when he might have done something else. . . ."

The reality of that conception is Proustian in its complexity, if we can conceive of a Proust whose first impulse is ethical, as Hemingway's (and Krebs') is, both here and without exception, in all his fiction.[8]

The most brilliant effects in *A la Recherche du temps perdu* emerge from Proust's juxtaposition of past and present, and from his narrator's fine perception in the final volume that his life will have form and meaning through his writing all the events that Proust has written for us, his collaborators. Memory, then, is all-important, and memory is almost as prominent in Hemingway as it is in Proust. Hemingway does not make novelistic capital of it, like Proust, but it is very much there in both his practice and his pronouncements on style. At the same time, both writers are vivid to us because of their ability to render wonderfully sensuous accounts of nature. "Big Two-Hearted River" can be read with profit alongside passages of natural description in *Au Côté du chez Guermantes*. Each is far more than description; each is a product of memory. Hemingway differs radically from Proust, of course, in the burden he places upon irony; that, in turn, makes for excision and concision, as opposed to Proust's expansiveness. In both writers, all the resources of their style conspired to form a profound criticism of their world.

For a long time, Hemingway's critics have been preoccupied with the question of influences upon his style. Mark Twain, Sherwood Anderson, Gertrude Stein, Ezra Pound, and Ford Madox Ford have been cited repeatedly to prove the case for influence. Hemingway himself, to be sure, often acknowledged his debt to Mark Twain, particularly to *Huckleberry Finn*. His ungenerous maneuvers to disengage himself from the alleged influence of Anderson, Gertrude Stein, and Ford, however, inevitably made the case "for" them and "against" Hemingway all the stronger. From Sherwood Anderson, Hemingway is supposed to have

[8] One of Hemingway's many reading lists contains Proust's *Remembrance of Things Past*. Other writers on the list are: Maupassant, Stendhal, Baudelaire, Flaubert, Mann, Gogol, Dostoevsky, Tolstoy, Mark Twain, Melville, Hawthorne, Stephen Crane, and Henry James ("Madame de Mauves"). Lillian Ross, *Portrait of Hemingway* (New York, 1961), p. 18.

got his taste for "primitive" illiterate characters; we know that Anderson introduced him to Gertrude Stein. One can sense Anderson's touch in the early story "My Old Man" (1923). The subject of horse-racing, the use of a boy narrator, and the mystified tone all smack of Anderson. Hemingway falls beneath Anderson in that single story, however, when he endows the boy with the perceptions of an adult, giving us artiness rather than art.[9] Hemingway's rejection of Anderson is painfully explicit in his parody of, among other things, *Dark Laughter* in *The Torrents of Spring*, his least professional work.

From Gertrude Stein, Hemingway is supposed to have learned his simplified syntax, the clauses connected by "and" rather than subordinated in the traditional manner; she is also supposed to have taught him the trick of repetition of word and perhaps of idea. Together with Pound and Ford, she is further supposed to have taught Hemingway to excise the unnecessary, to eliminate adjectives and adverbs. One could make this stew of influence still more savory by suggesting that Péguy, whom Hemingway almost certainly knew about in his formative years, also used repetition, or that Jacques Rivière, "influenced" Hemingway when he wrote of style, "However difficult it may appear, when we fasten our eyes upon the object it always ends by inventing within us whatever is necessary to express it and to make it clear to others' eyes."[10]

Like some patterns in chinaware, Hemingway's style has been so widely imitated by inferior writers that it is hard for us to react to the original. It, too, may seem to have been debased, and we need to make the historical effort to feel the impact of the original before it had been widely but only approximately imitated. No list of influences can account for Hemingway's style—or for anyone else's. He of course learned from others, but the result was original if only because it was a style, not pastiche. As in a geological epoch, Hemingway's style may be separated into early, middle, and late strata, although some overlapping occurs.

In the early style, which extends through *The Sun Also Rises*, the sentences are short, mainly declarative, and the diction is simple and

---

[9] Hemingway met Anderson in Chicago in 1920. Anderson wrote publishers' puffs for both *In Our Time* and *A Farewell to Arms*. Hemingway reviewed *A Story-Teller's Story* for *Ex Libris*, Paris, in 1925. See John T. Flanagan, "Hemingway's Debt to Sherwood Anderson," *Journal of English and Germanic Philology*, LIV (1955), 507–520.

[10] Jacques Rivière, *Nouvelles études* (Paris, 1947), p. 79.

un-Latinate. With the sole exception of "My Old Man," all the short stories in *In Our Time* are narrated in the third person, but the illusion of objectivity is carefully maintained. Dialogue is dramatic, ironic, repetitive, and oblique. Understatement and humor reinforce the sense of a keen intelligence in command of an eye alert for facts and patterns in nature and in human conduct. At its best, the early style is capable of generating emotional effects seemingly out of all proportion to the few devices which, on the surface, appear to be at work. At its worst, as in "Today Is Friday," that style is false and sentimental; it begs for parody. The middle style has the attributes of the early style, but it is more supple and capable of a wider range. In it, Hemingway often used the subjunctive as well as subordinate clauses in place of the mannered, continual reliance on the connective "and." It is the style of *A Farewell to Arms* and the best of the later short stories: "The Short Happy Life of Francis Macomber" and "The Snows of Kilimanjaro." The late style, as we encounter it in *Death in the Afternoon* or in *Across the River and Into the Trees*, by contrast, is rococo. The sentences become long and often clotted, the irony heavier, the first person unliterary and personal in the non-fictional, while the fiction deteriorates into clumsy symbolism. Even in his late style, however, Hemingway often wrote paragraphs, pages, and occasional chapters as good as anything of his earlier, purer periods.

One may account for the popular success of Hemingway's style, or styles, in his ability to project through style the illusion that complex matters of conscience and conduct can be reduced to their elements, ordered, and so dominated. Hemingway seemed to have perfected that process, and inhabitants of an imperfect world admire perfection. In truth, the style is limited and flawed, although the flaws are artfully concealed and the limitations made to seem sources of strength. Unlike Fitzgerald's fiction, Hemingway's is outside or beyond history. In his selection of character and incident and in his prose style, the historical past cannot be evoked, not even in the occasional allusions to historical event. In place of history, Hemingway (like Proust, as was noted) gives us memory, but memory is quite another matter. The style is contemporary without being local or provincial; this accounts for its freshness and its attraction for people who themselves lack a sense of history, or who do not want the writer to thicken his context by an appeal to the historical consciousness. Hemingway's world, by and large, is the world of ever-unfolding present rather than past phenomena, even though the phenomena occurred in narrative time past. Thus a characteristic passage from Chapter XX of *A Farewell to Arms:*

> We four drove out to San Siro in an open carriage. It was a lovely day and we drove out through the park and out along the tramway and out of town where the road was dusty. There were villas with iron fences and big overgrown gardens and ditches with water flowing and green vegetable gardens with dust on the leaves. We could look across the plain and see farmhouses and the rich green farms with their irrigation ditches and the mountains to the north. There were many carriages going into the race track and the men at the gate let us in without cards because we were in uniform.

The anti-historical, descriptive "and" produces a vivid visual flow of images, but it can do little more. A related anti-historical device is Hemingway's use, in the two early novels, of a first-person narrator. Although that device imparts vividness and ensures the reader's involvement, the narrators keep us in the flow of the present, rigidly within the dramatic unfolding of the narrative; they do not permit us to range into the historical past. Hemingway, in fact, used the techniques of the short story in the novel, a form traditionally within and essentially "about" history. He occasionally alludes to actual people and events, as in *The Sun Also Rises*, when he presents the historical bullfighters, Juan Belmonte and Marcial Lalanda. Their historicity, however, violates Hemingway's carefully constructed illusion of reality, and the reader is conscious of the bump of violation.

Another limitation of Hemingway's narrators, particularly of Frederick Henry in *A Farewell to Arms*, is that they are unusual, even heroic men who are forced by the author into the position of recounting to us their own heroism; this is in itself a violation of character, for they are supposed to be sympathetic and reticent. Aware of the difficulty, Hemingway tempers their deeds with humor and understatement; yet at the same time, we may be put off by their eternal knowingness, their oppressive expertise. Henry knows weapons, wines, food, cities, architecture, painting, languages, surgery, tactics and strategy, bartenders, Count Griffi, horses, and the detailed coastline of Lago Maggiore in the dark. As a result, he ought to be insufferable; it is a tribute to Hemingway that for most readers he remains sympathetic to the end. Hemingway's main device for preserving our sympathy with his heroes is his skillful use of dialogue. His dialogue is apparently realistic and always dramatic

It usually reflects an attitude or set of attitudes toward the subject and toward life. It is allusive and oblique, hovering, economical, and eloquent without eloquence in the traditional sense. It has been almost universally praised, even though Hemingway's British characters, particularly those in *The Sun Also Rises*, speak a language that appears to derive more from P. G. Wodehouse's Bertie Wooster than from life. It is not true, as one of Hemingway's characters says, that the English use fewer words than the Eskimos.

Although there is a community of agreement about Hemingway's dialogue, there is none about other aspects of his work. That lack of agreement is rooted in confusion over what he was trying to do and what his subject matter actually was. The usual method of attack is to note the human limitations of his characters, the self-imposed limitations of his style, and finally, the resulting impossibility of philosophical or any other sort of profundity. In 1934, Wyndham Lewis spoke for a number of critics before and since in his villainous essay, "The Dumb Ox: A Study of Ernest Hemingway," in which he scorned Hemingway's selection of characters because he considered them "empty of will," people "to whom things happen."[11] Two years later, John Peale Bishop was to expand the theme, when he wrote of Hemingway's characters:

> It is because they have no will and not because they are without intelligence that the men and women in Hemingway are devoid of spiritual being. Their world is one in time with the War and the following confusion, and is a world without traditional values. That loss has been consciously set down.

Again,

> Byron's tradition is sinister and romantic, Hemingway's manly and low-brow.[12]

Behind such comment lies a snobbish contempt for a kind of character and a kind of human being, whether boxer, gangster, sportsman, soldier, or bullfighter. Who is to say that such people are not worthy of a writer's attention? That attitude is not only indefensible, it is also founded upon a misreading of Hemingway's texts and a misunderstanding of his themes and literary procedures.

[11] Lewis' essay appeared twice in 1934; first in *Life and Letters* (April, 1934), then reprinted in Lewis' book, *Men Without Art* (London, 1934), pp. 17–41.

[12] John Peale Bishop, "Homage to Hemingway," *Collected Essays*, (ed.) Edmund Wilson (New York, 1948), pp. 39–44.

Only if Hemingway's work is read as naturalistic is it possible to interpret his characters as Wyndham Lewis and John Peale Bishop would have us do. Hemingway, on his part, was perfectly willing to encourage the naturalistic interpretation in his game of hide-and-seek with the public. His techniques, in turn, do look naturalistic to the casual eye: his selection of "low-brow" characters, his illusion of fidelity to common speech, his emphasis upon sexuality, his scorn for received ideas and accepted social institutions. Behind the apparent naturalism, however, is a conception of human experience that has nothing whatsoever to do with naturalism. Hemingway's most memorable characters seem to be men "to whom things happen," but they are also men who cause things to happen. Argument arises over what exactly those things are. They are, briefly, spiritual in nature but expressed in lay terms. Hemingway selects his characters for their possession of qualities which interest him: they are men on trial, men at the end of their tether, men often in ultimate situations which force the protagonists into a declaration, through action, of their first principles. War, sport, and the performing art of bullfighting accordingly are valuable contexts for such a writer, and Hemingway spent his career in working out their implications. His conception is religious, not philosophical, because the nature of his heavily disguised dialectic is spiritual rather than logical, specifically Christian but not theological.[13]

In his early short stories, Hemingway was concerned with the ethics

[13] A remark from a memoir concerning Ludwig Wittgenstein may well apply to Hemingway: "It seems to me that there are two forms of seriousness of character. One is fixed in 'strong principles'; the other springs from a passionate heart. The former has to do with morality and the latter, I believe, is closer to religion." Georg Henrik Von Wright, "Biographical Sketch," in Norman Malcolm, *Ludwig Wittgenstein, A Memoir* (London, 1958), p. 19. R. W. B. Lewis, in his critical biography of Hart Crane, has this to day; "Crane believed that poetry was redemptive of human life, that it was the major modern source of revelation; but unlike [Wallace] Stevens, Crane felt that poetry was not an absolute replacement of a belief in God, . . . Like Hemingway, Crane sought religious values in human actions and temporal actualities; but where Hemingway and his characters made the grand tragic mistake of seeking religious substitutes in the natural world, Crane saw the divine *within* that world, energizing and illuminating it." Lewis' criticism is just, although he does not take into account the differences between Crane's medium, lyric poetry and Hemingway's prose fiction. Hemingway's apprehension may be seen as closer to Crane's than Lewis would allow, and not entirely confined to "seeking religious substitutes in the natural world." We are driven back upon the question of Hemingway's literary naturalism. See Lewis' *The Poetry of Hart Crane* (Princeton, N. J., 1967), p. 282.

of individual behavior, but one could not yet describe his concern as religious. By the time of *The Sun Also Rises*, however, he had taken a new and interesting direction, one that he continued to follow with varying degrees of keenness until his death. It is instructive to consider *The Sun Also Rises* side by side with T. S. Eliot's *The Waste Land*, which Hemingway obviously had been reading. Eliot's dominating image of a land laid waste, deriving from the medieval legend of the Fisher King rendered sterile by a curse, provides the background for his depiction of the despair of a soul searching for the way to redemption. Despair in the poem is specifically modern, tied to contemporary London. Eliot provides resonance for his theme by ranging into history and into non-Christian cultures and rituals for examples of the possibilities of regeneration in the past. Eliot's characters are empty and flat, in particular, their small lusts banal and distasteful. Tiresias, the man-woman who is both yet neither, with his gift of prophecy, is all too appropriate.

In Hemingway's novel, Paris rather than London is the waste land, while the curse that has devastated the land and its inhabitants is the recent war. The majority of Hemingway's characters are as banal as Eliot's, and for the same reasons. They exist only to feed paltry appetites; they are unnatural. Hemingway adapts the Fisher King analogy to his purposes in the character of Jake Barnes, made impotent by his war wound, narrator and moral measure of the conduct of all. Like Eliot, Hemingway emphasizes sexuality through Barnes, his Tiresias. Paris abounds in homosexuals, the essence of sterility. Brett Ashley is a nymphomaniac and an alcoholic with whom Barnes is in love, and it is witness to Hemingway's power that the situation is not ludicrous. Campbell, Brett's fiancé, is a bankrupt spendthrift and an alcoholic. But where Eliot escapes from banality into history, Hemingway escapes into nature and into the art and ritual of bullfighting. The trout fishing episode in Navarre contrasts dramatically with the scenes in Paris, Hemingway's "rats' alley/Where the dead men lost their bones." Pamplona, the fiesta of San Fermin with its drunken dancing in the street, and particularly its bullfighting, provides Hemingway with contrast to his many scenes of the waste land. Romero, the young bullfighter, stands outside the waste land, saved by the ritual in which he has a central part. He is lured by the sexual availability of Brett, who is called a "Circe," and he is the occasion of her redeeming act of renunciation of him in Madrid, at the end of the novel.

It is further tempting to see Count Mippopopulous, with his arrow wound, as Hemingway's Madame Sosostris, and to discover actual lines of Eliot's poem that Hemingway might have had in mind in certain scenes: Barnes, on the beach at San Sebastian after San Fermin, miserable and let down, recalls "On Margate Sands/I can connect/Nothing with nothing." But it is not necessary to drive the parallel to inordinate length. The element that cannot be seen in quotation or allusion to events from either work is the religious element proper. Both works are religious in the same way—allusively, privately, surprisingly. Neither work is exclusively Christian; unalloyed despair works against such a conclusion. But the spiritual nature of the poem, together with the qualities of the novel which have survived the passage of time, enforces such a conclusion. *The Sun Also Rises* survives in spite of many references that are local and dated, in spite of some of the slang that is merely quaint. It survives for its specifically religious impact, a quality that criticism customarily has been blind to. The much-quoted dialogue between Brett and Jake Barnes at the conclusion omits the overtly religious expression. Brett, age thirty-four, has voluntarily given up Romero, the bullfighter, age nineteen.

> "You know it makes one feel rather good deciding not to be a bitch."
> "Yes."

The quotation usually stops there. But Hemingway went on:

> "It's sort of what we have instead of God."
> "Some people have God," I said. "Quite a lot."

To return to the question of will in Hemingway's characters, we may now see Jake Barnes as a specifically Christian hero who works against the standards of conduct of his time, who measures and indeed judges conduct, and whom others respect, admire, and follow. Those same qualities are even more apparent in Frederick Henry, of *A Farewell to Arms*. In that novel, the continuing dialogue between the priest and Henry points to a specifically Christian reading, to Henry's continuing awareness of Christian salvation and of the theme that he, and later Catherine Barkley, are beyond the Christian pale. Hemingway contrives the scenes of war in such a manner that the war is monstrous, inhuman, and horrible. Henry's desertion is not only very much a product of his will, it is the only possible act that he can take and preserve self-respect. In context, the contrast between the public world—the war—and the private world of human love, leading to Catherine Barkley's death in childbirth, has an exalted, would-be spiritual aspect. It fails, but the impulse is similar to that in the earlier and better novel. *The Sun Also Rises*, with its passages of ritual and its saving level of spiritual meaning, has elements of universality. *A Farewell to Arms*, most brilliant in patches, suffers from a lapse in taste. The love affair is novelettish, improbable, and no amount of stylistic brilliance can save it from its surprising vulgarity.

Hemingway's short fiction abounds in religious motifs, such as the little boy of "Fathers and Sons" who thinks he ought to pray at his grandfather's tomb, and the nun in "The Gambler, the Nun, and the Radio" who wants to become a saint. The best of that fiction is not overtly religious, however; it is spiritual in the sense that *The Sun Also Rises* is spiritual. One thinks here of the superb "The Snows of Kilimanjaro" and of what is perhaps Hemingway's finest story, "A Clean, Well-Lighted Place." In that story, with the old man who has attempted to hang himself and who does not want to leave the clean, well-lighted café for his home, and the waiter who concludes the story with his version of the Lord's Prayer, substituting *"nada"*—nothing—for the nouns, we are presumed to have Hemingway's nihilistic, if not atheistic, denial of religion. Such is hardly the case. What we have, rather, is a conception of religion common in Spain, particularly in the philosophy and fiction of Miguel de Unamuno and in the fiction of Pío Baroja.[14] It is a conception in which consciousness of death is constant and vivid, together with despair at the human lot. Despair, according to the Roman Catholic Church, is a sin, and both Unamuno and Hemingway are sinful and even heretical in their depiction of souls in despair. *"Nada,"* then, becomes an exclamation of despair, but not a denial of God or a negation of religion. Unamuno's re-telling of the legend of Cain and Abel in *Abel Sánchez* (1917), in which Joaquíun Monegro, the Cain figure, says, *"La humanidad es lo más cochino que hay"* (Humanity is the most vile condition there is), is parallel to Hemingway's *"nada."* Unamuno, like Hemingway, was obsessed by the possibilities and the limitations of human will in human affairs. It is not by chance that both writers have

---

[14] It may be relevant, although undue importance might be attached, that Hemingway visited Baroja in 1956 on his death bed in Madrid, told him that he had learned from him, and that he, Baroja, rather than Hemingway, should have been awarded the Nobel Prize. The best account is that of J. L. Castillo-Puche, *Hemingway entre la vida y la muerte* (Barcelona, 1968), pp. 319–326.

been claimed for existentialism,[15] Unamuno with far greater justification than Hemingway, to be sure.

The epigraph to *Winner Take Nothing* reads, "Unlike all other forms of lutte or combat the conditions are that the winner shall take nothing; neither his ease, nor his pleasure, nor any notions of glory; nor, if he win far enough, shall there be any reward within himself." It comes as no surprise to learn that Hemingway did not find his epigraph in a Renaissance book of rules for gambling, but that he wrote it himself.[16] It is perhaps the finest and most accurate brief description of Hemingway's heroes, of what he set out to do in his best work and what in the main he accomplished. It is also a profoundly religious sentiment, not the religion of popular Christianity, but the purer conception of an Augustine or a Loyola. And like many other austere conceptions, the epigraph conceived as a religious expression is open to accusation as the deadly sin of pride and to the suspicion of heresy.

Hemingway's religious bent does not in itself make him a better writer, nor does it give him a fuller claim to historical permanence. It does serve a valuable critical and historical purpose, however: it helps to explain that what some critics have read as symbolic force in his work is spiritual or quasi-religious force. That force helps to produce Hemingway's effect of "simplicity," directness, and what there is in him of universality. At the same time, the religious motif disposed of claims that he is a symbolist.[17]

At his best, in the work up to the early thirties, Hemingway is a symbolist only in the sense that every successful imaginative writer is one, creating images and characters that take on a life and meaning of their own as they are interpreted according to the private experience of a large variety of readers. (When Hemingway set out consciously to write symbolically, as in *The Old Man and the Sea* (1952), the results were painful and unworthy. The overt identification of the old man's agony with that of Christ crucified becomes a parody of Hemingway's genuine religious bent; it stands as a depressing reminder of his artistic decline.)

---

[15] John Killinger, *Hemingway and the Dead Gods* (University of Kansas Press, 1960), tries to link Hemingway to Nietzsche, Camus, and Sartre.

[16] Carlos Baker, *Hemingway: the Writer as Artist* (Princeton, 1956), p. 142.

[17] Carlos Baker's central claim for Hemingway "as artist" in *Hemingway: the Writer as . . .* is that a continuing set of symbols are consciously manipulated throughout much of the fiction. Caroline Gordon, "Notes on Hemingway and Kafka," *Sewanee Review*, LVII (Spring, 1949), 214–226, also sees Hemingway as a symbolist, but not enough of one to be as good as Kafka.

Hemingway's style, like Unamuno's, works against the religious interpretation. With its profanity, its apparent avoidance of the abstract, its
humor, it becomes another source of irony in the disparity between
what is announced and what is said, between the secular and the religious
interpretation of a sequence of events. Readers' reluctance to interpret
the work in terms of religion, their preference for symbolism, is evidence
of a basic anti-religious set of mind in the United States in the twenties
and later.

The book on bullfighting, *Death in the Afternoon* (1932), represents a
turning point in Hemingway's career. Here for the first time the style
often becomes clogged, beery, and self-indulgent, and we have the first
intimations of self-parody. Without the persona of narrator, Hemingway
can oppress us with his knowingness, his superiority, his suspiciously
frequent assertions of expertise. The style and manner are that of *The
Green Hills of Africa* (1935), yet contemporary criticism was kinder to
the early book than to the later one. Subject matter may account for the
difference: almost everyone has some notion about shooting an antelope,
but almost no one has a clue to the proper *lidia* to a bull. Reservations to
the contrary, *Death in the Afternoon* is valuable in itself and for its illumina-
tion of Hemingway's earlier and better work.

Hemingway has the great distinction of having been the first literate
non-Spanish person to perceive and to record with any authority that
bullfighting is neither a sport nor a circus spectacle, but an art. Second,
and more to the point, Hemingway saw the relationships between
bullfighting and prose fiction, and wrote convincingly about them.
Characteristically, he never actually defined those relationships in the
abstract, yet he made it clear that he was aware of them and that they
were valuable to him. Ostensibly, *Death in the Afternoon* is a complete
manual of bullfighting for the spectator, a series of discussions about
reading and writing, and a declaration of Hemingway's aesthetics in
terms of bullfighting. As a writer looking not for a useable past but for
a useable present, Hemingway found that bullfighting offered objective
material that was intrinsically interesting. As we have already noted, the
ritual element in bullfighting attracted Hemingway's religious impulse
and gave him a useful plane of reference. Finally, bullfighting was a
natural subject for a writer interested in men in ultimate situations, in
threats of violence, and in the individual dignity and satisfaction possibly
for the man who performs well in the ultimate situations.

Hemingway's very title, however, *Death in the Afternoon*, identifies a serious flaw in the book and in his conception of bullfighting; very possibly it reflects a flaw in his literary performance, too.[18] In the abstract, bullfighting is an art because of its unique relationship to nature and to reality. The bullfighter, like the writer, creates an entity that was not there before he began his work. As a result of talent and discipline, he dominates himself, and through self-domination, the bull, thus recombining all the elements involved—ritual, the particular animal, and himself—into a new reality.[19]

Hemingway seems to have known this, but as a writer he was more interested in the bullfighter than in the bull or in the other elements that make the art of the man possible. He emphasized gorings and deaths, consequently, out of all proportion to their incidence and importance to bullfighting. His judgments of individual bullfighters were sometimes ludicrously unfair, and his conception of what is basically a classical art was romantic. He looked for heroes and villains where none were, and his search distorted his much-vaunted technical knowledge, which was weaker than he knew. A literary parallel to his emphasis on death is the novelettish quality previously noted as a flaw in *A Farewell to Arms*, which is present even more embarrassingly in the late fiction. Bullfighting is heady stuff, by nature flamboyant and spectacular. When Hemingway was able to control his fondness for that side of it, he produced some of his finest short fiction. But when he indulged his propensity for romantic extremes, he lost control of both his style and his subject, as in two-thirds of *For Whom the Bell Tolls*.[20] The whole world of bulls obviously suggested to Hemingway a manner of containing violence through literature; thus he could write *The Sun Also Rises*, the finest war novel we have, without once taking us to the war. Bullfighting suggested further human attitudes and deeds that he could admire, no mean gift in a world where so little seemed admirable. In the process of taking from bullfighting what was useable, he gave us that neglected art, a munificent bonus to his imaginative work.

[18] I once asked a Spanish *matador de toros* if he knew Hemingway's *Muerte en la tarde*. He had never heard of the man or the book, but he laughed. When I asked why, he said that bullfighters do not go into the ring with a bull in order to die, but to live, and that my writer had it all wrong.

[19] See John McCormick (with Mario Sevilla Mascareñas), *The Complete Aficionado* (New York and London, 1967), chapter 1, "Toreo as Art."

[20] Castillo-Puche quotes a hostile Spanish newspaperman who said of *For Whom the Bell Tolls*, "*Oyó campanas sin saber exactamente dónde.*" "He heard bells without knowing exactly where from." *Hemingway entre la vida y la muerte*, p. 359.

The subject of bullfighting may help to explain the vexing question of Hemingway's influence. His defenders are frequently embarrassed when it is pointed out that Hemingway's stylistic influence in the United States has been clearest upon the most sentimental kind of newspaper feature story writing and upon detective-gangster (what used to be called "pulp") fiction. In general, the best writers do not have the poorest imitators. Why, then, should Hemingway be the exception? In large part, one suspects, because the image of the man rather than the image of the work has been imitated. Readers of *Death in the Afternoon* often come away with the notion of a tough American swaggering in the *callejón* at the *plaza de toros*, cutting a fine figure as he advises the bull-fighter which horn the bull favors, and perhaps guiding the surgeon's hand in the infirmary after the *cornada*. Hemingway's influence, that is to say, often is not a case of influence at all, but of imitation, and imitation of an attitude rather than of a literary style.

Abroad, Hemingway has fared rather better in the matter of influence, genuine or fancied. In *The Condemned Playground*, Cyril Connolly contrasted the difference in relationship to the reader between English novelists and American novelists, led by Hemingway. Connolly admired the "intimacy" that the American set up, writing for men of his own age and time, an intimacy, however, that may descend to "dogginess, but which in general brings out everything that is natural, easy and un-repressed" in the writer. "English novels seem always to be written for superiors or inferiors, older or younger people, or for the opposite sex.[21] Hemingway's influence, or "presence," has been variously reported in the writing of Graham Greene, Evelyn Waugh, Christopher Isherwood, the early Aldous Huxley, and strangest of all, D. H. Lawrence.[22] In France, Hemingway's mark has been seen upon writers so diverse as Montherlant, Prévost, Camus, and Sartre. Of such judgments, one can only remark the gross disparity in the quality of much French criticism between work on native writers as against work on foreign writers. In Germany, the comparative simplicity of the prose of Wolfgang Borchert, Heinrich Böll, Gerd Gaiser, Bastian Müller, and Siegfried Sommer is alleged to be Hemingway's responsibility. With far greater justification, Mario Praz has demonstrated with discrimination Hemingway's

---

[21] Connolly's essay, "Defects of English Novels," was written in 1935. Quoted by D. S. R. Welland, "Hemingway's English Reputation," in *The Literary Reputation of Hemingway in Europe*, (ed.) R. Asselineau (New York, 1965), p. 34.
[22] Welland, "Hemingway's English Reputation," p. 35.

influence upon the prose of Elio Vittorini, Giuseppe Berto, and Alberto Moravia.[23]

The whole question of literary influence at home or abroad is of interest not for its accuracy, but for its wild inaccuracy. When commentators begin to find "influence" in strange places, we know that we are in the presence of an important literary event. In Hemingway's case, that event may be defined as the confluence of several sources of literary energy which had been coming into existence for a century in both the United States and Europe. His work was immediately available to a wide public because it appeared, superficially, to be an advance upon a familiar process in narrative, the process of the naturalist, but a naturalist who spoke immediately, in all his dogginess, to both literary and nonliterary people. Style, or better rhetoric, was the vehicle of that popularity, but rhetoric as Delmore Schwartz conceives of it in his comparison between Jane Austen and Hemingway. In fact, Hemingway was not a naturalist, although he rang changes upon naturalism that were to serve him well in his depiction of manners and morals. He did indeed "use conversation for the sake of a kind of rhetoric," but that conversation was charged with moral and frankly religious meaning. To a traditional European concern with behavior he added an American interest in process: in how hay is made, how lumbermen mark trees, how trout are caught, how bulls are fought. These concerns made him neither a naturalist *manqué* nor a primitive, as his hostile critics would have it, but a realist *exalté*, a writer whose distinction is that he did all that was possible with his training and talent. His rejection of Gertrude Stein and Sherwood Anderson was part of his rejection of history itself. He was forced by his time, by that great violence, to turn away from writers who looked back and from a history for which he lacked taste and flair. But in so rigorously limiting himself to the present, he entered history, both as an artist and as a legend. However much we may dislike the legend, we cannot ignore the artist.

[23] Mario Praz, "Hemingway in Italy" in *The Literary Reputation of Hemingway in Europe*, pp. 108–123.

4

The
Romantic
Warriors

O monde, je veux ce que tu veux. Tout ce qui arrive arrive justement.—ALBAN DE BRICOULE, in *Le Songe* of Henry de Montherlant. In 1926, Régis Michaud collected in book form a series of lectures that he had given at the Sorbonne on contemporary American novelists. In the Foreword, he remarked that postwar American writers were no longer

> . . . wealthy bourgeois with time on their hands, nor graduates of the great universities, neither scholars nor professors nor professional globetrotters. . . . Most of them are "self-made men," literary parvenus, born of the people, very autochthonous, very American even though they may be of mixed national stock. Many if not most of them made their start in journalism.[1]

The comment is interesting for neither its accuracy nor its acuity—the entire book is a tissue of inaccuracies—but for its typicality. Europeans generally and the French in particular were by turns appalled and fascinated by what they saw, or thought they saw, in the post-war United States, and scarcely a year passed without a volume of profound superficialities by a French professor or Academician. Michaud implies that the wealthy bourgeois—for whom we may understand Henry James or Edith Wharton—is long departed, to be replaced by literary parvenus like Ernest Hemingway (whom, incidentally, Michaud identifies at one

[1] Régis Michaud, *Le Roman américain d'aujourd'hui* (Paris, 1926), p. 3.

point as "George" Hemingway). Michaud, Georges Duhamel, Bernard Faÿ and many more could not make up their minds whether to be delighted or horrified by the new American literary departures from what Michaud called "the accepted laws of decorum, perspective and harmony."

Michaud and the rest, however, cannot be criticized for lapses when American observers since the twenties have been preoccupied with drawing an impassable barrier between Palefaces—the school of Hawthorne and James—and Redskins—the school of Cooper and Mark Twain.[2] No matter how easy and attractive that thesis may be, it is wrong. One may find a good deal of Paleface in an alleged Redskin like Hemingway, while the entire post-war school of novel writing in America was a complex mixture of tradition and experimentation. A similar phenomenon took place in Europe. It is rewarding to compare writers on both sides of the Atlantic to determine, more precisely than is possible from the strictly national point of view, the components of the "new" novel and their relationship to the past. I shall return to Hemingway in order to round off our view of the previous chapter, and shall compare him with the writer often called "the French Hemingway," Henry de Montherlant. If we say that Hemingway derives from Byron, we may also say that Montherlant derives from Byron by way of d'Annunzio. Born in 1896, Montherlant fought in World War I, fought bulls as an *aficionado práctico* (one who faces bulls for love, not money), placed soccer, ran the 100 meters, wrote mediocre verse, fine novels and good plays, was versed in classical literature, a student of history, a member of the French Academy, and a citizen who has contempt for people who call him "the French Hemingway."

Even more than Hemingway, Montherlant has been the subject of critical debate, but more often on political than on literary grounds.[3]

---

[2] The terms are Phillip Rahv's, from his essay "Paleface and Redskin," in *Image and Idea*, first published in 1949. By 1961, Rahv's Palefaces and Redskins had turned into Harold Rosenberg's Redcoats and Coonskins in *The Tradition of the New*.

[3] Montherlant was accused of having collaborated with the Germans during World War II. He did not. He probably encouraged the charge through his advocacy in the twenties of reconciliation with Germany (along with Rolland, Romains, and Rivière) and through his almost despairing pessimism about the state of France at the outbreak of World War II. Montherlant told me that his apartment in Paris was ransacked twice by the Gestapo during the occupation. Then there is the famous (in France) episode of *Le Solstice de Juin*, published in 1941. It was first suppressed by the Germans, then authorized, when Montherlant's German translator, who had been appointed assistant director of the German Institute in Paris, intervened. The

Montherlant has used autobiography extensively in his fiction; hence it
may not be impertinent to examine aspects of his life. Three years older
than Hemingway, Montherlant was educated by the Jesuits, obtaining
his baccalaureate in 1914. By the age of sixteen, he had learned enough,
and that is a lot, about bullfighting to kill a *novillo* (a three-year-old bull)
at a festival near Burgos. After the war, he was gored in the lung while
caping a bull at the ranch of Samuel Flores near Albacete. In 1916
Montherlant volunteered for the infantry, and in 1918, like Hemingway,
he was greviously wounded in action. Precocious, like Hemingway, but
far more prolific, he published his first book, *La Relève du matin*, in 1920.
In 1922, his novel *Le Songe* appeared, and in 1924, *Les Olympiques*, perhaps
the finest writing in any language about sport. 1924 also marked the
publication of the moving *Chant funèbre pour les morts de Verdun*. From
1925 to 1933, Montherlant travelled and lived abroad, mainly in Algeria
and Morocco. In 1932 he completed a long novel of that region, *La Rose
de sable*, but he withheld it from definitive publication for political
reasons until 1968.[4] With the appearance of *Les Bestiaires* in 1926, his
first novel to be widely popular, of *Les Celibataires* in 1934, and of his
tetralogy *Les Jeunes filles*, between 1936 and 1939 (*Les Jeunes filles* and
Pitié pour les femmes, 1936; *Le Démon du bien*, 1937; and *Les Lépreuses*,
1939), his reputation as a novelist was assured. His later reputation as a
playwright, from the 1940's to the present, was so brilliant that it has
virtually eclipsed his fame as a novelist, a situation from which Montherlant
would derive grim satisfaction.

Lucid where Hemingway was silent or at best allusive; aloof, aristocratic, proudly solitary where Hemingway posed as the unshorn, un-
bathed, democratic man of the barrooms; learned, intellectual, a man of
letters, and an Academician where Hemingway affected the anti-
intellectual, the two writers might seem to have little in common other
than superficial biographical accident. The truth lies in the work; I
want therefore, to compare the two novels of World War I, *Le Songe*
and *A Farewell to Arms*, and to look briefly at *Les Bestiaires* (translated as
The Matador) in relation to some of Hemingway's writing about bullfighting.

French have always resented Montherlant's disdain for literary fashion, together
with his pretensions to aristocracy. Where the foreigner finds his claim to aristocratic
Castillian blood amusing, the French find it insulting.

4 In his *Avant-propos* to the definitive edition of *La Rose de sable* (Paris, 1968),
Montherlant gives a full account of the tortuous publishing history of the novel.

Our common phrase, "war novels," is particularly unsatisfactory when applied to either *Le Songe* or *A Farewell to Arms*. Both writers' true subject is the residue of war experience rather than the immediate trauma that subsequent experience cannot be conceived of *as* experience until it is extreme. The war determined the kind of artists they were. Their subject was not the war itself but the impact of extreme experience upon men and women. In both novels we find an interesting insistence upon the experience itself, an anachronistic conception of the heroic, and careful attention to the context of the experience in order to gain our sympathy for characters who might, without such attention, appear ludicrous. Neither novel has a plot. We recall that Hemingway begins *in medias res* with Frederick Henry in the ambulance service, attached to the Italian army on the Austrian front. He is wounded during an attack and sent for convalescence to Milan, where he has a passionate affair with the Scottish nurse, Catherine Barkley. Upon recovery, he is ordered up to the front again. In the retreat from Caporetto, Henry deserts, joins his now pregnant mistress, and makes his way with her to Switzerland, where she dies in childbirth.

We meet Montherlant's hero, Alban de Bricoule, in Paris in the middle of the war. Because of recent unsuccessful minor surgery, he has been assigned to non-combatant duty in Paris, but he "envies" his lycée classmates their deaths and determines to volunteer for combat. We also meet Dominique Soubrier, a young athlete in whom Alban is interested. She returns his interest warmly and comes to fall in love with him after he has gone to the front as an infantryman and she to duty as a nurse in a hospital not far from the lines. The bulk of the narrative has to do with Alban's reaction to combat, to his comrades, and to himself, whom he observes with total objectivity. He humiliates Dominique in the course of what develops into a cruelly comic assignation and returns to his company at the front.

Banal in dry outline, neither novel is so in fact. Hemingway's distinction, and his limitation, is that he sacrifices so much to the creation of drama. Character is mainly a product of drama and is revealed through action. The significant exception, however, is the scenes between Henry and the priest, in which Hemingway develops the religious theme beyond the limits of mere drama. Within the conventions that Hemingway sets up, Frederick Henry is a fully developed character, but it comes as a shock, some three-quarters of the way through, to learn that he had studied architecture in Rome. Hemingway tells us that fact only because of the demands of the narrative: Henry needs a suit of civilian clothes to escape the military police after his desertion. Hemingway's technique makes inordinate demands upon dialogue and description, since he forbids himself any manner of psychological analysis. The pressure of those demands creates his famous mannerisms and invites the charge of simple-mindedness. Beneath it all, his attitude to war is one of fascinated horror. He seems to say that desertion is proper because war is hell, while his descriptions of action are so perfect and so clearly the product of his devotion to process that the novel finally seems, paradoxically, a novelette. This is to say that Hemingway's kind of drama is insufficient to sustain the intellectual burden that the subject and the writer's irony encourage us to perceive.

Unlike Hemingway, Montherlant stands firmly within the great French tradition of psychological analysis. Montherlant's originality— and he is an original—lies in his thought, his loathing for received opinion, and his disdain for fashion, but not in departure from long-honored tradition. In conception, he is closer to the eighteenth century of Choderlos de Laclos than to the twentieth century of Gide, Camus, or Sarraute. In *Le Songe*, as in all his fiction, attitudes toward experience are crystal clear and intellectually enunciated; drama, the stuff of the novel, is invented only to support the enunciated position. Thus, a few pages into *Le Songe*, we know exactly where we are: Alban not only envies the deaths of his friends, he finds extraordinary virtues in war (so does Hemingway, although before the horrible Colonel Cantwell of *Across the River and into the Trees* he does not admit it). In the garden of his suburban home, Alban thinks of what the front must be:

> A dugout, a place of misery, of death. . . . But purified! all simplified! The simplicity of action, above all the action of war! If I were to establish any degree of intellectual or social influence, what patience, labor, how many stumbling-blocks in my way, what cleverness,—and I would be discussed, not supported, by those whom I love; my best friends might well become my adversaries; and who could reassure me that I would be following my own line (*être "dans le vrai"*), deliver me from doubt? But here! To stand at the parapet, to go have a look and return, to pull a trigger, that is something clear, direct, that upon the moment may confer a splendid glory. Here values are esteemed, classified; everyone agrees about their identity. What superiority! What peace![5]

---

[5] Henry de Montherlant, *Le Songe* (in *Romans et oeuvres de fiction non théatrales*, NRF, Bibliothèque de la Pléiade, Paris, 1959), pp. 9–10. Montherlant's ellipsis.

It is Montherlant's form of irony that Alban's revery, based on intuition rather than knowledge, is not really punctured by experience at the front, as we might reasonably expect. Rather, it is sustained, and we begin to see that Montherlant is constructing a "superior" man derived by way of Barrès from Nietzsche.[6] Alban discovers, in his admiration for Dominique as athlete, "an irreconcilable opposition between the order of sport and the order of the heart" (p. 21), something of which is also implied in many of Hemingway's men. Alban goes off to the front with a sense of relief, glad to leave Dominique, seeing the life of action as *"le bain dans l'élémentaire, l'anéantissement de l'intelligence et du coeur"* (Awash in the elementary, the annihilation of mind and heart [p. 21.]). And on his way to the front, he remembers in lyrical fashion walking along the tramway to the football field, drops of water falling upon him from the trees, mud underfoot, but above all, the anticipation of not having to think: *"ne pas penser!"*

> Not to have to cover up the gaps in his culture and the weakness of his mind, not to have to give the reasons for his judgments, not to have to be critical; to contradict oneself, to be incoherent! the thousands of questions on which one has no opinion! [p. 30].

Sport is the opposite of all that, and so is warfare, in which "Knowledge and intelligence and genius burn in a splendid *auto da fé!*" Once at the front, Alban joins his friend, Prinet. Prinet says, "It is bad, here." Alban answers "with hauteur, 'Is it your idea that I submit myself to mediocre tests?' " (p. 31).

After being under fire for the first time, Alban reflects that

> "When the whistling of the shells came down on me, and when at any moment I might have been blasted into eternity, I had not a single religious

---

6 In his three essays on Barrès, Montherlant acknowledges an intellectual debt to the older man but denies purely literary influence. See *Essais* (NRF, Bibliothèque de la Pléiade, Paris, 1963), pp. 265–285. Montherlant often quotes Nietzsche in his essays and journals. There is undoubtedly a strain of d'Annunzio, too, in Montherlant's egotism-cum-eroticism. He has said that he read d'Annunzio in the French translation of Georges Hérelle, and that his youthful works, including *Le Songe*, were influenced accordingly. Unpublished letter to Mr. L. Spitalnick, May 10, 1966. In March, 1963, Montherlant published an article, "Hommage à d'Annunzio," in which he says that before reading *Il Fuoco* in 1915, he had been a "prisoner of Flaubert, but that d'Annunzio untied the cords." Again, "My first two books, *La Relève du matin* and *Le Songe* are full of *Il Fuoco* to the point of intoxication."

thought, nor did I repent a single action, nor had I any impulse toward those I love." Since the day he had decided to go to the front, he had not once been caught up by the idea of death, he had written to no one, nor had he made his will. [p. 76].

The theme is expanded in a scene between Alban and Dominique, who has sought him out just behind the lines. She asks when he will return from the line, and he answers in two days.

"May fate [*fatalité:* untranslatable] let it come to pass!"

"What!" he said, wounded because he had caught her out in the crime of failing to be intelligent, "I am here at my own request, by my own decision and wilfulness, and you call that fate! It is my own will that constitutes fate," he added. . . . "Furthermore, I am not going to die; my passions will keep me firmly on the earth. But after all, what a lot of tales about death! Why be sad because you are going to meet Plato and Marcus Aurelius again! I have admired all that is noble; there is no pleasure that I have not known; I shall not be shocked if I am obliged to give up the game. I have gorged my hunger." [p. 89].

The most central statement of Alban's and Montherlant's neo-stoicism occurs in a conversation between Prinet and Alban in a trench. Prinet asks if Alban would really give up his life if it were demanded of him.

"I would do it, if I had to, by the sacraments that I received yesterday morning! I do not know the point of my sacrifice, and at base I think that I would be sacrificing myself to something that is nothing, and perhaps senseless, without a witness, without desire, renouncing life and the sweet odor of humanity, I throw myself into the indifference of the future only out of pride at having been so free. In the *Iliad*, Diomedes hurls himself upon Aeneas, although he knows that Apollo has rendered Aeneas invulnerable. Hector predicts the ruin of his city, his wife's imprisonment, before returning to fight as though he believed in victory. When the horse with the gift of prophecy announces to Achilles his approaching death, 'I am fully aware of it' the hero answers. But instead of crossing his arms and awaiting death, he rejects it and kills still more men in battle. That is how I have lived, knowing the vanity of things, but acting as though I were their dupe, and playing at being a man in order not to be rejected as a god. Yes, let us lose one in the other— my indifference and that of the future! After having pretended to fear death when I did not fear it, pretended to suffer when I never suffered, pretended to wait when I waited for nothing, I shall die in pretending to believe that my death has a purpose, but persuaded that it serves nothing and proclaiming that all is just." [p. 110].

One may remember at this point a different kind of rhetoric: ". . . the winner shall take nothing; neither his ease, nor his pleasure, nor any notions of glory; nor, if he win far enough, shall there be any reward within himself." But first, how does Montherlant prevent his Alban de Bricoule from being a monster of egotism and absurdity, posing as he does in the guise of a Homeric hero, inhumanly conscious and approving of his every thought and breath? Part of the answer is that Montherlant does not, not for lack of control, but because, unlike Hemingway, he is not interested in making his characters charming. He prefers to outrage us. But then, he gradually displaces our outrage by wit, elegance, and truth. In part, his technique is to portray as admirable those impulses that our culture says are evil: approval of warfare, of egotism, of the most anti-social attitudes.

Seemingly in spite of himself, Montherlant also describes a range of human reactions within his main character that we may not suspect. The death of a German prisoner of war, together with Alban's decent, human reaction denies his egotism and his philosophical self-preening. And when his comrade, Prinet, is missing in action, his vow "not to use his intelligence for three years" is an amusing combination of the human and the inhuman. That vow is at odds, however, with a basic philosophical position which Alban tries to maintain throughout the novel, one which is summarized in Alban's thoughts at the point where he learns that Prinet has been killed. He momentarily resents the fact that he, Alban, suffers at the knowledge of his friend's death, while external nature is indifferent. Then he accuses himself of sentimentality: "Foolish pronouncements about *the indifference of nature*! What do we expect? That the trees drop their leaves every time a human being dies?" (p. 165) Thus Alban lulls his grief, finally telling himself, "*O monde, je veux ce que tu veux. Tout ce qui arrive arrive justement*" (World, I want what you want. Whatever happens, happens justly. [p. 166]). In this manner, Alban maintains his earlier position, the very Montherlantian position of willing the inevitable. From the outset, Alban has asserted the primacy of his will; to Dominique about volunteering for the front lines, to Prinet on the same subject, and to himself throughout. Alban wills himself into the war rather as Frederick Henry wills himself out of it

But we next have a typical reversal of field, what Montherlant calls "alternance," to identify his personal philosophy.[7] Immediately after Alban's lyrical acceptance of events—"*O monde* . . . ,"—German bombers appear to work over the French position, and Alban is horrified to find himself terrorized and craven with cowardice. He violates all his announced virtues. He prays, he makes vows, he promises God to endow entire communities if only he is spared. He imagines himself dead, like Prinet. Then comes the final self-betrayal: he will do anything to be evacuated from the line. He will lie, cheat, kill if necessary, anything to save his skin. The bombers finally depart, and in the morning, as his comrades talk over who has been wounded and who killed among them, Alban turns himself in to the field hospital with a superficial wound that he had received earlier, and has no difficulty in being evacuated to the rear. The novel ends where it began, with the ambiguous affair between Alban and Dominique. Alban finally rejects her, seeing her as an Iphigenia, a sacrifice to save a soldier's life as he returns to the front. This is in contrast to Hemingway's conclusion, to the too neat death of both Catherine Barkley and her child.

Brief quotation and translation are unkind to Montherlant. It may not be clear that he and Hemingway arrive at similar positions through different but parallel literary avenues. Each has an apocalyptic vision of the modern world that he creates and re-lives through the experience of war. Hemingway's style, with its vividness and its visual quality, is superior, however, to the lyricism of Montherlant, whose highly charged *beau style* is at odds with his matter. Partly because of his style, partly because of his apocalyptic vision, and partly because of idiosyncrasy, Hemingway has been widely accused of anti-intellectualism. And so he is, although his anti-intellectualism is based upon a highly intellectual apprehension of experience. Montherlant, with his classical allusions, his extensive psychological analyses, his choice of an intellectual young man as hero, is nevertheless at least as anti-intellectual as Hemingway, if not more so. His anti-intellectualism is of that romantic variety that substitutes instinct for rationality and places blind faith in the superiority of art to any other pursuit.

Both writers essentially agree about the place of nature in relation to human affairs, although they appear to disagree on the evidence of *Le Songe* and *A Farewell to Arms*. Where Alban de Bricoule reminds

[7] See Montherlant's essay "Syncrétisme et Alternance," 1925, in *Essais*, pp. 237–245. This highly romantic philosophy of polarities seems to come straight from Swedenborg by way of Ralph Waldo Emerson.

himself that the leaves will not fall for any man's death, Frederick Henry sees a conspiracy to kill off the good, a conspiracy so huge that it must include nature as well as human society. At the same time, in both *A Farewell to Arms* and the rest of Hemingway's fiction, the best times and the best people are natural; lyricism and happiness are reserved for nature and for activities pursued in nature—hunting, fishing, love-making, rather than in society. On the evidence of *Les Bestiaires* and *La Rose de sable*, Montherlant agrees with that view, although he disguised his romanticism with a great deal of intellection and irony. Both writers pose the question of action versus contemplation, and both choose action as being superior; this, of course, is the romantic choice. Both devise heroes who live most fully when life is endangered, heroes who gravitate to extremes of experience. And for both writers, love next to death— but love in the extreme form of eroticism—is fundamental to their version of human relationships. Their ultimate romanticism lies in the conjunction, in both novels, of eroticism and death. Eroticism for both Hemingway and Montherlant may be defined as a focussing upon experience for its own sake, as against experience lived in society or experience having results beyond the superior individual's own con- sciousness. For the eroticist, love becomes aggrandizement of self and assertion of the individual will, rather than a merging of wills in which the individual will is gratefully abandoned. Both Hemingway and Montherlant are Byronic in their romanticism, never Wordsworthian.

These matters are even more clear in the two writers' work on bullfighting, because in bullfighting the element of the will is obvious— no law or convention forces any man to face bulls—and because in treating so exotic a subject, every motive of the writer stands out in stark relief. In *The Sun Also Rises*, the love-death theme is present not only in the emphasis upon the danger of bullfighting to the honest bullfighter, and in the Brett Ashley-Pedro Romero affair, but also more subtly in our continuing awareness that the action of the novel belongs to the war, was necessitated by the war, and in a sense is parallel to the war. At the same time, as we have seen before, bullfighting is a world apart from that of the waste land characters, and a better one in which purity and a kind of innocence are possible. Death and innocence, or openness, are the themes of two of Hemingway's short stories, "The Undefeated" and "The Capital of the World," in which an aging matador and a young waiter both meet their deaths in working according to their meticulous and exigent view of the proper rules of bullfighting.

Hemingway also emphasized death in the inter-chapters of his first book, *In Our Time*, by describing the death of the historical bullfighter, Maera. In each instance, the victim has willed his death by engaging the bull (or the simulated bull, in the waiter's case, in "The Capital of the World") according to an austere, interior view of himself and his conduct that has little or nothing to do with the public view of him. Thirteen of the sixteen brief inter-chapters of *In Our Time* deal with either war or bullfighting. Hemingway thus forces our attention to that aspect of bullfighting—its danger to the point of death—that is in reality residual, not central. He thus distorts one art, that of bullfighting, to the enhancement in the art of fiction of his obsessive theme—continuity of the consciousness of death.

In *Death in the Afternoon*, Hemingway equated bullfighting and death with an insistence that becomes grotesque. It is rather like a book on automobile design in which the author gives most of his attention to accounts of spectacular accidents and deaths on the highways. By including his neo-Jacobean meditation, "The Natural History of the Dead," a *tour de force* that would have charmed Poe, Hemingway makes possible the very accuracy to which in theory he is committed. As noted before, his countinuing emphasis upon gorings, wounds, gangrene, surgery, and death is a distortion of bullfighting, in which danger is only one among many elements. The result is a peculiar document, valuable for biography but personal in exactly the wrong way as literature. It represents a breach in a fine sensibility that was to widen as the years went by.

Montherlant, on the other hand, in his curious novel, *Les Bestiaires*, emphasizes the bullfighter in all his psychological reality rather than the abstract ethic and the objective performance. He writes from the inside, Hemingway from the outside. Montherlant characteristically constructs a Prosper Mérimée-like romantic surface, then proceeds to break it up. We meet an adolescent, pre-war Alban de Bricoule, who on school holiday in Spain is invited to a bull ranch near Seville. There he is introduced to his host's daughter, Soledad, who at first seems ugly and unpleasant to him. He comes to think of her as sexually available, however, and is flattered when she praises his handling of a savage horse and his ability with the cape. Seeing her at a distance across a room, he falls suddenly and passionately in love "with her wrists." Soledad, more interesting than most Spanish girls of fiction, plays the Spanish game by teasing Alban on, apparently promising herself to him if he will face

Mal Angel, her father's difficult three-year-old bull (*novillo*), in a benefit performance. At this point, we gratefully leave Mérimée for Montherlant. Alban agrees to take part in the benefit, but he cannot deceive himself. He tells Soledad that he fears the *novillo* and that he is neither old enough nor sufficiently experienced to dominate it. She is asking him to risk his life, he remarks, and he wonders whether she is worth it.

Soledad has said that any Spaniard would face Mal Angel or any other animal for her without hesitation. The struggle between Soledad and Alban now takes on a quality that only D. H. Lawrence, among writers in English, has apprehended. Yet Montherlant, unlike Lawrence, does not create a cult of inter-sexual strife. He uses the theme to mount an attack upon romanticism, while he supports the attack by a valid conception of what it means to the individual to face a difficult bull. For Hemingway, fear is cowardice and disgraceful. For bullfighters in real life, and for Alban, fear is a condition of the art, completely human and necessary to a good performance. In spite of his fear, Alban decides almost with humor that he will face the bull but that he will forget about Soledad. He knows that she is moved not by love but by romantic egotism. On the day, after a fearfully bad performance to his first animal, Alban is able to dominate Mal Angel. He then returns joyfully to Paris, to his recently widowed mother, and to school, like the schoolboy he is.

Insofar as bullfighting is concerned, Montherlant in this novel out-Hemingways Hemingway; *his* knowledge is genuine, a product of application and performance rather than of observation in the service of obsession. The novel is authoritative where bulls are concerned and almost a triumph in the affair between Alban and Soledad. It is badly weakened, however, by the burden of idea that Montherlant imposes. He ransacks anthropology and comparative religion for references to bulls, a violation of which Hemingway would have been incapable.[8]

Although we may see coincidence as responsible for certain parallels between Hemingway and Montherlant, the similarities are too frequent and striking to be coincidental. By placing Hemingway alongside Montherlant, it may be be possible to demonstrate the former's equivocal response to his own literary tradition, a tradition which in his own mind

---

[8] In his novel *Le Chaos et la nuit* (1963), Montherlant again put bullfighting to a most interesting use: what he sees as total decadence in bullfighting supports the disillusionment with Spain and the entire modern world of an aging Spanish Loyalist who returns to Madrid to die.

was not exclusively American by any means. While Hemingway used techniques of the past to create manners, his denial of the past became a source of energy for the creation of his own technique based upon exclusion and excision. Montherlant was at peace with his own literary tradition, free to create an eclectic mixture of styles and free to philosophize in asides to the reader. It should be noted here, however, that much of Montherlant's philosophizing, like that of Thomas Mann or Hermann Broch in their novels, represents thought after the event, as we have seen Alban de Bricoule "willing" the inevitable and so giving himself the illusion of independence. It is a form of fictional rationalizing which has little to do with philosophy as a discipline.

Thus, we may question the many European and American attacks upon American writing for lacking "thought." Both Montherlant's thought and Hemingway's lack of it come down to the same point: a questioning of accepted modes of thought in light of the extraordinary shambles that society was in after the First World War. Nor is it coincidence that both writers, looking for themes worthy of their attention, should have gravitated to the margins and extremities of human experience. Conditioned by the extremity of war, they took satisfaction in its peacetime equivalents: sport, bullfighting, eroticism, and violence. The point of balance in their work is the self of the central character, more or less autobiographical, conceived as heroic and presented in varying degrees of irony. Their irony was enforced by their awareness of the outmoded romanticism of their view of the self and of the will; the end of their romantic quests was always a private, not a public triumph, an equivocal triumph that could be interpreted as a defeat. Such a view, in turn, was impressed upon them by their common awareness of post-war society. Politics entered their minds hardly at all; a considerable distance existed between the generations and between individuals of the same generation. Their main characters are heroic isolates who hope to escape their isolation in love, which for them is eroticism; in sport; or in bullfighting, which they see as non-intellectual and therefore desirable. Rationality is unbearable. Hemingway approximated religion, while Montherlant substituted a private paganism for his early Catholicism. Both finally despaired.

In style they are far apart. Montherlant, like Fitzgerald in America, defined his time to his contemporaries according to his views, but he used the modes at hand. He was not interested in formal experiment, but he combined many traditional French voices into his own voice. André

Malraux (whose novels are strikingly similar to Montherlant's) called it a "royal" style: *"l'union fort rare de l'ironie avec une écriture royale."*[9]

We may hear the French seventeenth and eighteenth centuries in Montherlant's style, together with Chateaubriand and Stendhal. Hemingway not only defined his time to his contemporaries, but in addition created a pattern of thought, of action, even of speech. This is at once his distinction and another dimension of his limitation, for such patterns move beyond literature into sociology, where they soon become outmoded. That has happened to Hemingway, and only now is the literary portion of his work emerging in uncertain purity to a deserved permanence.

[9] Pierre Sipriot, *Montherlant par lui-même* (Paris, 1953), p. 184.

5

*Lewis
and
Svevo*

To re-read in bulk the writing of the American 1920's is to induce a state of literary vertigo at the difference between the best work of the time and much of the work which was held up to public admiration as the best. There is a special awfulness that defies the historical imagination about novelists like Sinclair Lewis, Theodore Dreiser, James Branch Cabell, and Joseph Hergesheimer; poets like Edna St. Vincent Millay, Carl Sandburg, or Vachel Lindsay; playwrights like Susan Glaspell and Arthur Cram Cook; critics like H. L. Mencken, George Jean Nathan, Stuart Pratt Sherman, and William Lyon Phelps. How could they, we ask, at a time when not only Americans of lasting merit were at work, but also Yeats, Joyce, Svevo, Kafka, Rilke, Mann, and Broch. What, if anything, did these writers of the American twenties have in common, apart from three names?

The answers are complex and only obliquely literary, but essential to one's understanding of the period. Some part of the answer has already been seen in the response of nationalistic criticism to Sherwood Anderson. The case of Sinclair Lewis is even more revealing, for Anderson was gigantic compared with Sinclair Lewis. Lewis (1885–1951) was the particular creature of the 1920's, although he had published four pot-boiling novels before 1920 and had written a great deal of women's magazine short fiction. After the twenties he continued to publish a novel every year or two, in spite of the fact that with each succeeding book he slipped farther away from the position he had maintained in that decade. His considerable reputation both in the United States and in Europe rested upon *Main Street* (1920), *Babbitt* (1922), *Arrowsmith* (1925), and to a lesser degree upon *Elmer Gantry* (1927), *The Man Who Knew Coolidge* (1928), and *Dodsworth* (1929). In 1930 he became the first North American to receive the Nobel Prize for literature, winning out, we are told, over Theodore Dreiser, to whom he is often mistakenly compared. With his wealth gained from writing, his small lecheries, his alcoholism and his talent for alienating his friends, Lewis sounds like one of Dreiser's less credible characters. His life is best forgotten, and so, too, his work. Thanks to his canonization by the Nobel Prize committee, however, Lewis' work is continually held up as exemplary, and his novels still appear on reading lists in schools and universities.

Lewis is popularly believed to have been an iconoclast, one who with admirable honesty went directly to the heart of small-town complacency in *Main Street*, stripping away layers of legend, sentimental folklore, and patriotic cant to give us the wounding but necessary truth. He is supposed to have done the same for the small city in *Babbitt*, adding to his theme the dishonesty of American salesmanship, the banality of American daily life, the non-existence of any of the ideals so loudly and frequently professed. *Arrowsmith* is presented as a novel cutting two ways. Lewis not only exposed the materialism and incompetence of American medicine, he also constructed a heroic portrait, in Martin Arrowsmith, of the dedicated research scientist, the selfless hero of the twentieth century who defies his money-grubbing colleagues in the cause of abstract truth. In *Elmer Gantry* we find again the old Lewis, excoriating the hypocrisy of established religion in America, whether Protestant, Catholic, or Jewish, seeking with unerring eye and keen mind the inconsistencies, the pretensions and the hollowness of religious congregations throughout the land. Whatever the subject, Lewis' many admirers found in his novels accuracy of ear, precise portrayal of characteristic American types and attitudes, and a masterly ordering of an attack upon the fundamental American ethos. His masses of readers, masochists all, agreed with the predominant critical view.

That generous view of Lewis is preposterous and always was. *Main Street*, Lewis' least embarrassing novel, may serve as a text. At the outset, one may wonder why the novel is dedicated to James Branch Cabell and Joseph Hergesheimer, two writers with whom Lewis had nothing in common but whom he regarded as properly "literary" as he emerged from the back alleys of the women's magazines to stride down the boulevards of literature. It is ominous that he should have chosen the two writers whose pseudo-historical fiction, made up of whimsy and syntactical posturing, was least likely to survive the decade which at one level affected a taste for such things.[1] Before beginning the narrative proper, Lewis wrote a brief preface, assuring the reader of the universality of his theme and scene. Its tone, a mixture of jocularity, condescension, and seriousness, is typical of Lewis in the throes of an idea. It must be quoted:

> This is America—a town of a few thousand, in a region of wheat and corn and dairies and little groves.
>
> The town is, in our tale, called "Gopher Prairie, Minnesota." But its Main Street is the continuation of Main Streets everywhere. The story would be the same in Ohio or Montana, in Kansas or Kentucky or Illinois, and not very differently would it be told Up York State or in the Carolina hills.
>
> Main Street is the climax of civilization. That this Ford car might stand in front of the Bon Ton Store, Hannibal invaded Rome and Erasmus wrote in Oxford cloisters. What Ole Jenson the grocer says to Ezra Stowbody the banker is the new law for London, Prague, and the unprofitable isles of the sea; whatsoever Ezra does not know and sanction, that thing is heresy, worthless for knowing and wicked to consider.
>
> Our railway station is the final aspiration of architecture. Sam Clark's annual hardware turnover is the envy of the four counties which constitute God's Country. In the sensitive art of the Rosebud Movie Palace there is a Message, and humor strictly moral.
>
> Such is our comfortable tradition and sure faith. Would he not betray himself an alien cynic who should otherwise portray Main Street, or distress the citizens by speculating whether there may not be other faiths?

Whatever this may mean, it characterizes Lewis' intellectual quackery and displays his fatal fluency. He had, in fact, no historical knowledge or interest, but he wanted his novels to be universal. Both here and in a similar preface to *Arrowsmith*, it is apparent that Lewis' historical allusions are not the illuminations of matters to come that they pretend to be, but rather a flaunting of the writer's depth and breadth of vision.

---

[1] Mark Schorer writes that in 1920, Hergesheimer asked Lewis to read a set of proofs. When Lewis ventured suggestions, Hergesheimer said that he "cared only for the word of Conrad and Gosse." *Sinclair Lewis: An American Life* (New York, 1961), p. 259.

Main Street is the narrative of a foggy-minded, idealistic young woman who attends a sectarian college in St. Paul, Minnesota, at the turn of the century. She becomes a librarian, meets Will Kennicott, a medical doctor from Gopher Prairie, a small Minnesota town, marries him, and goes there to live. The bulk of the novel has to do with the crippling limitations of the small town, the combination of vulgarity, boyishness, and blindness of the men, not excepting Kennicott himself, and of the clannish, petty back-biting of their wives. Carol Kennicott, appalled at what she finds when she arrives as a young bride, has visions of reforming the town, of bringing "beauty" into the dessicated lives of the townspeople. She of course fails, spends two years in Washington during the First World War, and returns, defeated but not beaten, because she assures us that she is still honest with herself.

Lewis purports to give us an anatomy of life in a midwestern village at a given moment in recent history. What he in fact gives us is a zoo filled with the nastier animals of creation. His town banker, grocers, manufacturers, and clergymen are portrayed with the venom of a small-town boy getting his own back. It failed as a literary rendering because of Lewis' lack of control and ignorance concerning what he really is writing about. Lewis cannot write satire, because satire assumes a standard his subject cannot meet. He writes burlesque, instead, sometimes so foolish in its extremity that it had a certain vigor. He sacrifices literary effectiveness by never knowing when to stop, never realizing that the cartoon has reached the end of the strip, never failing to explain, to repeat, and to explain his joke once again.

Although the more extreme figures in Lewis' zoo create momentary interest when his broad current of fraudulent foolishness is running strong, his sympathetic characters remain lifeless and embarrassing. Lewis must have hated women in order to write about them as he did. Carol Kennicott, like the horrible Leora Arrowsmith, is presented in diminutives; she is forever girlish, coy, small, cute, a toy rather than a woman. (The women whom we are supposed to dislike, like Tanis Judique in *Babbitt*, have the lumbering, contralto charm of the six-footers whom Groucho Marx used to dance with in the movies.) "It was a frail and blue and lonely Carol who trotted to the flat of the Johnson Marburys for Sunday evening supper." No one ever walks in Lewis' novels; they trot, slide, bounce, scamper, flit, or pounce. And they never speak their thoughts; they bleat, yammer, rage, nicker, bay, pipe, gloat, or croon. Carol Kennicott's unhappiness results from her appetite for beauty, we are told. She wants to transform Gopher Prairie into a neo-Georgian New England village, to reconstruct the "rest-room" in which farmers' wives wait for their husbands to conduct their business, and teach her own husband to enjoy early William Butler Yeats. She fails, and Lewis writes of her failure:

> That was her last effort to harvest the April wind, to teach divine unhappiness by a correspondence course, to buy the lilies of Avalon and the sunsets of Cockaigne in tin cans at Ole Jenson's Grocery.

Whenever Carol Kennicott entertains a flight of fancy, Lewis gives away the Maxfield Parrish-Balaban and Katz quality of his mind. On her way to Washington after finally having separated from Kennicott, she tells her young son that they are going to find

> beyond the blue horizon rim . . . elephants with golden howdahs from which peep young maharanees with necklaces of rubies, and a dawn sea colored like the breast of a dove, and a white and green house filled with books and silver tea-seats.

The men in *Main Street* whom we are to regard as sympathetic are as hard to swallow as the women. Guy Pollock, the ineffectual lawyer who shares Carol's view of the town but not her optimism about reforming it, is even more gray, shadowy, neuter, and dog-like than Lewis knows. Miles Bjornstam, the town handyman, village atheist and radical, is totally theatrical, present in the novel to provide verisimilitude, but lacking any vestige of psychological reality. He reads books by Byron, Tennyson, Stevenson, and Thorstein Veblen, and when Carol visits him on a winter's day, he says things like, "Yeh, I'm probably a yahoo, but by gum I do keep my independence by doing odd jobs, and that's more'n these polite cusses like the clerks in banks do." In the portrait of Erik Valborg, Carol's would-be lover, Lewis makes a conventional association between incipient homosexuality and "sensitivity."

Lewis' basic difficulty in *Main Street*, as in all his fiction, is that he makes subject and process pass for idea. When Kennicott asks his wife what she is after, she answers, "Oh, conversation! No, it's much more than that. I think it's greatness of life—a refusal to be content with even the healthiest mud." Although Lewis is using his character's vagueness he is also giving away his own vagueness of purpose and of execution. He lacks imagination and inventiveness. It is not a literary idea to burlesque the small midwestern town, what Lewis called the "village virus"; in any case, George Ade and Ring Lardner did it earlier and better. For lack of idea, Lewis' characters never change; they merely endure episodes and display their quirks and tics for our amusement. They come on the page, stumble through an episode, and return to the card file until Lewis needs them again. The nearest Lewis comes to an idea in *Main Street* is Carol Kennicott's notions of freeing herself and the people she likes from their slavery to inadequate modes of behavior enforced upon them by the small town. Lewis uses almost the identical idea in *Babbitt* and *Arrowsmith*. What form that freedom should take, however, is never defined, and whenever Lewis tries to define it, he lapses into his late-Victorian purple prose. He suspects the motif of freedom and burlesques that, too, but the burlesque is half-hearted and seems to cover up uneasiness.

Lewis boasted to all and sundry about his methods of composition in *Babbitt* and other novels. He would do research on the subject, whether real estate, popular religion, or bacteriology, write thousands of words of physical description of scenes, biographies of characters, then in short order write the text of the novel essentially as it would be published. Such a method suggests the notebook naturalism of the late nineteenth century, but Lewis lacked even the dubious idea of that school. His careful attention to background was not a Zola-like product of a philosophy of environment and heredity, but a substitute for inventiveness, a way of creating the illusion of authenticity, and another subject for burlesque.

There is even less idea in *Babbitt* than in *Main Street;* in its place is melodrama and psychological reversal. George Babbitt, first portrayed as a fool, snob, liar, petty tyrant, hypocrite, corrupt petty swindler of public money and self-deceiving, loud-mouthed bore is turned briefly into a political liberal, rebel, and seeker after truth. It is too much even for Lewis, however, and Babbitt soon resumes his earlier role as fool, snob, etc. The tedious descriptions of Babbitt's home and public life are so close to witless burlesque that they move off the sociological point. Lewis' much praised ear for colloquial speech is abundantly evident in *Babbitt*. What we actually find, however, is the dialogue of a vaudeville skit. His characters speak essays, and his main device for suggesting the colloquial is to preface every speech with "Say," or "Well," and to end the last sentence with an exclamation point! This is the Sinclair Lewis who, in his Nobel Prize address, expressed impatience with discussions of style: "I am not exactly sure what this mystic quality 'style' may be, . . ."

Lewis' leaden irony about style is misplaced, for it calls attention to the fact that his impulses were sociological rather than novelistic. Like some sociologists, Lewis used the technique of bombarding the reader with data transferred bodily from his "research" notebooks. Thus the inordinate length and tediousness of his work, and thus its popularity with readers who honor what they think is fact and reality, rather than mere fiction. Yet the order of "fact" that Lewis selected lacks even sociological validity. His Gopher Prairie is not true to the historical midwestern village of the years 1910–1920, nor is his Zenith true to the historical reality of the small American city just after the First World War. In each instance, the truth is far more complex, at once more appalling and more interesting, than Lewis' method of burlesque indicated. His vaudeville Americans, Germans, Swedes, and English are true to a tendency in American life for only a brief period, and a recessive tendency at that. In place of the complexity of American life, Lewis saw little more than electric cigar lighters, hotel lobbies, items of dress, and repellent social institutions of a generation of American businessmen. His own remarkable intellectual vulgarity allowed him to be content with parodies of American speech. His hunger for money and his training in the *Saturday Evening Post* school of writing made him distrust literary style and instilled in him a permanent belief that melodrama and tragedy are indistinguishable.

By the time he wrote *Arrowsmith*, the various components of Lewis' literary personality had fallen out of relationship, never to be reassembled. In the earlier novels, venom and energy had helped to compensate for simple-mindedness. *Arrowsmith*, however, is partly Lewis' response to the criticism that he was merely destructive and lacked positive standards. Martin Arrowsmith is presented as a modern hero, the scientist who selflessly struggles with unswerving faith against all the temptations of a corrupt society—domesticity, wealth, fame, and success in his chosen field. Lewis actually wrote the scenario for a lesser film production, where in spite of his "research" and his collaboration (which he repudiated) with a young scientist, Paul de Kruif, he succeeded in misunderstanding the methods of modern science and in creating once more a burlesque where he had intended tragedy. His medical doctors are variations upon George Babbitt; his New York and Chicago are proof of his lack of sense of place; his characters, beginning with Martin

Arrowsmith, are cardboard cutouts; his bubonic plague has all the evoked danger of rain in the park. One can only agree with the scientist who wrote of the novel:

> If an epidemiologist on a plague study talked and behaved in the manner of the hero of *Arrowsmith*, he would not only be useless, but he would be regarded as something of a yellow ass and a nuisance by his associates.[2]

Arrowsmith is useful in that it indicates more clearly than the other works Lewis' fascination with process. Because of that fascination he was a good naturalist, American style. This is how Arrowsmith begins, as a student, to work without supervision:

> The room was dark, thick dark, but for the gas-mantle behind his microscope. The cone of light cast a gloss on the bright brass tube, a sheen on his black hair, as he bent over the eye-piece. He was studying trypanosomes from a rat —an eight-branched rosette stained with polychrome methylene blue; a cluster of organisms delicate as a narcissus, with their purple nuclei, their light blue cells, and the thin lines of the flagella.

Lewis' respect for process (trypanosomes! flagella!), which is allied to his collection of data, helps to explain his popularity, but only partially. His apparent iconoclasm should remind us that the 1920's in the United States and England also elevated Lytton Strachey to curious heights as an iconoclast, in part the result of reaction to the war and to the peace. For supposedly serious social criticism, however, there is little in Lewis' work of politics or of any other serious pursuit.

Although it may be unfair, Lewis' concentration upon the middle class, his narrative technique, and some of his devices of humor suggest comparison with an incomparably better writer, Ettore Schmitz (1861–1928), better known by his pen name, Italo Svevo. A citizen of Trieste who became wealthy in the paint business, Svevo wrote little and probably would have remained unknown had he not been James Joyce's student of English in 1906. Svevo's *Una Vita* (1893) had gone unnoticed, as had *Senilità* (1898), which Joyce read and remembered when Svevo's finest novel appeared in 1924, *La Coscienza di Zeno* (*The Confessions of Zeno*), which he then helped to publicize. Like Sinclair Lewis, Svevo satirized the middle class, but lovingly and without Lewis' unrestrained

---

[2] Hans Zinsser, *Rats, Lice, and History*, quoted by Mark Schorer, *Sinclair Lewis*, p. 417.

burlesque. Svevo knew that he was looking into himself; Lewis did not, until it was too late, and then in his novels of the 1930's and 1940's he became the strident defender of the middle class he had denounced in the 1920's.

Lewis' narrative technique consisted mainly of a mosaic of vignettes, rarely more than a printed page in length, which he numbered within a chapter to construct a loose formal pattern. The result is not a smoothly flowing narrative, but rather the expansion of moments of consciousness, of specific segments of time. It is most successful in *Babbitt*, where the technique is appropriate to Lewis' fascination with objects and processes; in *Main Street* and *Arrowsmith*, the fragmentary time-conscious technique works against sustained narrative, and, as a result, against our awareness of the passing of months and years. Lewis emphasizes segments of time because of his interest in the objects and furnishings of middle class life; Svevo, in his different way, emphasizes fragments of time in his concentration upon states of boredom, memory, and awareness of self. These, too, are allied to the encompassing theme of the bourgeoisie, but Svevo's resulting texture is far richer than Lewis'. Lewis always narrates in the third person, with frequent ironic addresses to the reader and occasional fragments of reported interior monologue. Svevo in *Zeno* creates an elaborate texture through various devices: the novel has the frame of a psychiatrist's report (and it is a satire upon psychiatry); we are within Zeno's mind, but aware of at least two Zenos: the young man to whom things happen, and the mature Zeno, who remembers and relives events past. This complex method makes possible degrees of irony and sensibility far beyond Lewis' capabilities.

Both Zeno and Babbitt are smoking men who think they would like to stop the filthy habit. Babbitt, over a period of a week or so, simply keeps saying, "Rats! I got to quit smoking!" while he locks his cigars in a file cabinet. Zeno, a hypochondriac, spends days, months, years, a lifetime, enjoying his last cigarette. Lying in bed with a sore throat and fever, Zeno smokes away, but the doctor tells him to stop. He has one "last" smoke, then continues to smoke his way in secret through his illness.

My father would come and go, always with a cigar in his mouth, and say from time to time:
"Bravo! A few days more of no smoking and you will be cured!"
It only needed that phrase to make me long for him to get out of the room

instantly so that I might begin smoking again at once. I would pretend to be asleep in order to get rid of him quicker.[3]

The novel is punctuated with Zeno's proud noting of the date and "Last cigarette!"

When Babbitt is attracted to the widow, Tanis Judique, the affair is described in comic strip terms in keeping with the widow's name, and Babbitt's pangs of conscience are those of an eight-year-old boy who has been stealing fudge. Zeno's affair with Carla, on the other hand, is amusing, fully real, and fully human. His pangs of conscience are beautifully and at the same time satirically rendered; the whole episode is a masterpiece of delicacy. In the same vein, Arrowsmith's simultaneous engagement to two girls and his luncheon invitation to both of them to discuss the matter is as close to subtlety as Lewis ever came, yet the episode seems out of character and forced. Zeno, by contrast, who proposes first to the beautiful Ada, knowing he will be refused, then to her sister Alberta, who refuses him because she is becoming a playwright, and finally is accepted by the third sister, the wall-eyed Augusta, all on the same day, is successful. It is so even though the events are obviously the stuff of burlesque, because Svevo's narrative technique gives them surprise and depth. While remembering his proposal to the lovely Ada, Zeno's mind jumps forward to the present, years later, and to Ada living in Buenos Aires, ill, her beauty vanished, and no longer able to wound him or detract from his genuine happiness with Augusta. Similarly, his reluctance to marry the wall-eyed girl is such that on the day of the wedding, his father-in-law to be has to get him out of bed and lead him to the altar. It is the very stuff of burlesque, yet it is burlesque relieved by Zeno's gentle, slowly unfolding, and genuine love for his wife, a love she more than returns and which we know of as the memory of the wedding day unfolds.

Svevo was a great original, Lewis a writer deformed by apprenticeship in a worthless school. Svevo did all that Lewis set out to do and more, and in doing so, he joined the very small company of writers who could combine humanity with satire. It is unkind to compare him to Lewis, who occasionally catches and distorts surfaces with vigor and brilliance But on balance, never in the history of literature has so slight a writer been taken so seriously, rewarded so richly, or honored so highly.

[3] Italo Svevo, *The Confessions of Zeno*, trans. Beryl de Zoete (London, 1948), pp. 14–15.

Sinclair Lewis stands oddly alone with his ambition to write the Great American Novel, which he referred to as the "G.A.N." Schorer has found debts to Dickens, H. G. Wells, and Arnold Bennett, but it is hard to take those debts seriously. If Lewis imitated Dickens in his concept of character, he imitated the worst of Dickens. From the others, he took not their best characteristics but their worst: sentimentality, cosiness, pseudo-intellectuality, and melodramatic fantasy. Every now and again some young scholar will find a trace of Thorstein Veblen in Lewis, yet it is impossible to accept Veblen as an influence, even assuming that Lewis had read him. Lewis simply did not think in Veblen's terms, or in terms of any organized philosophy. He dedicated *Babbitt* to Edith Wharton, of all people. If we did not have the correspondence between the two writers about the dedication, we would have to think that it was the result of a drunken bet. Lewis' relationship to H. L. Mencken (of whom more later) was logical, but he was quite formed as a writer when he met Mencken. Lewis seems to have influenced none of his younger, better colleagues, with the possible exception of the strain of wild burlesque in Thomas Wolfe. Lewis' American popularity must be accounted for by his women's magazine touch, together with the extremes of burlesque that allowed the targets to say, "But I am not like that." His European popularity is all too clearly the result of anti-Americanism; Lewis said what many Europeans wanted to think about the country, and more. The awarding of the Nobel Prize must also be put down to anti-Americanism on the part of the Swedish committee.[4] Lewis' career after the Nobel award in 1930 unfortunately belongs more properly to the history of medicine than to the history of literature.[5]

[4] See Mark Schorer, *Sinclair Lewis*, p. 553, for evidence to support this view.

[5] The above account purposely ignores Lewis' more interesting and, in some respects, attractive, side. He belongs to the sociology of American literature, as does his later work. Only this would account for Mark Schorer's vast (814 page) study and for studies by younger men which, mysteriously, continue to appear after Schorer has said all·there is to say.

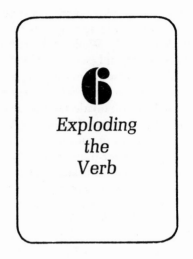

Exploding
the
Verb

Thus far, the discussion of prose fiction has been confined to writers identified as "retrospective"—Sherwood Anderson, Sinclair Lewis—and those identified as "prospective": Scott Fitzgerald, Ernest Hemingway. If the discussion has been even reasonably efficient, these and other writers' relationship to history proper, to American literary history, and to European writing has begun to define the nature of the period 1919–1932. Now it is time to consider the frankly experimental prose of that period before we move on to poetry and its special questions.

Experimentation in prose fiction needs to be approached with circumspection, if only out of respect for the generic demands, the possibilities and limitations of the medium. One could argue that the most egregious fallacy of modernism is the fallacy that concepts valid for one art are valid for all; that the arts progress as history unfolds, like Chinese tables; that all the arts are in the same stage of "progression" at any historical moment; and that a special cachet attaches to the writer who "experiments." The invention of the revolving stage, for example, made possible certain departures in the playwright's conception of his material. Bertolt Brecht comes to mind as one whose imaginative reach was extended and whose entire conception of reality was probably altered significantly by changes in stage mechanics. But the invention of the electric typewriter has not changed the writer's task in the slightest

Just as obvious is the fact or accident that the painter's teasings and play with his materials is hardly possible to the writer.

False as opposed to genuine experimentation might be thought of in terms of a town where all the houses are built without windows. The false experimenter is like the public health official who selects that town for an allergy study. Form and purpose, that is to say, coincide in true art; the merely mechanical experimenter would tear them apart in order to alter form. One result was that the world after 1918 on both sides of the Atlantic strove for a new classicism while retaining the purely romantic impulse to merge the arts in a grand salad. Berlioz triumphed over Lessing.

The unquestioned veracity and propriety of poetic experiment in the 1920's, together with the publication of a great variety of prose that seemed to derive from the same fountainhead as that of poetry, conspired to urge many writers to experiment. Not only did generic differences make the impulse suspect, but also the differences in rationale were enormous. For poetry in English, Eliot's essays of the early twenties, some of Pound's essays and pronouncements, together with a host of essays by poets as different as Robert Graves and William Carlos Williams, constituted a re-evaluation of the entire poetic tradition. Eliot's work alone, in his essays and in his editorship of the *Criterion* (for seventeen years, beginning in 1922), formed such a re-evaluation and left no doubt in his readers' minds about his rationale for poetic experiment, a rationale of immediate and overwhelming influence. In addition, discussion in the leading periodicals of the period in the United States—*The Dial, Poetry* (Chicago), *The Little Review*—as well as the many periodicals published in English in Paris and in other European cities from time to time, formed a continuing discussion, a continuing re-evaluation of the past, and a varying intellectual framework for the poetic experiment so fully in progress. Nothing of the sort was written of prose.

In place of Eliot's closely reasoned essays, there were Sherwood Anderson's maunderings in his autobiographical books, Hemingway's reading lists, Gertrude Stein's solipsisms, and Virginia Woolf's elegant digs and polite applause. Henry James' influence was at low ebb, his prefaces to the New York edition of the novels virtually unobtainable, while the American critics who might have taken on the task of re-evaluation of the past for prose were busy making their living at literary journalism or engaging in various kinds of special pleading. We have seen Van Wyck Brooks working over the American past, but with the

purpose of evoking a particular, pre-arranged response, his duck call
being answered by rabbits. H. L. Mencken, who congratulated himself
for his concern with fiction and history, was too bemused by his peculiar
reading of Nietzsche and his special wrath over the American present to
serve the purpose; in any event, he lacked both taste and scholarship.
Edmund Wilson produced fine literary reviews and, in 1931, his book on
symbolism, *Axel's Castle*. Kenneth Burke was only getting started, as
was Richard Blackmur. The criticism of prose, that is to say, lagged
well behind criticism of poetry. It still does.

The wealth of fine prose fiction in the period suggests that the work
precedes critical evaluation. More than forty years later, we are still
becoming really familiar with Joyce, Proust, Kafka, Mann, and Malraux;
we have hardly made the acquaintance of Broch, Musil, Svevo, Baroja,
or Unamuno. The young prose writer of the post-World War I period
in the United States or elsewhere had, if he were even dimly alert, every
impulse to imitate living masters who seemed to experiment. What may
not have been so apparent is that the masters can never be imitated.
Then, too, criticism in the period neglected the distinction between
technical experiment and the manipulation of new material through
traditional techniques. Very often the latter was called experiment and
honored accordingly. The point has particular relevance for the United
States, where novelty of material was praised and where, as we have
seen, the concentration upon process had a hypnotic effect upon writers
as different as Hemingway and Sinclair Lewis.

One returns to the difference between Sinclair Lewis' burlesque and
Italo Svevo's gentle satire of the businessman. Lewis, who struggled to
be contemporary and bright, dates badly; his work has the deadly period
flavor that precedes burial. Svevo, who had no particular illusions about
experiment or contemporaneity, is sparkling and timeless. Neither
writer was experimental, but their methods of dealing with similar
material provide perspective upon innovation. Lewis' work dates because
it is basically mechanical, a product not of love but of a task he set himself to sweat through. Svevo wrote out of affection, if not love, for his
material, and his satire is directed more against himself than his sur-
roundings. Lewis shows off; Svevo never does, even though at base he
is a confessional writer. His material is the world, his world. He writes
of psychoanalysis not to satirize it *as* material or as idea, but because it
is there, and because as an artist he recognizes its value as a frame. His
use of psychoanalysis in *Zeno* is early enough to seem "experimental,"

but it is not; had he been a woman, Svevo might just as well have used childbirth rather than psychoanalysis. He is in the world, at ease there, and of it; the world is his inevitable material. He does not have to go out, notebook in hand, like Lewis, to uncover a world foreign to him. The world is a natural place for Svevo, and good, although frustrating and ultimately tragic. Lewis places himself obliquely to the world; he is only ambiguously in it, and never of it. Hence he ignores history and is caught up in the things of the world, and he must eternally and boringly be at work making lists and catching surfaces.

The great experimenters' relationship to the world may tell us something about them, about Joyce or Kafka, whom some writers tried to imitate; about Unamuno, who remains splendidly alone in his departures from the traditional forms of Spanish prose. The experimenters whom we honor have without exception been at home, Svevo-like, with the things of this world (which has little to do with the fact that they generally have been at odds with society). In terms of the art of fiction, as opposed to poetry, that has meant awareness of the world not only through personal vision, but also through traditional literary forms, through the work of writers who preceded them. Another way of putting it is to say that the poet moves from apprehension, or vision, to form; language for him is virtually a function of form.

The prose writer, however, cannot do that. Language for him is far more bound up in material and in the rhetoric by which his society recognizes material; thus the length and relative unwieldiness of prose as compared with lyric verse. Formal perfection in verse may be compared to that of a jewel; formal perfection in prose may be compared to that of a long road through mountainous terrain. The great experimenters, those civil engineers, have almost without exception started with traditional techniques: hence Joyce's *Dubliners*, Proust's very conventional early fiction, or Mann's *Buddenbrooks*. Tradition becomes a heavier drag upon prose than upon verse, if only because prose is closer to the surface of society, closer to our rational intellectual processes than verse is. What we recognize as prose experiment has come out of the fullest knowledge of the geology of the road. Only then has the experimenter seized upon the new form, or the variation upon an old form, to reach the end of *his* road.

It is crucial to this argument to emphasize that the basic image here is a departure from Stendhal's famous simile of fiction as a mirror in the roadway. It is rather the roadway itself that must be emphasized for our comprehension of *Ulysses* or *The Trial*, or, for that matter, *The Sun Also Rises*. The First World War, to reiterate, had smashed all the Stendhalian mirrors, and Stendhal did not really believe in mirrors anyway. But the smashing of the mirrors, the disappearance of the last shred of illusion that the mirror could reveal truth, accounts for the appearance of myth in fiction, for writers' welcome to Freud, and for the shift from the exploration of society to exploration of the self. If for no other reason, we read Proust. The entire process is there in his great work, and we may observe as in a laboratory the shift from the social to the personal, from the Guermantes set to the male bordello. But just as in Proust we are constantly aware of the mark of the seventeenth century upon his mind and style, so in Joyce's use of stream-of-consciousness we are aware of his study of Ibsen's naturalism, and of stream-of-consciousness as an ultimate development of naturalism. That is, we are just as aware of tradition as of novelty. For some reason, too much novelty in prose produces surfeit and awareness of unconscious comedy: see Amy Lowell's prose-poetry, or Thomas Wolfe's, or Virginia Woolf's.[1]

The history of the 1920's is littered with both genuine and pseudo experiments in prose. Since those two orders of writing are so often confused in history and criticism, it is to the point to try to sort out the American variety, always keeping in mind the European model or counterpart. Miss Katherine Anne Porter is an amusingly hostile witness. In one of her essays on Gertrude Stein, she comments that many Americans in Paris after the war "wished their writings to be as free from literature as if they had never read a book, as indeed too many of them had not. . . ." Miss Porter is firmly anti-*transition*, the magazine edited in Paris, and anti-Eugene Jolas, its polyglot editor. Noting that he was an Alsatian who spoke each of his languages with the accent of one of the others, Miss Porter also notes that he was hostile to language itself. She catches one quality of the period that scholars like to overlook—its aggressive phoniness:

(Jolas) issued frantic manifestoes demanding that language be reduced to something that he could master, crying aloud in "defense of the hallucinative

---

[1] The whole question of prose-poetry, of the limits of English prose, needs full exploration by a good literary critic well-versed in aesthetics. Why is prose-poetry in English self-conscious and worse, while we read Baudelaire's or Rilke's with pleasure? Wherever one turns from the 1920's on, one inevitably meets this teasing, and in English untouched, problem.

forces," the exploding of the verb, the "occult hypnosis of language," "chthonian grammar"; reason he hated, and defended the voice of the blood, the disintegration of syntax—with a special grudge against English—preaching like an American Methodist evangelist in the wilderness for "the use of a language which is a mantic instrument, and which does not hesitate to adopt a revolutionary attitude toward syntax, going even so far as to invent a hermetic language, if necessary."

And of Gertrude Stein:

> Miss Stein had no problems, she simply exploded a verb as if it were a soap bubble, used chthonian grammar long before she heard it named (and she would have scorned to name it), was a born adept in occult hypnosis of language without even trying.[2]

"Exploding" the verb may bring to mind William Carlos Williams' travesty, *The Great American Novel* (1923), the heroine of which is a little Ford car:

> Break the word. Words are indivisible crystals. One cannot break them—
> —Awu tsst grang splith gra pragh og bm—Yes, One can break them.

The operative word in the sort of thing that Miss Porter objected to is "free." Much of the anti-historical quality so prominent after the war relates to many writers' efforts not only to throw out all history, which had been made irrelevant by the war and by the oratory of the peacemakers at Paris, but also literary history, literary tradition, anything smacking of the past. The emphasis upon freedom derived from an obsession with the place of puritanism, generally misunderstood, in American history and current life. It led to the notion that any writer who wrote about sexual intercourse, who hinted or said that women had breasts and genitals, was not only free but experimental. Henry Miller is a pure, although gamey, product of that school of non-thought, while Joyce was read for years for the wrong reasons, because *Ulysses* had been censored for salaciousness. What we might call the fallacy of subject matter, of sexual matter in particular, led to the over-praise of D. H. Lawrence, to the judgment of even so good a critic as Edmund Wilson that *Lady Chatterley's Lover* (1928) is a literary work of the first rank, and to Lawrence's canonization by F. R. Leavis.

One of Lawrence's motives in *Lady Chatterley's Lover* for naming

[2] Katherine Anne Porter, *The Days Before* (New York, 1952), pp. 44–45.

common acts by common names was to *épater le bourgeois*, a motive he shared with Joyce. The French had known the joys of that particular chase since Stendhal, but in the United States, second only to Germany as the most bourgeois country the world has known, it required the vindication in the post-war prosperity of Thorstein Veblen and the election of oddities like Harding, Coolidge, and Hoover to the Presidency to bring about a reaction similar to that of the French. To be anti-middle class was the mark of all thinking men, but it was the special mark of the experimental writer. The 1920's, we can now see, marked a special point in American social history, the point at which that earlier folk-figure, the pioneer, turned into the middle class figure of satire. The pioneer in literature was basically sympathetic, as in the novels of Willa Cather. The middle-class character was not sympathetic, but a figure of cruelest fun, a Babbitt, or so "careless" as to be downright evil, like Fitzgerald's Tom Buchanan. So it was that the immediate post-war period, which appeared apolitical, in reality prepared the way for the political literature of the Depression years.

E. E. Cummings (1894–1962) went from Harvard into the Norton-Harjes Ambulance Corps in France. He was arrested in 1917 for anti-war remarks in a personal letter, judged treasonable, and sent to La Ferté Macé, a prison camp in northwestern France, where he remained for four months. That experience is depicted in *The Enormous Room* (1922), which for lack of a better term we may call an experimental novel. It is the first American novel in which the distinction between a fictional "I" and an autobiographical "I" is eliminated. Cummings thus ignored the entire objective tradition, all the Jamesian attempts to disguise the author's hand in narrative. In content and approach, Cummings' deliberately shocking accounts of prison life, with his emphasis upon filth, his loving treatment of his own and others' suffering, his strong suggestion of homosexuality, and his apparent inversion of civilized values, interestingly anticipate Jean Genêt. The enormous room of the title is the church-like space in which the men are confined; by extension, it is the war itself, although Cummings does not press that symbolic parallel. Cummings' nearest approach to an idea occurs in a scene between some of the inmates and the narrator, Mexique, who when asked what he thinks of the war, answers, "I t'ink lotta bullshit."

In place of a literary idea, Cummings produces a long series of poetic arias of ironic outrage. In the midst of the unspeakable, he pretends to enjoy his lot, and he expresses himself in the most courtly and literary language. The resulting irony is sometimes effective, but more often sophomoric and contrived. Lacking narrative and ironically avoiding any sort of novelistic tension, *The Enormous Room* becomes a series of expressionistic tableaux, each worked over with loving, narcissistic care. Many of these characteristics are clear in the address to Jean le Nègre, not least the anticipation of Genêt:

> —Boy, Kid, Nigger with the strutting muscles—take me up into your mind once or twice before I die (you know why: just because the eyes of me and you will be full of dirt some day). Quickly take me up into the bright child of your mind, before we both go suddenly all loose and silly (you know how it will feel). Take me up (carefully, as if I were a toy) and play carefully with me, once or twice before I and you go suddenly all limp and foolish. Once or twice before you go into great Jack roses and ivory—(once or twice, Boy, before we together go wonderfully down into the Big Dirt laughing, bumped with the last darkness).

If this has an Elizabethan air (like some of Cummings' early verse), other passages, with their alliteration, punning, use of exaggerated or exotic diction, give an even stronger intimation of the lamp and the book— the book being Burton or Sir Thomas Browne. For Cummings and for "poetic" writers of prose at large, intensity is all. But intensity at considerable length is tedious and ultimately defeats the writer's first aim: to catch and hold us. Despite its tediousness, however, Cummings' novel is far from negligible. Its vitality is undeniable, even though its content may seem tame stuff to a generation familiar with Auschwitz. The comparative benevolence of La Ferté Macé made possible a literary treatment; Auschwitz has produced nothing but documentary horrors that are a faint echo of the reality.

Like his friend Cummings, John Dos Passos (1896-1970) went to Harvard, then into the ambulance service in France, and unlike Cummings, into the army medical corps at the end of the war. Cummings was a poet born, but Dos Passos was a novelist. His first novel, *One Man's Initiation* (1920), as its title suggests, is a *Bildungsroman*, conventional in structure and expression of the outrage of the war felt by a young man of sensibility. It is not memorable, nor is the novel closest to it in conception, *Streets of Night* (1923), which deals with a Harvard undergraduate's repulsion at the crassness of life about him and his suicide. The theme of *One Man's Initiation* is taken up again in *Three Soldiers* (1921), just as the central character is repeated in the person of Andrews, who is one of the three soldiers. *Three Soldiers* is mildly experimental in that it shows Dos Passos is familiar with French *unanimisme* and capable of working out his own equivalent. He deliberately tries to avoid the personal and lyrical by shifting his narrative from Chrisfield to Fuselli to Andrews, the three of the title, men from the west coast, Indiana, and the east respectively, each different in background and sensibility and each in his own manner appalled at what he encounters in the army. Dos Passos' attempt to avoid the personal through the objectivity of *unanimisme* is defeated, however, by his obvious favoring of Andrews, the apprentice composer of music. Dos Passos is also defeated by his own rhetoric, which, like the rhetoric of *One Man's Initiation*, clearly derives from the Walter Pater-Algernon Charles Swinburne manner of registering human emotion. Chrisfield's and Andrews' desertion, as against Fuselli's stupid conformity, is literary and unconvincing, as is Andrews' final gesture of giving himself up to the military police, his sheets of music fluttering about him like birds, his death by firing squad more than likely. *Three Soldiers* was one of the earliest American novels of the war and, until Hemingway, perhaps the best.

One could ignore Dos Passos' early fiction if it were not that *Manhattan Transfer* (1925), one of the finer works of the period, would be inexplicable without our awareness of his earlier theory and practice. *Manhattan Transfer* stands out in the history of the American novel, for it is the first novel to attain complete objectivity outside the tradition of naturalism with its theoretical insistence upon objectivity. Furthermore, it is perhaps the only novel in English in which the theory of *unanimisme* may be said to function with any degree of success. In that sense, Dos Passos' urge to experiment in prose fiction was successful. The question of whether his formal experiment was consistent with his impulses as a writer, whether experiment was the proper outlet for his imaginative vision, remains to be answered. It is at once apparent that in *Manhattan Transfer*, Dos Passos had made the transition from self-indulgent *fin de siècle* prose to a style approximately suited to what he was about: the scrutiny of a city, rather than of individuals, over a period of twenty-five years. The city itself is the central character, and while Dos Passos works through the lives of many characters, no single one dominates, no Andrews steals the scene from Chrisfield or Fuselli. In sacrificing the emotional value of a central character, to say nothing of the emotional space that such a character takes up in our minds, Dos Passos created the necessity to substitute some other fictional characteristic.

What he substitutes, I suggest, is a series of manipulations of style and emphasis which inadvertently call excessive attention to the writer, who, ironically, is trying to eliminate himself, and to the dialogue, however disguised, that goes on between writer and reader in the traditional, non-experimental novel.[3] The style of *Manhattan Transfer* owes a great deal to Joyce's *Ulysses*. Dos Passos is unique in English for having been able to imitate Joyce without sacrificing his own voice and individuality. Joyce is present in the formal organization of the novel, the slipping from place to place and from character to character. He is present in the considerable use of interior monologue and in the brooding, somber tone of the whole, an effect perhaps not intended, but a result of similarity of temperament and mind between the two writers. Joyce may also be present in Dos Passos' penchant for naturalistic detail, although his stinking ashcan, spit-bedribbled New York is remote from Joyce's green Dublin. Dos Passos may be thought of as Joyce's American agent, for it was through him that many writers came upon Joyce's devices. Few American writers have been so widely imitated, and it is worth considering why.

In his earlier novels, a dream-like atmosphere is present, for Dos Passos does not seem to be in charge of his materials, but rather to drift along with them, submerged in them as in a dream. In *Manhattan Transfer*, he is in complete control. He gives us impressionist paintings of New York landscapes—gulls wheeling over the river, vistas of streets at dawn, crowds of city people—always keying in his paintings to the nature of one or more of his vast set of characters. He tries through description to give us a quality of character, but when he arrives at the character he gives us only dialogue, rigidly controlled descriptions of their actions, and interior monologue, all techniques of the objective writer. Occasionally his characters glance off one another, Dos Passos' way of establishing unity and of relieving his excessive reliance upon the visual. Dos Passos appears to run up and down the social scale, from bums on the Bowery, to unemployed war veterans, to ward-heeling politicians, to Congo, the ex-sailor turned bootlegger, to young men just (thrown) out of college, to Ellen Thatcher, the actress, to the elegant Jimmy Herf and his mother.

[3] The same objection can apply to abstract painting. There comes a point in the process of abstraction when the viewer is forced back upon the painter; to accede to that force is a form of emotional suicide, a sacrifice of the self that one may be reluctant to make for any mere artist.

Such variety, in Dos Passos' case more evident than real,[4] emphasizes his reaching out for a collective unity in keeping with the philosophy of *unanimisme*. He departs basically from *unanimisme*, however, in his naturalistic pessimism. As noted in Chapter 2, the French *unanimistes* were a special product of pre-war optimism, and their work lost its impact with the onset of the war. Dos Passos' work is never a celebration of life, as Joyce's in part is; it is always somber, low-keyed, peopled by characters who have failed, are failing, or are about to fail. They often commit suicide or otherwise come to bad ends. The prevailing pessimism, often sentimental and humorless, is occasionally relieved by a purple patch of lyrical description, shocking in the context of the dominant minor key. Although *Manhattan Transfer* has a tone of despair and the trappings of Spenglerian pessimism, it lacks a theme. We never know why Dos Passos' people despair, why they go to their deaths or into a featureless future wanting a vague something and neurotically dissatisfied. The earlier novels were sustained by the anti-war theme, but in *Manhattan Transfer*, the occasional satire and the dissatisfaction of the characters amount to a large communal itch. The satire does not point and specify, as it will later do. The occasional joke that someone cracks is just a joke. Technique, plus experiment in style, is all. Here for the first time we get Dos Passos' Germanic compounds, which were picked up by *Time* magazine, where they belonged in the first place: "purple-gray," "musicroll," "tentshow." The distance and the control suggest expressionism or Brecht's extremity of expressionism through *Verfremdungseffekt* (the playwright's deliberate alienation of the audience's emotional participation). Dos Passos might have had in mind an expressionist mask when he described Stan Emery, walking down a street, drunk, and "a policeman's ballbearing eyes searched his face as he passed."

For all its finish and polish and its sustained brilliance, *Manhattan Transfer* fails, I think, because Dos Passos withholds his people from us, and in so doing, distorts the genre of the novel, whatever that may be, beyond tolerable limits. He ends up in an uninteresting area between fiction and painting, forced to increasingly self-conscious attempts to sustain his effort. One of the most serious and interesting American writers, he appears as anti-intellectual and almost as anti-artist in his

[4] Dos Passos cleverly suggests that he is including all of a given society, both in *Manhattan Transfer* and in the later trilogy, *USA*. He never presents, however, the very wealthy, Negroes, artists who are not frauds, or intellectuals who are not phony.

unwillingness to investigate his characters' inner motives, to say nothing of why he believed society is in the state of disintegration that he portrays. In his novel, we see not life, but the illusion of an illusion of life, one which in different guise we have seen in Sinclair Lewis: it is a life of surfaces, without history, without any realized motor impulse toward either a philosophy or a fulfillment that is recognizably human. In *Manhattan Transfer*, we know only that the past, apart from the war, does not exist, that the present is intolerable, and that the future has even less reality than the past. Dos Passos' New York is thus more waste than any land of T. S. Eliot's, for regeneration through sacrifice is not even considered.

It is not the waste land aspect of *Manhattan Transfer* that others imitated, but rather what appeared to be Dos Passos' technique for making everyone's experience available. On the face of it, if one is liberated from the necessity of creating character, then virtually anyone can be a novelist. When it was discovered that Joyce was concealed in the bushes, too, the technique took on special cachet. In the United States, Dos Passos' influence, like Hemingway's, has been confined to minor and negligible writers who, more than forty years after *Manhattan Transfer*, write rigidly controlled descriptions of towns, gulls, sparrows, streets and, once in a while, people. Abroad, Dos Passos' imitators are more distinguished; they include Jean-Paul Sartre in his cycle, *Les Chemins de la liberté*, and Carlos Fuentes in Mexico. Those imitations are tribute to a deceptive writer who concealed in his method discipline of observation and a fine sense of selection. *Manhattan Transfer* was widely read in the 1920's; it promises to stand up better than Dos Passos' later and more engaged work.[5]

[5] Sartre and Fuentes were, of course, influenced by *USA* as much as or more than by *Manhattan Transfer*. My point in including them is to strengthen the argument that without *Manhattan Transfer*, *USA* would probably have been a very different kind of work.

Sinclair Lewis' verdict on *Manhattan Transfer* is interesting. He reviewed it for the *Saturday Review of Literature* (Dec. 5, 1925). That review, "Manhattan at Last," was published as a pamphlet in 1926 (by Harper & Bros., N.Y.). Almost always generous to young writers, Lewis said that *Manhattan Transfer* was greater than anything by Gertrude Stein, Proust, "or even the great white boar, Mr. Joyce's 'Ulysses' " (p. 3). Lewis found none of "Dickens' hypocrisy, arising from self-doubt" (pp. 7–8) and wrote of the style, "a thousand divinations of beauty without one slobber of Beauty-mongering." He also admired the absence of "ego-mongering" (p. 11). D. H. Lawrence also reviewed the novel, contriving to link its success to Dos Passos' treatment of sex (in *Calendar* [April, 1927], IV).

William Faulkner (1897–1962) began slowly and even limpingly, like Dos Passos. His early fiction, *Soldiers' Pay* (1926) and *Mosquitoes* (1927), were frankly experimental in the pejorative sense, while his later novels of the years to 1932, although altogether denser, more ambiguous and highly complex, were not experimental in the sense that the word was defined at the beginning of this discussion.[6] One lingers briefly over Faulkner's early, inferior work not to detract in any way from his later fine achievement but to indicate the distance he moved and to show how conventional he was at the outset of his career. *Soldiers' Pay* and *Mosquitoes* are alike in their defects, and their defects are the reverse of Faulkner's later virtues: certainty of tone and the most absolute sense of place in American writing. Some of that early uncertainty may be charged to Faulkner's use of devices and turns of phrase, some learned from Sherwood Anderson and others from Joyce. Conventional enough in form, the two early novels show Faulkner trying on various things in the search for his own voice and theme, pushing out into the unknown, just as a matador experiments with a bull fresh from the corrals before making up his mind about what he can and cannot do with it.

In *Soldiers' Pay*, one of the soldiers is Donald Mahon, and his pay is a frightful wound in the head from having been shot down in his plane over the western front, amnesia, a return to his home in Georgia, and death. The subject suggests starkest tragedy, but Faulkner chooses to treat it by turns jocularly and half seriously. Mahon, unaccountably on an American train after discharge from an English hospital, is picked up by Private Joe Gilligan and Margaret Powers, a young widow, and shepherded back by them to Georgia and to his father's house. Faulkner's first difficulty is that he attempts a central character even more difficult than the idiot, Benjy, in *The Sound and the Fury*. Mahon has not only lost his memory, but his speech is made up entirely of phrases like "Yes," "No," and "Carry on"—the latter apparently because he had served in the R.A.F. Mahon goes blind, too, toward the end. Yet Margaret Powers falls in love with him on sight, and Joe Gilligan is devoted to him, acting as batman and bodyguard until Mahon's death.

Margaret Powers is the first in Faulkner's long line of unconventional, attractive, mysterious women whom all men love immediately. She is

---

[6] Faulkner's fiction of the period included *Sartoris* (1929), *The Sound and the Fury* and *As I Lay Dying* (both 1930), *Sanctuary* and the short stories, *These Thirteen* (both 1931).

la belle dame with a ration of *merci*, Helen of Troy, Hertha, and Jocasta in modern dress. Faulkner loves her dearly, and so do all young men in the novel. She contrasts with Cecily Saunders, the young tease of the Georgia town, who rejects Mahon when he returns in spite of the fact that she had been engaged to him before his departure. She symbolizes aggressive provincialism as opposed to the tragic wordly knowledge of the good characters. Gilligan is by turns a Faulknerian joke and sympathetic; Faulkner never really makes up his mind about him, and like most of the characters, he remains shadowy.[7] The most convincing character is Emmy, a poor girl from the wrong side of the tracks whom Mahon had seduced before going off to the war. Her remembered idyll of Mahon as a boy is deeply sentimental, and also mechanical, in that it shows Faulkner trying to give his hero a background.

In a novel abounding in partially realized characters, none is more preposterous than Januarius Jones, who is presented as classical scholar, obese fool, faun and satyr; fauns, satyrs, and the Great Pan inhabit much of the second-rate fiction of the period.[8] Jones is a stage prop who takes up too much space and whose presence reflects how very "literary" the novel is. " 'I will try any drink once,' [Jones] said, like Jurgen." Faulkner was never to repeat that particular kind of echo. But this, and Jones' question to the rector, Donald Mahon's father, "Could you put a faun into formal clothes?" mark the boundaries of Faulkner's experiment and his unresolved difficulty in reconciling his war theme with the domestic theme of the post-war Georgia town. The inordinate amount of space given to Cecily Saunders' flightiness is surprising in the writer whose best work is architecturally so right, whose sense of construction by 1929 was so certain.

Soldiers' Pay fails through the difference between Faulkner's projection of the single most challenging fact of his time, the futility of men's suffering and death in the war, and the trivial side excurions into jokes and satire that disperse one's belief in his serious theme. *Mosquitoes* is

7 William Van O'Connor sees Margaret Powers and Gilligan as frankly modelled on Jake Barnes and Brett Ashley of Hemingway's *The Sun Also Rises*. The idea seems far-fetched, for among other reasons, *Soldiers' Pay* was published on February 25, 1926, but *The Sun Also Rises* not until October 22, 1926. The two had not then met. In "Faulkner, Hemingway, and the 1920's," *The Twenties*, (ed.) Richard E. Langford and William E. Taylor (Deland, Florida, 1966), p. 97.

8 The period taste for the fauna of mythology seems to be related to anti-puritanism, the affectation of paganism, and the refutation of Christianity. Such an association is the complete reverse of Hawthorne's in *The Marble Faun*.

the other way round. Conceived as a protracted tall tale, it turns momentarily into grotesque horror, then resumes its earlier character. Faulkner still had not found his geographical region; placed in New Orleans and on Lake Ponchartrain, the novel has only a slight relationship to its setting. A group of New Orleans "bohemian" characters are urged to a cruise on the lake aboard Mrs. Maurier's yacht. She is straight out of the comic strips, and so are most of the other characters, bohemian or not. The yacht runs aground. Patricia, the Cecily Saunders of this novel, and the cook, David West, go ashore to elope; they almost die of exhaustion before returning to the yacht. For the rest, Dawson Fairchild (Sherwood Anderson) talks and talks and talks, and Faulkner works over joke after joke.

It is all formless, inept, and boring. Happily, there are neither fauns nor satyrs, but Faulkner had been reading T. S. Eliot. At intervals, we hear in the flat Mississippi voice unsettling poetic flights—"Spring and the cruelest month were gone"—and other minor echoes from Eliot. Gordon, the sculptor, has sessions of stream-of-consciousness which, although ineffective in the novel, are interesting to the future reader of *As I Lay Dying, The Sound and the Fury*, and all the later works in which Faulkner showed that he was one of the few writers who could command that particular narrative device.

Faulkner made almost all his mistakes in his first two novels. By the time of *Sartoris* he had found not only his region, Yoknapatawpha County, and most of the themes which would occupy him for the next thirty years, but he had also reached the border of the prose style and the narrative techniques that remain peculiarly his own. *Sartoris* is transitional, although the transition was swift and much of it had been accomplished in the writing of that work. Like many other writers, Faulkner found his enduring subject in his own region—northern Mississippi—and in his own family. Colonel Sartoris is modelled in part upon Faulkner's great-grandfather, Colonel Falkner. But in recovering his own family past, Faulkner was not merely using history. Rather, in *Sartoris* and more fully in succeeding novels, he was gradually uncovering a philosophy of time and simultaneously, in a peculiarly American manner, establishing a truth about the American relationship to history. The two themes, time and historical apprehension, are related and intertwined, so much so that Europeans have difficulty in sorting them out.

That difficulty is most apparent in the novels which Europeans most fully admire. Albert Camus, for one, whose fineness of grain is unparalleled in the modern period, wrote that *Sanctuary* and *Pylon* (the two novels of Faulkner's later period that seem to most American critics inferior) are masterpieces.[9] Malraux, who had the distinction of recognizing Faulkner almost before anyone else, European or American, wrote in his preface to the French translation of *Sanctuary* that it "is the intrusion of Greek tragedy into the detective story."[10] And Jean-Paul Sartre, in a philosophical essay of 1947, "Time in Faulkner: *The Sound and the Fury*," after a convincing analysis of Faulkner's manipulations of time in that novel, comes to the tendentious conclusion that Faulkner's metaphysics are faulty because there is no provision in them for a future. All is historical, all in the past; Quentin Compson's suicide itself is in the past when, through Faulkner, he re-lives his last day of life. There is a hint of political attack in the interpretation and an echo of the fatuous political interpretations of Faulkner by Americans in the Depression years. Sartre further discovers that we have been where Faulkner takes us before: in Proust. The confusions of chronology, as opposed to their mechanical order, the emotional ordering of events in Quentin's mind, are the order of Proust's mind as well. But the significant difference between Proust and Faulkner, for Sartre, is that where Proust discovers salvation in time, in the recovery of time past, for Faulkner the past is never lost, however much he may want, like a mystic, to forget time. Both writers emphasize the transitoriness of emotion, of the condition of love or misery, or whatever passes because it is transitory in time. "Proust really *should have* employed a technique like Faulkner's," Sartre legislates,

> . . . that was the logical outcome of his metaphysic. Faulkner, however, is a lost man, and because he knows that he is lost he risks pushing his thought to its conclusion. Proust is a classicist and a Frenchman; and the French lose themselves with caution and always end by finding themselves. Eloquence, a love of clarity and a rational mind led Proust to preserve at least the appearance of chronology.[11]

What is interesting in Malraux's and Camus' statements is their singling out for special comment the two novels beyond Faulkner's

[9] In *Faulkner: A Collection of Critical Essays*, (ed.) Robert Penn Warren (Englewood Cliffs, N. J., 1966), p. 295.

[10] *Faulkner: A Collection of Critical Essays*, p. 274.

[11] Jean-Paul Sartre, "Time in Faulkner: *The Sound and the Fury*" in *William Faulkner: Three Decades of Criticism*, eds. Frederick J. Hoffman and Olga W. Vickery (New York, 1963), pp. 229–230.

apprenticeship that are not concerned with history, novels that are, accordingly, least characteristic of him, although more readily available to the European, perhaps, than *Sartoris* or *The Sound and the Fury*. Sartre, on the other hand, sees what an American would call history in Faulkner solely in terms of metaphysics, in terms of Proustian time. That element of time is of necessity present in Faulkner, for one cannot perceive or write historically without being involved in problems of time. Generally speaking, the order of precedence for the European is time→history; for the American, history→time. The European, that is, perceives history as a philosophical problem and addresses it in metaphysical language. The American sees history in terms of perception, consciousness, apprehension of self. With the exception of Henry Adams, Americans do not write philosophies of history; that is a task for Europeans. The European is at ease with history. He can take it or leave it as circumstances warrant. When he actually confronts history, he becomes a Vico, a Hegel, a Carlyle, a Dilthey. When the American confronts history, he has the illusion that he is confronting himself, which is to say that he treats history through art rather than through philosophy. History for him is recent and urgent. Just beyond the tall buildings is the illusion (not the reality) of wilderness; just back there in the family album are pioneers or immigrants. No distinction need be made, for both pioneers and immigrants were people who began anew with the illusion of re-birth. History breathes down the American's neck, and when he becomes uncomfortable, he says *Good-Bye, Wisconsin* like Glenway Wescott, or like Faulkner he writes of fourteen-year-old boys in the American South for whom

> . . . not once but whenever he wants it, there is the instant when it's still not yet two o'clock on that July afternoon in 1863, the brigades are in position behind the rail fence, and guns are laid and ready in the woods and the furled flags are already loosened to break out and Pickett himself with his long oiled ringlets and his hat in one hand probably and his sword in the other looking up the hill waiting for Longstreet to give the word. . . .[12]

Such a vision is not history, of course, but a romantic vision of history which may perform an equivalent function if one is not fussy about facts or if one is more interested in using history than in philosophizing about it.

Criticism needed twenty or more years to discover that Faulkner

---

[12] Faulkner wrote Pickett's or Jeb Stuart's charge many times, from *Sartoris* on; this, from Chapter 9 of *Intruder in the Dust* (1948) is quoted for its brevity.

was not a Negro-hating southern regional Fascist, interested mainly in violence, madness, and the more lurid crimes, but a writer whose vision was historically encompassing, compassionate, and universal. This is not the place to comment on Faulkner's total canvas, but it is essential to note that as early as 1931, it might have been apparent to critics that there *was* a canvas in view, rather than fragmentary and hysterical moments of intensity. That canvas was historical, but historical in an American, Faulknerian manner. The hints of a larger frame were present in *Sartoris* (1929), and by the time *The Sound and the Fury* and the short stories of *These Thirteen* appeared in 1930–31, Faulkner had given ample evidence of what he was about. In sharp contrast to his first two novels, *The Sound and the Fury* demonstrated experiment at ease, experiment that justified the seemingly inordinate demands which Faulkner made upon his readers. At the same time, the novel began to make clear the nature and dimensions of Faulkner's historical vision.

I think *The Sound and the Fury* is not only Faulkner's finest work, but also among the very finest novels of the past one hundred years. In form a ring-and-book treatment of Candace Compson's loss of virginity and her subsequent pregnancy and marriage, the novel is in fact a history of the Compsons, of the South, of black-white relationships, a social satire, and a haunting meditation upon time and human destiny that transcends all of these individual elements. Faulkner's view of history is implicit on every page, in every character, and in every formal device. By beginning the circular narration in the mind of Benjy, the thirty-three-year-old idiot, Faulkner achieves the high degree of intensity necessary to his second narration, that of Quentin on the final day of his life. Faulkner also constructs a symbolic reading of southern history through his "mad" re-telling of a mad family's destruction.

Benjy as symbol, however, is not the gratuitous symbol-mongering of *A Fable* (1955) (Faulkner's worst book, rivalled only by *Mosquitoes*), or of Hemingway's *The Old Man and the Sea;* Benjy is in every sense natural and wonderfully right. Without Benjy's love for Candace (Caddy), without his sense of her loss—and if the novel has a single theme, it is that of loss—we could not accept Quentin's passionate attachment to Caddy and his resulting suicide by drowning in the Charles River, near Boston. Quentin is the Compsons' last hope—the Compsons, who have produced generals, Confederate of course, and governors, whose wealth has been dissipated by folly and drink, whose square mile of land has been reduced almost to nothing, the final sale being that of

Benjy's pasture to pay for a year at Harvard for Quentin. Quentin is a frail hope, for his life is dominated by Caddy and by a John Knox-like Presbyterian sense of sin such that he confesses to his alcoholic father an incest that he has not committed in the hope of "saving" Caddy from her own sexuality. He can no more save her than, in a crucial passage, he can cut her throat with his pocket knife—at her urging. Although Caddy is the focus of Quentin's despair, she is only part of a larger and overwhelming sense of the fate of a culture that kills him.

After the high tragedy of Quentin's death, the low comedy of Jason Compson's narration of these events is necessary relief. Jason, every inch his miserable, snivelling mother's boy, is the Snopes principle at work among the once noble Compsons; the Snopeses, of course, represent the redneck, poor white trash who take over the South from the exhausted first families. Always happy with a tall tale, Faulkner, in the tale of Jason's self-undoing through stealing from his own mother and his niece, produces one of his tallest and most successful. Having had an exalted, Shakespearian narration through Quentin, we welcome Jason's account for bringing us back to sub-normalcy, to the killing, practical viewpoint that Faulkner associates with money-making, carpetbaggery, the Snopes family—all the dominant trends of the post-Civil War South. Jason, too, is observed historically. The fourth and final account is technically Faulkner's, who writes in the third person, but emotionally it belongs to Dilsey, the old Compson family servant, who with her own family has served the Compsons throughout their adversity, whose moral judgment is impeccable, whose humanity attains greatness. In her suffering the silliness of "Miss Cahline" (the Compson children's mother), in her love for Benjy and Quentin, Caddy's bastard daughter, in her strength and her humility, Dilsey is a black saint, a most memorable tribute to Faulkner's awareness of the obscenity of black slavery and its meaning for the modern South.[13]

The Sound and the Fury is as fresh as the day it was written. It has the marvelous immediacy of other works that seem tied by theme to their time but are not: *Middlemarch* or *Le Rouge et le noir* or *The Con-*

---

[13] We need to look to his fiction, to *The Sound and the Fury* above all, for Faulkner's view of race relations in the South, rather than to his later editorializing either in interviews or in non-fiction on the matter of civil rights. Faulkner's public pronouncements, more than those of any other modern writer, must be distrusted, in particular the interviews after he was awarded the Nobel Prize in 1950. It would seem that Faulkner had been either ignored or stupidly interpreted for so long that he spent the final famous years of his life in evening the score.

fessions of Zeno. Why should that be? We may well ask. Most obviously because the novel has scarcely a flaw, because the form and the meaning are inseparable, because the complexity of narration is justified by an intellectual process which makes inevitable the changes in time, tone, and focus. Because the characters without exception are sharp, unforgettable, more real than reality yet imagined and fictional, and because Faulkner is not afraid to love and to hate them. He can take sides without writing melodrama: He loves Benjy, Caddy, Dilsey, Quentin, and Jason Compson senior; he hates young Jason and his unpleasant mother.[14] He is one of the few writers who has ever created memorable children without being cute or sentimental.

These qualities alone, however, do not sufficiently account for his achievement; they account only for his role as experimenter. Faulkner's distinction in his best work lies in his uncanny ability to unite two apparently mutually hostile elements: pictorial realism and transcendent symbol, or, dread word, myth. He could do this because of the nature of southern history and because his energy derived from the southern American inability to leave history to history, to the past; and it derived from Faulkner's perception of how the past pervaded the present, creating for him an apocalyptic, if not tragic, prospect. Unlike Yeats or Eliot or Hemingway, who invented a mythology of their own or took from cultural anthropology symbols with which to create a mythology, Faulkner knew either consciously or in his novelist's bones that southern history itself provided a useable mythology. All he needed to do was to talk to neighbors and go to his own family records to uncover material for a lifetime of fiction. The myth was the familiar one of the unvanquished, of the gentlemen out of Scott who went off to the Civil War to defend a civilized, humane way of life, their oiled ringlets

---

14 Faulkner, characteristically, has evoked some of the finest criticism and some of the most deplorable. Critical comment on his young women, however, has been almost uniformly wrong. Repeatedly, critics have seen his girls as identical and virtually interchangeable, constructed on the principle of the vicious Temple Drake in *Sanctuary*, and all as examples of his personal hatred for the sex. Faulkner assuredly was interested in flappers, a type that he put to good dramatic use. But he loved Caddy. His love is reflected in hers for Benjy and Quentin, in her respect for her father, and obversely, in Caroline Compson's luxuriating in her own disapproval of her daughter's behaviour. Faulkner saw sexuality, male and female, as a rich subject for study, but to say that all his girls are nymphomaniac or some other kind of maniac is to join the camp school of Leslie Fiedler (*Love and Death in the American Novel*), in which all American writers are homosexual or worse, and all American novels the product of redolent sexual neuroses.

flowing in the wind, only to be beaten but not conquered by a civilization of bastard mechanics and greasy machines. It was a myth of chivalrous gentlemen brought up on the Greek and Latin classics, men too essentially fine to survive the machinations of a lesser, northern breed whose ways were imposed on the South by force of arms. It was a myth of the happy darky, devoted to his master to the point of death, a slave yet free in his protection from the harshness of life, with which in any event he could not cope.

As another southern writer has shown,[15] the First World War put an end to the elegiac view that the South held of itself, a view that Faulkner knew to be false, yet honored for that small portion of it that was noble and honorable. The world war pushed and hauled the South screaming and kicking into the 1920's. Faulkner hated the process, hated the new cities of the "new South"; this is why he needed Mississippi, not the Georgia of his first novel, or the New Orleans of his second, and why he had to invent the world of Yoknapatawpha County. The "new South" was a product of history as progress. Faulkner's South was a product of a much older conception of history, as old as Vico, a conception of history as spiral or circular, in which the past not only illuminates the present but might well *be* the present. No European wrote like Faulkner; no European needed to, not even the Germans, who in the twenties shared the post-Civil War southern American myth of themselves as the unvanquished. The Germans were logical, too. They had perfected, in Ranke, the formula that truth about the past can be scientifically recovered. Faulkner's experimentation produced not only great fiction, it produced the truth that the truth about the past is as varying as Benjy's (an idiot's) and Quentin's (a suicide's) and Jason's (a petty crook's) and Dilsey's (an illiterate's) view of it.

William Faulkner's fiction makes it clear that we need to distinguish between what is commonly called the historical novel, and fiction in which history is used to make a philosophical point or to construct a literary idea about the past, the present, or both. We are assured that American readers between 1919 and 1932 maintained an active interest in their own past, since no fewer than 123 historical novels were published.[16] The use of the adjective "historical" to describe what is usually

[15] Robert Penn Warren, "Introduction: Faulkner: Past and Future," *Faulkner: A Collection of Critical Essays*, pp. 2–4.
[16] Ernest E. Leisy, *The American Historical Novel* (Norman, Oklahoma, 1950)

either costume romance or naturalistic abuse of popular error about the past is unfortunate. The professional historical novelist is usually a historicist, but not a historian. He believes that history can teach us, while he would make the lesson palatable through plot and historical artifact. Perhaps the distinction between historicist and historian, between historical novelist and the writer who necessarily is involved in historical matter, will be clearer through a brief discussion of Glenway Wescott's and Thornton Wilder's fiction of the later twenties.

Wescott (born 1901), as noted before, held a vision of the past as a greener, finer time than the bleak American present. His central characters, accordingly, look for refuge in Europe, occasionally returning to the midwestern scene of their childhood to confirm the past vision and to reaffirm their intolerance of the contemporary reality. The first narrative in *Good-Bye, Wisconsin* (1928) is related by that prototypical Wescott character, the midwesterner who becomes an expatriate, returning to Wisconsin in mid-winter for a visit. Wescott seems to say that the expatriate can indeed go home again, although he cannot *be* at home again once he has returned. Wescott emphasizes the going, the journey itself, and the importance of coming to terms with the re-engaged reality of one's past. His rationale for registering such experience appears as follows:

> What may be called honest portrayal of a period of transition, of spiritual circumstances changing for an entire race, requires a fastidious realism, minute notation of events in their exact order, and the special sobriety of doctors or of witnesses at a trial.

This is the reverse of Faulkner's flow of drunken rhetoric, but the purpose is similar: the reconstruction of the past and the demonstration through fiction that the past is never past. Bayard Sartoris returns to Mississippi from the First World War in order, among other things, to sit on his heels drinking moonshine with the countrymen. Wescott's precious

---

and Frederick J. Hoffman, *The Twenties* (New York, 1955), pp. 156–157. Hoffman's list of "notable" historical novelists includes Joseph Hergesheimer, Emerson Hough, Edgar Lee Masters, Margaret Wilson, J. P. Marquand, James Boyd, Martha Ostenso, Stark Young, O. E. Rölvaag, Evelyn Scott, Kenneth Roberts, Elizabeth Madox Roberts, Edna Ferber, T. S. Stribling, and Leonard Ehrlich. Almost without exception, the novels produced by this array of writers are hackwork. Faulkner is not included, nor is Thornton Wilder. The omission of Ellen Glasgow is surprising. Willa Cather, Caroline Gordon, and Glenway Wescott are on the list, and only they wrote work of literary (as opposed to historical) merit.

young man, on his way home by train from residence abroad, wears gloves and a Basque beret and uses a cigarette lighter while he reads Thomas Mann's *Hochstapler Krull* and Gide's *Les Nourritures terrestres*, all the while shrinking from contact with the young working men in the railroad car. For him, "The Middle West is nowhere; an abstract nowhere." It is a place in which, he supposes, there is "less love-making than anywhere else in the world. . . ." His ruminations combine past and present, Europe and America. Wescott indulges in the self-conscious classicism of the period with an epigraph from Plutarch; his young man reflects that

> It is the Greeks and Romans and the traditions preserved in Europe by the translators of Plutarch and by Montaigne and Goethe which, if one is an American, exasperate the imagination. Traditions of the conduct of life with death in mind. . . .

That tradition which he would wrench from the past is classical and intellectual, not local, and certainly not midwestern. The narrative ends with the young man comparing the port of Milwaukee in midwinter to the Hudson, the Pool of London to Marseilles, Naples, and Villefranche —all the pleasanter places he has recently visited.

This repeats the powerful theme of *The Grandmothers* (1927), in which Alwyn Tower reflects that in reviewing the past, he had broken "an instinctive law for Americans";

> Never be infatuated with nor try to interpret as an omen the poverty, the desperation, of the past ; . . . Upon pain of loneliness, upon pain of a sort of expatriation though at home. At home in a land of the future where all wish to be young; a land of duties well done, irresponsibly, of evil done without immorality, the good without virtue. Maturity, responsibility, immorality, virtue are offspring of memory; try not to remember. America had as yet nothing worth remembering—no palaces, no enchanting antiquity, . . . The past was by nature tragic. No tragic arts ought to flourish; tragedy was treason, the betrayal of state secrets to the enemy, even the enemy in one's self. Memory was incest . . . . [Chapter 15, Conclusion]

Apart from the idea of the past as tragic, the viewpoint here is the exact reverse of Faulkner's, for the good reason that Faulkner wrote from a complex affection, Wescott from a complex dislike of his native scene. But neither writer, not even Faulkner at his most romantic, was interested in the costume drama of the past. Both on occasion created the trappings, but their purpose is far more interesting than anything of Kenneth Roberts, Edna Ferber, or the other boilers of the historical pot. In using the past, writers such as Faulkner and Wescott create documents for the historian. The historical novelist, on the other hand, simply ransacks, selects from, and mis-uses the historian's reflections upon the documents.

While Faulkner was being ignored and Wescott was being read by only a handful of people, Thornton Wilder (born 1897) was making a considerable reputation on the basis of three novels: *The Cabala* (1926), *The Bridge of San Luis Rey* (1927), and *The Woman of Andros* (1930). In all three works the historical imagination is at work, although it is least prominent in *The Cabala*. The quality of that imagination is fanciful and directed to a Christian interpretation of events which, when draped with historical trimmings, creates the appearance of philosophical profundity. Always a good craftsman, Wilder uses his prose style and narrative skill to disguise the shallowness of his characters and the second-hand nature of his thought. In Wilder's first novel, the cabala of the title is a group of aristocratic, wealthy Romans whose power and influence lead outsiders to believe that they form a cabal for some obscure, even malign, purpose. We infer through the young American who narrates the various episodes that the cabal actually consists of the ancient Roman gods, living out their days in frustration and neurosis. In the end, on his way home by ship, the narrator discovers to his surprise that he prefers "the shelf of Manhattan" to Rome, and the ghost of Virgil appears to reassure him that "The secret is to make a city, not to rest in it." This novel, reminiscent of Norman Douglas' whimsy, was called "Proustian" in its day,[17] even though its content would have been entirely acceptable to the boosters of Sinclair Lewis' Zenith.

Wilder moved to legendary eighteenth-century Peru for the setting of his next novel, which, fittingly, won the Pulitzer Prize for 1927. Elegantly turned, *The Bridge of San Luis Rey* is the tale of the lives and deaths of five travellers who are killed when the bridge of the title, which spans a canyon, collapses. The characters are colorful although never quite human, their stories mildly interesting, and the reflections upon providence, actual and implied, unparalleled in banality. The novel is a costume romance, although its prose is more competent than that of

[17] By Edmund Wilson, surprisingly. "Thornton Wilder," (1928) in *A Literary Chronicle*, pp. 102–108.

most of the genre. The theological-philosophical reflections are intended
to provide a frosting of thought.

The Woman of Andros is still another example of the pseudo-classicism
so dear to the period. Purporting to be an analogue to the *Andria* of
Terence, the brief novel is remote from Terence, being indeed no more
than an involved web of narrative to demonstrate that the classical world
needed Christianity to give form and meaning to its better instincts.
Perhaps indebted to Walter Pater or Anatole France, perhaps even to
Lew Wallace, Wilder improves upon his masters through his brevity,
polishes his prose with care, and again provides a dish that every believer
in watered-down Christianity could savor.

Wilder's fiction is discussed only because it is useful in reminding us
of what happened when a writer did not rebel against the past and did
not experiment in any sense. Wilder's safely orthodox religious ideas
contrast dully with Hemingway's vague, heterodox, but deeply felt
attitudes. Religion apart, Wilder may remind us of Ellen Glasgow and
twenty other conventional historical writers. His craftsmanship is superior,
but the banality of his work is apparent when we place it against
Faulkner's or Fitzgerald's in the United States, or in Europe against
André Malraux's first novel, *La Voie royale*, published in 1927, the year
of Wilder's Pulitzer Prize triumph. Wilder, nevertheless, has been
remarkably lucky; he continues to be regarded as a modern master,
mainly for his plays. His novels are still treated with a remote respect.
He represents a kind of American writer who appears in every generation
with what looks like novelty and high art, capable of pleasing a wide
range of people. English lacks a word for such writing, but German is
precise with *Kitsch*. Wilder is an American monument to the fact that
there is no *Kitsch* like historical *Kitsch*.

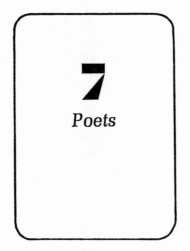

7

Poets

Poetry, which in the modern period means lyric poetry, makes particular demands upon the comparative historian's tact. At first glance, poetry would seem to be the most national of arts, since poetry by nature depends for full success upon the exploitation of words, of language, as opposed to the exploitation of ideas in prose. Words, language, in turn, belong to locality, to the individual and specific place which is radical, rooted in the lives of specific peoples. Ideas are the reverse; the more valid, the more prompt they are to assume generality, universality, even abstraction. I have tried to show that thematic comparisons in fiction (Hemingway–Montherlant) may be capable of enlarging our understanding of the total fiction quite beyond the theme of comparison. If thematic comparison is successful, it succeeds in spite of language, in spite of the fiction writer's necessary base in his own language. Thematic comparison in poetry, however, has only the most general validity; it has nothing of the central efficiency of the technique as applied to prose.

One might be tempted to conclude that the poetry most firmly rooted in the local, the most national poetry, is the finest. Such is not necessarily the case. We have seen the special urgency with which American critics and editors called for a native literature, together with their essential vulnerability to the Sherwood Andersons and the Sinclair

Lewises who emerged, they thought, in answer to their call. That special urgency produced in poetry inflated claims for Edgar Lee Masters; more seriously, it confounded popular vulgarities with genuine poetry. It accounts for Carl Sandburg's having been regarded as a poet, and for Vachel Lindsay's and Stephen Vincent Benet's reputations. Among the genuine poets, nationalistic criticism accounts for scholars having tracked down in Hart Crane's poetry every echo of Melville and Emerson, and for ingenious proofs that Wallace Stevens belongs not to the line of Mallarmé and the symbolists, but with Hart Crane, to the line of Walt Whitman. Not against the nationalistic view but in addition to it, the comparative historian of the post-World War I period would note that much of Eliot's and Pound's distinction lay in their efforts to free both American and English poetry from nationalistic bias, and in their insistence that our tradition is not merely linguistic, but one that also includes classical, medieval, and Renaissance literature, both Continental and English. At the outset, one would further remark that the period has such interest because it produced in the poetry of Pound, Eliot, Hart Crane, Stevens, and others the opening up of horizons, the vivid awareness by these poets of the entire tradition. And to the nationalist, one would for the moment reply that Hart Crane has more in common with Rilke and García Lorca than with Vachel Lindsay or Carl Sandburg. What Crane and those Europeans share is intensity. Their intensity is based in a common apprehension of human life in nature, an apprehension by turns apocalyptic and joyous, an apprehension that was missing from the poetry of the later nineteenth century, with the exception of France after Baudelaire.

In the sense that experiment defines the poet's attempt to use language freshly, to cultivate his perceptions and to present them originally, even within the demands of strict pattern, poetry has always been experimental. The idea of experiment has had particular impact, however, since romanticism, with its emphasis upon individuality and its exaltation of originality. What happens to poetry when the concept of experiment is lacking was all too obvious in America between the completion of Whitman's best work between 1865 and 1870, and the appearance after 1912 of a large and varied group of excellent poets. The interim produced a dismaying abundance of verse, not poetry, of genteel cliché. British verse, stricken by an attenuated and bloodless aesthetic, seemed hearty by comparison with American; England had Hardy, Yeats, and even

Kipling. America had Ella Wheeler Wilcox and Edward Rowland Sill.[1] The great example of French experiment from Baudelaire to Corbière made no useable impression on the English-speaking world until Pound, Eliot, and Wallace Stevens. That rather deadly period for America and England was a tribute to the triumph of romanticism, followed by its domestication. An increasingly prosperous and numerous middle class had learned not only to live with some of the equipage of romanticism, but also to weep over it and to feel literary. A generation of poets needed to howl in the desert—the young Yeats, the young Frost, Edgar Lee Masters, Edwin Arlington Robinson, Thomas Hardy—before the movement of 1912 could get properly underway.

Because of the contrast between late romanticism even at its best and the theories and practice of imagism, the unwary reader is likely to make too much of the imagist movement, to find in it a neatness and finish that it may not have possessed. In the profusion of magazines between 1912 and 1914—Harriet Monroe's *Poetry: A Magazine of Verse* (1912), Margaret Anderson's *Little Review* (1914), Harriet Shaw Weaver's *The Egoist* (1914), or Wyndham Lewis' *Blast* (1914)—one may find a cohesion and a firmness of outline that is historically false.[2] Against a natural desire to see something, for once, in history, possess distinct profile and coherence, against Pound's announcement that "our opportunity is greater than Leonardo's," must be placed the evidence in Pound's own letters of his recurring despair that anything of merit would come out of the new movement, his awareness that so many would-be poets lacked the intellect and the discipline for their work. Many if not all of the fond pronouncements of Amy Lowell (the "demon saleswoman," according to Eliot), Pound, the various lady editors, Wyndham Lewis and the rest were publicity designed to gain money from potential backers in Chicago or London. Against the perhaps unduly wide dissemination in literary history of pronouncements and manifestoes must be placed our knowledge of Stevens' sense of isolation as a poet in an insurance company, Eliot's early struggles, or the fact that William Carlos

[1] See Warner Berthoff, *The Ferment of Realism* (New York, 1965), pp. 263–285, for a sound review of the period.

[2] Harold Bloom's splendidly tendentious essay, "Yeats and the Romantics," an argument against the notion of a sudden experimental revolution in modern poetry and a plea for the awareness of the place of the romantic tradition in Yeats in particular, is pertinent. In *Modern Poetry: Essays in Criticism*, (ed.) John Hollander (New York, 1968), pp. 501–520.

Williams had to pay for the publication of his first three books of verse. Whether the movement of 1912 was actually a movement is relatively unimportant. What is important is that a remarkable group of writers born in the twenty years between 1879 and 1899,[3] who knew each other either personally or through their work, and who shared if nothing else a conviction about the futility (for them) of the late Victorian tradition in poetry, produced a body of work that promises to be read for a long time. While avoiding stress upon the idea of a single movement, then, one may make certain groupings among those poets that are valid and that may aid in the construction of a workable historical view.

It is not too much to say that without Ezra Pound, the modern movement in poetry might never have taken place. His varied influence upon that movement is incalculable. Since from the outset he posed and often wrote as an auto-didact, like many other American writers, it should be noted that Pound was educated quite elaborately. He was born in Idaho and brought up in Pennsylvania and New York. He was educated at Hamilton College and the University of Pennsylvania. He went to Italy in 1906 to work on an advanced degree. He taught briefly at Wabash College, Indiana, then left the United States in 1908, first for Venice, then for London. After the First World War he went to Paris and in 1925 moved on again to Rapallo, where he remained until the confusions of World War II.

As a student of classical and romance languages, Pound early on began his life-long task of trying to adapt to English the measures and

---

[3] Wallace Stevens, 1879–1955; William Carlos Williams, 1883–1963; Ezra Pound, born in 1885; Marianne Moore, born in 1887; T. S. Eliot, 1888–1965; John Crowe Ransom, born in 1888; Hart Crane, 1899–1932; Allen Tate, born in 1899. A second group: Sara Teasdale, 1884–1933; Elinor Wylie, 1885–1928; John Gould Fletcher, 1886–1950; Hilda Doolittle, 1886–1961; Robinson Jeffers, 1887–1962; Conrad Aiken, born in 1889; Archibald MacLeish, born in 1892; Edna St. Vincent Millay, 1892–1950; E. E. Cummings, 1894–1962. Some Europeans: Guillaume Apollinaire (Wilhelm Apolinaris de Kostrowitski), 1880–1918; Juan Ramón Jiménez, 1881–1958; Oscar Loerke, 1884–1941; D. H. Lawrence, 1885–1930; Gottfried Benn, 1886–1956; Georg Trakl, 1887–1914; Guiseppe Ungaretti, born in 1888; Paul Eluard (Eugène Grindel), 1895–1952; Robert Graves, born in 1895; Edmund Blunden, born in 1896; Eugenio Montale, born in 1896; Federico García Lorca, 1899–1936. The Europeans who tended to dominate poetry during this period were born somewhat earlier: the great trio, Yeats, 1865–1939; Valéry, 1871–1945; and Rilke, 1875–1926. In England there was A. E. Housman, 1859–1936; and in Spain, Antonio Machado, 1875–1939.

the intellectual discipline of Greek and Latin, and to try to work in the tradition of Dante and the Provençal poets rather than in his native English tradition. By 1912 he had attained a certain authority in England, and to a lesser degree in the United States, by virtue of five books of verse and his prose study, *The Spirit of Romance*.[4] For Pound, always desperately on the alert for places in which to publish his protegés', his friends', and his own work, the distance from London to Chicago, where Harriet Monroe had founded *Poetry*, was as nothing. Although Miss Monroe had the acumen (and the social connections) to raise sufficient money to guarantee the existence of her magazine for five years, her literary taste was uncertain, and to Pound, distressing. He woofed and barked at her heels for two years, acting as London correspondent and guiding to the magazine most of the young and soon-to-be-distinguished poets in English, to say nothing of William Butler Yeats, Rabindranath Tagore, and translations from many countries. Even after Pound ceased to take an active hand in the affairs of *Poetry* he continued to publish his own verse in it. The magazine continued to influence the shape of American poetry until the 1950's, not only through the verse that it published, but also through its articles and reviews. In the early years, Pound's mark was everywhere evident; it was to remain evident for as long as the magazine was an active force in American intellectual life.

Always difficult, interesting, and quirky as only an apparently self-taught man with a message can be, Pound gave himself wholly to the cause of reform in the arts, with the supreme art of poetry foremost. He made it his business to know and in an unselfish way to use everyone even remotely approachable. His published letters are a small measure of the attention he gave to young writers who came to him for advice and encouragement. His attempts to free T. S. Eliot from banking have long been known; only with the recovery of the manuscript of *The Waste Land* in 1968 can we assess the full extent of Pound's editing of that poem.[5] Pound's urging of Yeats into his penultimate, great period as a poet was

---

[4] Pound wrote vigorously and often. His published work before 1932 includes, in verse: *A Lume Spento*, 1908; *Personae*, 1909; *Exultations*, 1909; *Provença*, 1910; *Canzoni*, 1911; *Ripostes*. 1912; *Lustra*, 1916; *Quia Pauper Amavi*, 1919; *Umbra*, 1920; *Hugh Selwyn Mauberley*, 1920; *Poems*, 1918–1921; *A Draft of XVI Cantos*, 1925; *A Draft of Cantos 17–27*, 1928; *A Draft of XXX Cantos*, 1930. In prose: *The Spirit of Romance*. 1910; *Pavannes and Divisions*, 1918; *Instigations* 1920; *Indiscretions*, 1923; *Antheil and the Treatise on Harmony*, 1924; *Imaginary Letters*, 1930; *How to Read*, 1931.

[5] Donald Gallup, "The 'Lost' Manuscripts of T. S. Eliot," *Times Literary Supplement* (no. 3480, November 7, 1968), 1238–1240.

enough to ensure Pound's place in history. Pound discovered Robert
Frost and urged Frost's first book of verse upon a London publisher.
He praised D. H. Lawrence long before Lawrence was known; he
helped Hemingway to be published, as well as Hemingway's enemy,
Wyndham Lewis. He recognized Joyce and Picasso and Kandinsky
early. He was grateful for two good lines among a young poet's fifty
bad lines; he was a foster-poet, a foster-father, and a force for aesthetic
good. The attempts to be a force for economic good, the anti-Semitic
rant, and the Italian Fascistic persona were still mercifully far in the future.

Pound's activity as publicist for the arts extended to his association
with the Imagists and his attempt to save Imagism from the ravages of
Amy Lowell. The history of Imagism has been written many times,
therefore it need not detain us. Interpretation is called for, however.
Imagism is interesting not for the verse it produced, most of which was
negligible, but because it served as a point of diffusion for literary ideas
and aesthetic influences present before World War I, which in conjunction produced the outbreak of experiment.

The official philosophy of Imagism, such as it was, was supplied by
T. E. Hulme (1883–1917). Hulme's influence and high reputation among
such men as Pound, Eliot, and Herbert Read are hard to account for on
the basis of his posthumously published work, *Speculations* (1924) and
"Notes on Language and Style" (1925—both edited by Read). During
his lifetime, Hulme published only a translation of Bergson's *Introduction
to Metaphysics* (1913), a translation of Georges Sorel's *Reflections on
Violence* (1916), some articles in the *New Age*, and, significantly, during
the war, some articles on military tactics which amounted to an intellectual defense of militarism. Pound published five Imagist verses by Hulme
in *Ripostes*. He was killed in action near Nieuport, Belgium, in 1917 at
the age of thirty-four. Hulme projected various grandiose philosophical
works, but he left little in the way of clarity or consistency in the posthumously published notebooks. He loathed romanticism, holding it
responsible for literary decadence, as did Irving Babbitt and the new
humanists in the United States. Hulme tried to repudiate all philosophy
since the Renaissance, yet he reserved admiration for Bergson and Sorel.
He admired in both the element of irrationality; Bergson's notion of
reality as a flux rather than an absolute attracted him, as did Sorel's
apocalyptic vision of revolution. Herbert Read wrote that Hulme wanted
to rehabilitate pre-Renaissance philosophy.[6] This seems to me quite

---

[6] Herbert Read, "Introduction," T. E. Hulme, *Speculations* (London, 1949), p. xiv.

wrong. If there is any consistency whatsoever in the notes as published, it is in an impulse toward and beyond what Hulme called the "neo-realism" of G. E. Moore and Bertrand Russell, both of whom he had encountered in his two brief periods at Cambridge. Hulme admired Husserl's early work, just as he admired Worringer's, Moore's and Russell's; in his tortuous expressions of image, language, and logic, he occasionally reminds one of the later Ludwig Wittgenstein. Hulme's interest in the study of propositions, his conviction that there are no ultimate principles, is Wittgenstein-like, although he utterly lacked Wittgenstein's clarity, force, and charm. His only pre-Renaissance affinities were his appreciation of dogma and a certain allegorical cast of mind. He identified himself, accurately, as a dilettante of philosophy. His aesthetic reads as Bergson's might have done if Bergson had had horrifying visions of Dante's hell.

Hulme's central metaphor for physical and metaphysical dissolution was "Cinders," the title he gave to his notes, his *Weltanschauung* (he used the German noun deliberately, to distinguish between a world outlook and a philosophy). The world, he wrote, is a plurality, not a unity, and "This plurality consists in the nature of an ash-heap." "In this ash-pit of cinders" certain patterns exist, by which Hulme means symbolic communication. "Cinders" equals death—for Hulme, lack of organiza-tion. What is interesting here are not the ideas, which are banal, but the images, the literary dressing, the flow of purposefully dreary, unpleasant scenes: "A landscape, with occasional oases. So now and then we are moved—at the theatre, action, a love. But mainly deserts of dirt, ash-pits of the cosmos, grass on ash-pits." Again ,"Illness and a reversion to chaos. . . . Walking in the street, seeing pretty girls (all chaos put into the drains; not seen) and wondering what they would look like ill." Of men laughing in a bar, Hulme wrote, "but wait until the fundamen-tal chaos reveals itself." The words "ennui" and "disgust" are often in Hulme's notes, Baudelaire-like. Again, "Philosophical syntheses and ethical systems are only possible in arm-chair moments. They are seen to be meaningless as soon as we get into a bus with a dirty baby and a crowd."[7] One recognizes Hulme's images of disgust, despair, and ash-heaps in at least two places: Pound's *Hugh Selwyn Mauberley* and, of course, Eliot's *The Waste Land*. In passing, one remembers Eliot's insistence that the atmosphere of *The Waste Land* did not derive from the war but from other sources.

[7] *Speculations*, pp. 219–229.

If we note the date of Hulme's death, 1917, it is at once clear that whatever his limitations, he possessed a prophetic capacity to which his talented friends reacted. Two wars have fully vindicated the ash-pit aspects of Hulme's thought, while in the Poets' Club, which he founded in 1908, he impressed upon Pound and "H. D." (the American, Hilda Doolittle, who married Richard Aldington) his anti-romantic views. Believing that he had punctured romanticism in terms of aesthetics and logic, Hulme wrote, "I prophesy that a period of dry, hard, classical verse is coming."[8] That dry, hard, classical verse was to be exemplified by Imagism, fortified by the examples of Japanese *tanka* and *hokku*, a verse in which exactness of diction was to be substituted for the abstractness of English nineteenth-century verse and all ornament and comment eliminated. This implied a justification of free verse, since traditional forms in verse were also ornament, a kind of comment that detracted from the fundamental image. Hulme gave the new movement leadership, a philosophy of sorts, and a tone. His own despair shaped his prose and contributed to its hectoring, bullying quality which was also present in Pound, particularly in Pound's essays on economics and society of the 1930's. (It is Wyndham Lewis' tone, too, as well as H. L. Mencken's, Sinclair Lewis', and Bernard De Voto's.) If Hulme was a humanist, he was a brutal one; man for him was no more than a strident ego. It is difficult to reconcile his lapses into intellectual vulgarity ("A nonmuscular man is inevitably physically a coward") with his influence upon so meticulous a nature as T. S. Eliot's. That he contributed to the side of Eliot and Pound that some critics have called "Fascist" is unmistakable. Of his anti-democratic thought, one could quote Hulme against himself: "All clear cut ideas turn out to be wrong."[9]

Pound seems to have recognized that the issues brought into prominence by Hulme and the Imagists were exactly those issues which needed to be debated if poetry in English were indeed to move away from its early-twentieth-century anemia. The issues included not only the primacy of the image, in itself rather unimportant, but also the issue of free verse, poetic diction, freedom of subject matter, and concentration of effect. Pound remained with the movement as long as it needed him and as long as it proved wise for him as a working poet. Then, in 1914, after publishing his anthology, *Des Imagistes*, he was ready to give way to Amy Lowell, who began to put together the first of three annual Imagist

---

[8] From "Romanticism and Classicism," *Speculations*, p. 133.
[9] *Speculations*, p. 225.

anthologies.[10] One suspects that Pound may simply have found Imagism too romantic for him. In spite of Hulme, Imagism as it developed—with its emphasis upon cadence and stress, upon a necessarily *individual* vision, upon freedom from traditional restraints on subject matter and formal pattern, upon the language of everyday speech—was close to the romantic aesthetic. No poet of the period became the neo-classical artist that Hulme had prophesied—certainly not Eliot. The nearest to an exception was Pound in parts of the early *Cantos*, but even there his remoteness, as it has been called,[11] offsets his admittedly splendid "classical" effects. Pound's effect upon his friends, upon poetry, and upon history is subtle, and it is something more than the sum of his poetry or his activities on behalf of the arts or his friends. He did not need Imagism nearly so much as Imagism needed him. He came to poetry from youthful studies in Latin, particularly the Latin of Catullus, Horace, and Martial. To these he added knowledge of Italian, the Troubadours, and Browning. The resulting eclecticism in style led to pastiche and predisposed him to experimentation. He recognized the possibilities in free verse, which, as Herbert Read said, he did not invent but reform. Most important in the years before 1912 was Pound's (together with R. W. Flint's) awareness of developments in French poetry. In Rimbaud, Gautier, and the later symbolists—Verlaine, Jammes, Paul Fort, Corbière, Elskamp, Mallarmé, Maeterlinck, and Verhaeren—Pound discovered useful models for some of the effects which he would try to bring into English. As for verse, there were the *vers libristes* with whom Pound was in touch through Rémy de Gourmont: Jules Romains, André Spire, Vildrac, and Duhamel. Pound corresponded with Gourmont until his death in 1915 and knew Gourmont's *Livre des masques* and *Problème du style*, the latter a lucid source for poetry in France and England of the period.[12] Pound and Eliot, who was discovering for himself the usefulness of some of the same French models, thus between them by their practice (and in the case of Pound, through theory) negated the rondeau-ing and rondel-ing of the English *fin de siècle* and put English poetry back in touch with

[10] The first, in 1915, included verse by Aldington, H. D., John Gould Fletcher, R. W. Flint, D. H. Lawrence, Amy Lowell herself, but nothing by Pound.

[11] A. Alvarez, "Craft and Morals," *Ezra Pound: Perspectives*, (ed.) Noel Stock (Chicago, 1965), p. 51.

[12] These lists are Herbert Read's, whose reminiscence of Pound of the early period is most valuable. In *Ezra Pound: Perspectives*, p. 12, Pound did not admire Mallarmé as much as Read might suggest; he found Mallarmé's translation of Poe's "The Raven" absurd.

France as it had not been since the eighteenth century. This, in itself, was an achievement.

Pound's other major revolutionary act, one that took him beyond Imagism into the *Cantos*, was his study of Chinese, first through the work of Ernest Fenollosa and later through his independent "translations." Fenollosa was an American oriental scholar who died in 1908; Pound was his literary executor. His literary remains were extensive, but Pound centered his attention upon one essay, "The Chinese Character as a Medium for Poetry," which Pound published in 1918. In that essay an aesthetic appears that has dominated English poetry for at least fifty years, together with a rationale for Pound's own subsequent work as a poet. Fenollosa notes the concreteness of the Chinese character, not only in nouns, but in verbs, conjunctions, and pronouns. Abstractions too are concrete, because what is purely abstract in English is concrete in Chinese through metaphor, the logical extension of the concreteness of the individual character. Abstraction exists, but it reveals its roots in direct action, in the tangible. "But the primitive metaphors do not spring from arbitrary *subjective* processes. They are possible because they follow objective lines of relations in nature herself." Metaphor reveals nature and is the substance of poetry. The mind moves from the known to the obscure; "The beauty and freedom of the observed world furnish a model, and life is pregnant with art." Medieval logic is responsible for the notion that art deals with the general and the abstract; art and poetry are rooted in the concrete, in nature. Because poetry is more concrete, it is superior to prose. Poetry needs active words, those which express vitality, motive force. The danger of English lies in "its hard parts of speech," its satisfaction with nouns and adjectives. Yet English has strength in its transitive verbs. Such verbs have power because they recognize nature as a "vast storehouse of forces". Shakespeare's language is superior for his "persistent, natural, and magnificent use of hundreds of transitive verbs."[13]

Pound followed with his translations from the Chinese in *Cathay* (1915) and in his use of Chinese characters in some of the *Cantos*. Fenollosa's remarks, however, account for more than the overt use of Chinese. From that language and from Fenollosa's aesthetic came Pound's habit of striking juxtapositions, his efforts to convey the sensations of force and energy, and the conscious creation through such groupings of overtones which provide both intellectual power and musical felicity.

[13] Quoted in Read, "Exra Pound," *Ezra Pound: Perspectives*, pp. 15–16.

Pound's Chinese leads to the once agitated question of his competence as a translator of the many languages in which he worked. Specialists have squirmed over some of his renderings, and to the hostile eye, an unmistakable air of the bogus lies over much of Pound's verse. Pound is often strident and occasionally repellent, but he is never bogus. His translations, as Hugh Kenner has remarked, are "transposition, not recreation."[14] That is to say, Pound was not attempting the system of equivalences, 'of word-for-word renderings, which might satisfy the scholar whose ultimate authority is the dictionary. Transposition is the process of bringing into modern English poetry as much as possible of the diction, rhythms, and concentration of the original without violating poetry or committing sins against diction in the interests of dictionary accuracy. Pound's use of language, whether we call it "presentation," as he does, translation, transposition, or re-creation, has a distinction that cannot be brushed aside in quarrels about accuracy. His practice pertains to his view of what poetry is, who the poet is, and of the poet's relationship to the past, to tradition, and to history.

Octavio Paz, the Mexican poet and diplomat, is hostile to Pound's entire poetic attitude. Paz sees Whitman and Pound as poets who proclaim a "universalism," but a North American universalism:

> Both declare that the United States has a global vocation. Whitman Americanizes freedom and believes his country to be the chosen seat of "comradeship." Pound fills his *Cantos* with Chinese ideograms, Egyptian hieroglyphs and Greek and Provençal quotations. Pound's method resembles that of the Roman conqueror plundering the gods of the vanquished. To appropriate an alien god or a foreign work of literature is to perform two similar magical rites; in both cases the intention is to create not a universal museum of plunder but a sanctuary for still efficacious idols.
>
> The rite is one of homage but also a sacrilege, a rape. The god is ousted from his temple and the text from its context. . . . There is a sort of grandiose and affecting rapacity about this ecumenical greed Americans have. Other countries have simply destroyed the idols and works of literature of those they have killed and humiliated.

After discussing his objections to Pound's theory of translation in detail, Paz continues:

> My objection is not merely aesthetic—Pound is a great poet in spite of everything—it is moral too. Pound's theory is not only naïve, but it is also—

---

[14] See the witty essay by Hugh Kenner, "Leucothea's Bikini: Mimetic Homage," *Ezra Pound: Perspectives*, p. 29.

and this must be said even if it sounds shocking—barbaric and arrogant. The barbarism and arrogance of the conqueror; Rome, not Babel.[15]

Paz's remarks are as valuable as they are wrong: valuable in that they go directly to the aspect of Pound that one must understand in order to read him at all, wrong in that Paz misses the reason for Pound's "rape" of the past and assigns in its place a characteristically Mexican nationalistic indignation. It is as though he confuses Pound with the CIA or the Department of State. Like the American fiction writer, the American poet of the World War I period was even more clearly faced with the question of his relationship to literary tradition, whether American or English or beyond the confines of his language. At the same time, he needed to make his peace with history, to decide whether to acknowledge history or to try to write a-historically, confining himself to an endless present. Such problems are not exclusively North American, but because of American self-consciousness, itself a product of history, they took on particular urgency for Americans. In the case of fiction, we have seen two directly opposed strategies: Hemingway's and Fitzgerald's. Pound's use of the past is not really like Whitman's, whose historical reference was soft and wheezy. The *Cantos* are Pound's version of *A la Recherche du temps perdu*, his *Ulysses*, his *Aufzeichnungen des Malte Laurids Brigge;* that is, like Proust and Joyce and Rilke, his vision became inexorably involved in time and history. He is no more a rapist of the past than Proust of Venice, Joyce of Gibraltar, or Rilke of Denmark.

Second, Pound's use of ideograms and all the rest of his linguistic paraphernalia is an intimate part of his effort as an American poet to come to terms with literary tradition. He was not content, like the Imagists, with "objective," a-historical, extra-traditional images. He did not, or not for long, share their view that all poetry had to start anew in every generation. Hence his efforts to encourage the young to master their metier, his plaintive call (taken over from Ford Madox Ford) that they write verse at least as well as prose, his insistence that they know what had been written in the past and exactly what it was they were challenging. His verse, accordingly, is filled with echoes of the past, with quotations, allusions, translations, approximations, while at the same time he is able to give, at his best, a fresh and personal intonation by means of poetic craftsmanship and intellectual perception.

[15] Octavio Paz, "The Word as Foundation," *The Times Literary Supplement* (No. 3481, November 14, 1968), 1284.

Finally, Paz is wrong because he takes no account of Pound's craziness. By this, I do not mean mental aberration or any form of neurosis or psychosis. I mean simply what one small boy means when he says to another, mildly, "You're crazy." It is a quality native to North America, like maize. With any other sort of humor it is hard to define and better left undefined. It is often found in good poker games. E. E. Cummings had it in abundance; Faulkner had it; Eliot did not have it; Wallace Stevens had it; William Carlos Williams and Marianne Moore are full of it. Neither the French nor the Italians nor the Spanish have it; it is not a romance characteristic. The only German who has something approximating it is Robert Musil, and the only recent Englishman with the same approximation to it is Evelyn Waugh. Aldous Huxley tried to simulate it in his early novels and failed. Hemingway had it, although he became afraid of it. Pound has it. It comes out, among other places, in his "Amurrican" talk, where it is universally unfortunate. It is indeed barbarous in his verse. It is more subtly present in his principle of juxta-position, in his fantastic motion from Greece to the Renaissance to Thomas Jefferson and back again. American craziness is an important literary quality, one that puts off foreign critics like Octavio Paz. It is deep in the American language and a valuable adjunct to poetry. It may look barbarous, but it is civilized. It is in danger of disappearing through the efforts of non-writers in the 1950's and 1960's to appropriate the principle of spontaneity as an exclusive principle.

Humility rather than arrogance marks Pound's use of the past. Not only his criticism and letters, but also his poetry indicates a love for the Provençal poets, for Dante, for the *Shih Ching*, for Chaucer. What may sound like arrogance when he writes that Vergil is useless, having no story worth telling, that Milton is "poison," that Goethe is a man who comes off his perch only in the lyrics—all that is a product of historical (and polemical) passion, of love for the poets whom he admires and finds useful for the living, writing poet of the twentieth century.

Pound's achievement as a poet is hard to assess. It is too soon. We cannot yet see the *Cantos* in perspective, and for too many critics, bio-graphy gets in the way. Pound's unfortunate later history, embracing the inevitable political controversy, obscures the literary issue. One can say that *Cathay, Hugh Selwyn Mauberley,* and the first thirty *Cantos,* Pound's best work up to 1930, constitute a body of poetry as important as that of any of his contemporaries except Yeats. Pound and Yeats had in common a rare capacity to continue to learn, so that their work became better as they grew older. Pound began with pastiche and translation, then moved on through polyglot study to perfect a wonderfully varied and subtle poetic voice that is completely his own, yet firmly in and of tradition. There are few effects in verse which he did not eventually master, and yet (and with Pound there is always the nagging "and yet") he fails to convince, finally, in the sense that Eliot or Yeats can convince. Part of the difficulty lies in the circumstance that Pound is forever striving for effects; his most successful lines and even full poems are somehow stage-managed, and managed in such a way that we are deliberately allowed to see the weights hanging down from the flies. Pound produces a strange imbalance between diction, rhythm, and thought, as though the effort at continual control is too great, and the resulting strain makes itself felt.

In the *Cantos*, the striving for effect often produces nothing more than decoration; as much as a fifth of the *Cantos* are purely decorative. The main defect of the *Cantos*, however, is a virtue: ambitiousness. In the recurrence of themes, in Pound's juxtaposing the past and the present, his ambition for the *Cantos* is clearly epic. The *Cantos* fail as epic, however, for lack of narrative; by the same token, his history is only history in shadow. Both history and epic poetry demand narrative. The *Cantos*, nevertheless, are Pound's challenge to Dante, to Milton, to all that we honor of the past. They are a product of his didacticism, his repeated statement that a serious poet must first know the best that has been written, then try to do better. Without ceasing to be grateful for the fineness of many of the *Cantos*, early and late, one must nevertheless question whether any pattern, much less narrative, ever emerges from the hundreds of pages, or whether the pattern is simply an image of the poet's eccentricity or whimsy. When Pound becomes strident and hysterical, one is shocked, for he seems to violate his own standards, to take leave of the humanity he so obviously possesses. But it is ungenerous to carp. Pound did so much for us all by writing, talking, and acting. It does not, finally, matter whether he is greater or lesser than X or Y; what matters is that his qualities force the comparison in the first place.

Dominant (and domineering) as Pound was, his slightly younger friend, T. S. Eliot, was to dominate the period even more fully. Pound, always quick to recognize work of merit and generous in assistance, was responsible for Eliot's first publication, "The Love Song of J. Alfred

Prufrock," which Pound submitted to *Poetry* in 1915, even before meeting Eliot; Conrad Aiken, Eliot's Harvard friend, had acted as intermediary. Eliot was to be indebted to Pound for further assistance, but he was better equipped than many young poets to keep his independence before the Poundian hurricane.

Eliot's lifelong expatriation from the United States after 1914 tends to obscure his midwestern birth and childhood in St. Louis, Missouri. He attended Harvard in the class of 1910, then continued there as a graduate student and instructor in philosophy. In 1910 he lived in Paris, following courses at the Sorbonne and taking private lessons in French from Alain-Fournier. He read widely in French literature at that time, particularly the work of Baudelaire, Corbière, Laforgue, Verlaine, Gautier, and Rimbaud. In prose, he listed Stendhal, Flaubert, the Goncourts, Benda, and Maritain.[16] Eliot may have been in France again in 1912. He set off from Cambridge, Massachusetts, in 1914, with Conrad Aiken, for a prolonged European residence. When the war broke out in August, he was in Germany. He succeeded in reaching England, where he made his permanent home, becoming a British subject in 1927. He read philosophy for a time at Merton College, Oxford, and he completed a Harvard Ph.D. thesis on F. H. Bradley. He did not take his formal Harvard Ph.D. degree, however; possibly he did not wish to be known as "Dr. Eliot," in the line of Samuel Johnson's doctorate. Eliot became, by turns, schoolmaster; clerk in a branch of Lloyd's bank, London; assistant editor of *The Egoist*; editor of the *Criterion*; and editorial associate at Faber and Faber, publishers. He met Pound early in his London residence; he wrote poetry.

Biography matters in Eliot's case, for it indicates something of the intellectual solidity so lacking in Pound. Our historical comprehension of Eliot depends upon our awareness not only of the lyrical aspect of the verse but also of the intellectual control in all his writing. Pound may be seen as Eliot's John the Baptist, the forerunner who prepared the way (although Eliot would have retreated from the blasphemy of himself as Jesus Christ). Eliot did not need to be an Imagist because Pound, in a

---

[16] Until we have an authoritative biography, the chronology of Eliot's early travels will remain confused; there are as many dates as witnesses. I follow Wallace Fowlie in citing 1910 as Eliot's first residence in France, since that date is at least circumstantially validated in Eliot's later remarks and writings. Wallace Fowlie, "Baudelaire and Eliot: Interpreters of Their Age," in *T. S. Eliot: The Man and His Work*, (ed.) Allen Tate (New York, 1966), p. 305.

sense, had done it for him. He did not need to fight the free verse fight;
rather, he could put the argument back on the rails, noting that *vers* can
never be *libre*. This is in line with his linking of the English metaphysical
poets with Laforgue and Corbière in his essay "The Metaphysical Poets"
(1921). The former student of Babbitt at Harvard did not need Pound to
uncover for him flaws in the romantic aesthetic, nor, as a reader in
philosophy, did he need to repeat Pound's technique of historical mosaic.
He could, and did, move at once beyond mere juxtaposition to an integ-
ral, philosophical use of history. Eliot shared Pound's prejudice for
Dante over Milton, but in place of Pound's polemic he constructed
reasoned essays and fluent verse. Eliot's knowledge of French literature
was fuller and closer than Pound's; he wrote better than passable French
verse himself.

While Pound moved from Imagism to association with the noisy
Wyndham Lewis of the Vorticist movement and to Lewis' magazine,
Blast, Eliot joined the staff of the eminently rational *Egoist* and found
congenial company in the comparative gentility of Bloomsbury.[17]
Pound's *Hugh Selwyn Mauberley* of 1920 interestingly anticipates *The
Waste Land* of 1922. This is not for a moment to undervalue Pound's
influence on Eliot; Eliot himself certainly did not. It is, rather, to emphasize Eliot's independence, his apparent conviction that he needed to
go his own way at his own pace. He joined no group, and although he
was to contribute powerfully to the reformation of English poetry,
he was not, like Pound, a reformer. Pound was brittle; Eliot was
tough.

Although one can discern definite stages in Eliot's poetic career, his
poetry is more of a piece than that of any other poet of the period.
This is explained, in part, by the accuracy of his self-criticism; Eliot never
published work that was not his best. Also, he seems very early to have
taken a hard look at the world and formed a view that remained with
him throughout his life. It is a view best summed up by Stephen Spender,
who recounted a luncheon with Eliot in 1930: "I asked him what future
he foresaw for our civilization. 'Internecine fighting. . . . People killing
one another in the streets. . . .' "[18] The prophetic accuracy of that

[17] Eliot was never a "Bloomsberry," as they liked to call themselves. Bloomsbury
would have liked to swallow Eliot, but Eliot, wisely, kept his distance. See Michael
Holroyd, *Lytton Strachey*, Vol. II (London, 1968), pp. 364–369, for a brief
account.
[18] Stephen Spender, "Remembering Eliot," in *T. S. Eliot*, (ed.) Tate, p. 49.

statement, more accurate than Eliot lived to know, suggests something of his hard-headed realism, his firm exception to the easy American optimism of the twenties, together with the imaginative power that he exercised in order to express his devastating conviction in poetry.

Prufrock and Other Observations (1917) contains some of Eliot's "lightest" verse, but even that verse, as in the title poem, is pervaded by an irony that derives in part from the vision of devastation. That irony also derived from Laforgue, particularly in "Prufrock," "Portrait of a Lady," "Preludes," and "Hysteria." Eliot, far more than Pound, wanted a technique for presenting contemporary scenes and people. Since he repudiated the obvious romantic technique of working through his own individuality, he found Laforgue's mingling of tones, genres, and epochs especially useful. The voice, however, of the first book of verse was unmistakably Eliot's, and it was to remain Eliot's throughout his career. With *Poems* (1920), the verse is more regular than in the early volume, in response, according to Pound, to his and Eliot's reading of Gautier's *Emaux et camées*. "Gerontion," one of Eliot's finest poems, dominates *Poems* and further reflects his mastery of the dramatic monologue. This, in turn, suggests the example of Browning, either direct or through Pound, who ranked Browning highly. "Gerontion" was proof that Eliot not only had found a technique for using history but had mastered it. He had also, in *Poems*, invented Sweeney, the Boston Irishman who was to reappear in Eliot's work, by turns comic and sinister, mindless, muscular, the special work of the sub-world, the flesh, and probably the devil.

Hugh Selwyn Mauberley was published in the same year as Eliot's *Poems*, 1920. Rather than paralleling *Poems*, *Hugh Selwyn Mauberley* is more profitably seen as anticipating *The Waste Land* of 1922. Both poems are long and ambitious, both experimental for their time, and both depict a common mood and landscape. It is the landscape of Hulme's "Cinders," the landscape of a ravaged world. Pound's abrupt changes in verse form and tone, from witty rhyme to the unrhymed catalogue of Part IV, are superficially like Eliot's formal changes from part to part. Pound's purposeful mixing of classical allusion, contemporary event, and tags of Latin and Greek reappears with embellishment in *The Waste Land*. Pound's cast of characters—M. Verog, Brennbaum, and Mr. Nixon (O prophecy)—are cousins to Madame Sosostris, Mr. Eugenides, Stetson, and Mrs. Porter.

Despite such similarities, the two poems are utterly different, for the good reason that the two poets were utterly different men. The nature of their differences may illustrate a good deal about poetry in the period, for both were genuinely representative. One basic difference is that in texture. Pound's poem is elegant, beautifully turned, finely controlled, but finally aesthetic in the sense he hated, basically rhetorical in its condemnation of the age. We may sense that the poet wanted the age to be insufferable so that he could condemn it. For all his careful objectivity and public intent, Hugh Selwyn Mauberley is Ezra Pound in a cleverly attached false beard, and the poem is basically personal. The texture of *The Waste Land*, in contrast, is dense and rich. For one thing, more seems to be going on. That is illusory, of course, but an informative illusion. We return for partial explanation to Eliot's use of history, as first developed in "Gerontion."

Like Joyce, whom he admired, and like Yeats, whom he considered his peer, Eliot found that he was forced back upon history, if only to evade the naturalistic anecdote. Like Rilke and Proust, he was aware that for the writer, history is a function of time, inseparable from a working theory of time. Perhaps from the example of Laforgue, who seems out of scornful playfulness to have confused the traditional historical mix, or perhaps from his formal study of philosophy, Eliot in "Gerontion" and *The Waste Land* hit upon a manner of treating historical event that really was not new (nor did he ever suggest that it was). When Eliot's old man ranges in his mind from the coughing goat on the contemporary hill to battles which took place far in the past, or when the poet evokes Dido's and Cleopatra's grand sexuality and simultaneously causes Tiresias to see the contemporary seduction of a London typist, we are witnessing an interesting philosophy of history at work. Eliot engages the view of history as a spiral rather than as a straight line, history as recurrence rather than as linear causation.

Deriving from Giambattista Vico's *The New Science* (1725–1730), the idea of history as a series of related spirals (*ricorsi* in Vico) was powerfully attractive to the German romantics; following their lead, that idea turns up in a multitude of romantics in many countries. Thus it is interesting and ironic that the "classical" Eliot should have resorted to a view which the romantics had made peculiarly their own. On the other hand, Eliot's romantic eclecticism is more prominent than his classicism in his verse as a whole. Vico provides a logic, however illogical, for the movement within *The Waste Land* from the group at the spa in Part I, the cluster of images from myth and anthropology of fear and death, of sterile sexuality, on through the brilliant shifts in scene and time and imagery through the remaining parts. The process is clearer in "Gerontion" simply because that poem is briefer and less complex; the process, nevertheless, needs the length and complexity that Eliot devoted to it in *The Waste Land*. Pound's shifts in time and place in *Mauberley*, by contrast, seem willed and quite illogical: in comparison to Eliot, Pound is like a caller at a square dance who signals the changes in figures according to whim and perhaps the amount of beer he's had.

The other quality that distinguishes *The Waste Land* from Pound's poetry is its religious cast. Eliot obligingly identifies in Jessie Weston, Frazer, and the rest his quasi-religious sources. Only his metrical skill and the particular conjunction in the poem of images from anthropology, Christianity, classical literature, and contemporary life serve to identify the religious character of the poem. As was noted of Hemingway, so Eliot's religious bent at that point in his career is not readily assessable either as Anglo-Catholicism or as a quality even approximately Christian —but it is religious. The title of Part I, "The Burial of the Dead," suggests religious ritual, while the first two lines,

> April is the cruelest month, breeding
> Lilacs out of the dead land. . . .

with their gravity of rhythm and their portentous, ambiguous meaning are also religious. And when we have been over the ground and are more or less in command of the poem, we may observe that although its burden is despair, disgust, and the drying up of natural and human sources of fertility into death, Eliot's notation of such material carries with it a Christian sense of sin, a conviction of responsibility that is totally opposed to naturalistic determinism.

This is caused by the construction of the poem, the ordering of imagery, and by Eliot's interesting use of the dramatic first person. It is not correct to call the agent a narrator, for the poem is not narrated in the conventional sense of the word. Rather, the "I," the "we" of the poem, evokes now a congregation at a church service, now their pastor, who speaks for them to God. The "us" of "Winter kept us warm . . ." is the "us" of "Forgive us our sins." The unfocussed religious aspect of the poem resembles the unfocussed search of the uninstructed religious person, conscious of sin but momentarily ignorant of the way to grace and salvation. Eliot's later career as man and poet bears out such a reading, but even if he had ceased to publish in 1922, the interpretation would be justified by the text.

Eliot's religious leaning is missing from Pound's work. Pound remained American and very much of his time in his omission of religion. Katherine Anne Porter wrote that "this period [was] perhaps the most irreligious the world has ever known."[19] Eliot displayed his cool uninterest in current intellectual fashion, his characteristic impulse to go his own way, no matter how difficult or how isolated.

History and religion apart, a third quality of *The Waste Land* requires comment: its urban frame of reference. London is the city, but by extention it is any or every city, from Blake's London to Baudelaire's Paris to the cities of ancient Egypt. Eliot shows a roiling hatred for the city. He associates it with our special modern *Dreck*, with banal and contemptible people, with hasty and vividly unpleasant sex. The unpleasantness of the city accounts for much of the acute pain of the poem. That pain, registered upon the secular "I" of the poem, as opposed to the religious "us," is familiar not only in Blake and Baudelaire but in that strain of thought in romantic writing, in prose even more than in verse, which regards the city as tainted, evil, and unnatural; tainted because unnatural. It is present in Wordsworth, of course, and prominent in the American romantics—Hawthorne, Melville, Emerson, and Thoreau. Unlike the romantics, however, Eliot does not oppose to the evil city the ample bosom of nature. In his inability to do so lies his modernness and his despair. But it is worth noting his tie to the romantics through the theme of the city, his announced contempt for the romantics notwithstanding. It further indicates the nature of Eliot's experimentation: at many points, it was in and of tradition.

Eliot's finest single contribution to poetry was his view of tradition and the use to which he put it, both in critical theory and in practice. The poet Delmore Schwartz wrote acutely on this point. He contrasted Eliot's use of the past to Carl Sandburg's statement, "The past is a bucket of ashes." Schwartz then compared Eliot's to certain other poets' use of the past:

> When we compare Eliot's poetry to the poetry of Valéry, Yeats and Rilke, Eliot's direct and comprehensive concern with the essential nature of modern life gains an external definition. Yeats writes of Leda and he writes of the nature of history; Valéry writes of Narcissus and the serpent in the Garden of

---

[19] *The Days Before*, p. 79.

Eden; Rilke is inspired by great works of art, by Christ's mother and by Orpheus. Yet in each of these authors the subject is transformed into a timeless essence. The heritage of Western culture is available to these authors and they use it in many beautiful ways; but the fate of Western culture and the historical sense as such does not become an important part of their poetry.[20]

Schwartz' distinction is important, for it helps us to account for the immediate and lasting impact of *The Waste Land*. Through Eliot's projection of the past as living, not dead, his belief in the continuity of tradition, and his ability as poet to move beyond allusion to actual representation of past experience, whether as literary reference or as historical event, he made his poem immediate; painful in the proper, unsentimental manner; and urgent. He had solved, momentarily at least, the first problem of the modern poet: where to find a range of reference for language when all coherent systems of belief have gone out of a civilization. He did not invent new systems, like Blake and Yeats, nor write himself into silence, like Valéry, nor leave society, like Pound. His position, until his conversion to Anglo-Catholicism in the mid-twenties, cost him depths of suffering that appear in *The Waste Land* and even more prominently in *The Hollow Men* (1925). Many believe, with Herbert Read, that all Eliot's poetry from *Ash Wednesday* (1930) on was moralistic, not excluding *Four Quartets* (1943).[21]

Although it is true that Eliot's post-conversion poetry lacks the characteristic interior drama of *The Waste Land*, to call it moralistic is to call all religious poetry moralistic, including that of Dante, St. John of the Cross, Donne, and the rest of the English metaphysical poets. That is the company in which Eliot belongs. To exclude the emotions of religion from poetry is just as arbitrary as to exclude love, politics, history, or any other area of human experience. The dimension of failure in *The Waste Land*, if failure it be, lies in its willed complexity, which derives from Eliot's conscious theory of what modern poetry can and cannot be. That it is a willed complexity is clear from the purity and simplicity of Eliot's short lyrics of the period, particularly in "Marina,"

[20] Delmore Schwartz, "T. S. Eliot as the International Hero," *Partisan Review*, XII, no. 2 (Spring, 1945), 204–205. Schwartz died without releasing for publication a book on Eliot that he had substantially completed by 1951. That he published only a few chapters is a loss to both criticism and poetry.

[21] Even though *Four Quartets* lies outside the chronology of this volume, it is discussed here rather than in Marcus Klein's succeeding volume, since the poem logically belongs to the religious period of Eliot's work.

surely one of the finest lyrics in English.

"The Hollow Men," I think, is Eliot's weakest poem of an ambitious nature. In one sense, it is a prolonged footnote to *The Waste Land*, a repetition in stylized pattern of the despair and horror of that poem. But by now, the frightening figures are only spooks; the star and the rose and the dead land are not felt as intensely or rightly as the range of images in the earlier poem. The images of "The Hollow Men" demand elucidation beyond the simple irony of structure embodied in the nursery rhyme that gives the poem its form. But if it is weak for Eliot, it is still not *weak*. "The Hollow Men" is shocking in its despair and therefore successful; Eliot had obviously set out to shock. *Ash Wednesday* (1930), by contrast, represents a return to the elaborate manner and construction of *The Waste Land*, while it rounds off the development of spiritual apprehension that Eliot adumbrated in the earlier poem and carried forward in "The Hollow Men." At the same time, *Ash Wednesday* anticipates interestingly the matter and some of the imagery of *Four Quartets*, Eliot's final work as pure poet before he turned to verse plays.

Ash Wednesday is that rare thing, a modern poem depicting mystical experience, the struggle of a soul to entertain "the Word," to confront God. Such a poem could have been written only by one of the more intellectual saints or by a convert to Catholicism like Eliot. Poets born within the Church are rare enough, and when one occurs, his religious poetry is likely to be low-keyed, unexciting, often smug. *Ash Wednesday* conveys the despair that one had learned from the previous verse to expect, the excitement of the poet's discovery of a means to combat his despair, and most interesting of all, a rather Jansenistic holding of all the points of reference in uneasy balance; the sense of belief as struggle, daily renewed, requiring the believer's total attention, will, and faculties. The upshot is still a form of despair, but it is now bearable and suffused with Christian humility:

> Teach us to care and not to care
> Teach us to sit still
> Even among these rocks,
> Our peace in His will

Unlike the soft Catholicism of some painting and much verse which centers only upon the mystical experience, Eliot incorporates in *Ash Wednesday*, as in *The Waste Land* before and in *Four Quartets* to follow, a sense of secular history which is religious in that it shows the poet's humble awareness of the brevity of human existence. That truism is unforgettably registered in varying intensities and an astonishing assortment of images, from the three white leopards under the juniper tree to such a line as "The dreamcrossed twilight between birth and dying."[22] Eliot's relationship to faith and to his own existence in the world was rather like that of certain wealthy people who imply that their money is not really theirs; they are no more than surrogates until such time as they will leave the pain and responsibility of it to others. The nearest recent English poet to Eliot is Gerard Manley Hopkins, yet Hopkins' religious verse is ecstasy in relation to Eliot's protestant gloom. One must go to Gide in prose or to Claudel in verse and drama for a parallel, and the parallel remains inexact.

Four Quartets, written at the beginning of World War II, is at once a coda to a life and a career, a bitter-sweet look at the past, and a remarkable advance that was to mark an end. Eliot feared to repeat himself, he said; therefore, he turned to the theater. He did repeat himself, but to note the fact is not to accuse; we may be grateful for it. All the themes of the earlier verse reappear in the four long poems: the themes of time and history that dominate "Burnt Norton"; the themes of dissolution and dessication, despair, a tenuous hope for salvation, the folly and fear of men in the world. What is new, however, is the poet speaking in his own voice of his own career, addressing his own time out of his knowledge of the war and the threat of extinction. Without being confessional (in the recent Robert Lowell–W. D. Snodgrass manner), the poem takes the shape of the poet's own life, for

> Time present and time past
> Are both perhaps present in time future,
> And time future contained in time past.

That is Eliot's triumphant escape from confession. He provides a rationale for life and returns us to Vico, to the historical theory of *The Waste Land*.

Eliot's former note of horror is still with him; indeed, more than ever: his vision of the tawdry present is frighteningly powerful. He notes the

---

[22] According to Stephen Spender, an undergraduate at Oxford asked Eliot, " ' 'Please, sir, what do you mean by the line: ' " 'Lady, three white leopards sat under a juniper tree?' " ' Eliot looked at him and said: " 'I mean, ' " 'Lady, three white leopards sat under a juniper tree.' " ' "Remembering Eliot," p. 42.

                Eructation of unhealthy souls
                Into the faded air, the torpid
                Driven on the wind that sweeps the gloomy hills of London
                              ★   ★   ★   ★
                Not here
                Not here the darkness, in this twittering world.

Eliot's "darkness" is the darkness that would "purify the soul" and lead
it to the still point in time that contains revelation and hope. "East Coker"
begins with an echo of Ecclesiastes:

                Houses live and die: there is a time for building
                And a time for living and for generation. . . .

We next read the poet's conclusions about poetry and his view of the
near-futility of experience. Poetry is

                . . . the intolerable wrestle
                With words and meanings. The poetry does not matter.

Age provides no wisdom, far from it, for

                . . . the pattern is new in every moment
                And every moment is a new and shocking
                Valuation of all we have been. . . .

At the center of the poem lies the Dantesque:

                In the middle, not only in the middle of the way
                But all the way, in a dark wood, in a bramble,
                On the edge of a grimpen, where is no secure foothold,
                And menaced by monsters, fancy lights,
                Risking enchantment. Do not let me hear
                Of the wisdom of old men, but rather of their folly,
                Their fear of fear and frenzy, their fear of possession,
                Of belonging to another, or to others, or to God.

'Or to God." That is the burden and source of the poet's despair, as
well as of his Pascalian hope. The next section, Part III of "East Coker,"
begins:

                O dark dark dark. They all go into the dark,
                The vacant interstellar space, the vacant into the vacant,

'They" are the public men, the good citizens whom we bury, when
they die, but we bury nothing. What is necessary is for the soul to wait,
but without hope, without love,

. . . for love would be the wrong thing
. . . there is yet faith
But the faith and the love and the hope are all in the waiting.

This again is Eliot's despairing mystical vision, his look at the still point
to which the soul must arrive, his version of the Dantean journey to God.
The agony is even greater than in *Ash Wednesday* or "The Hollow Men,"
because now it is related to the lived life of the poet, to his art, and to
his conclusion that life and art are an exigent struggle predestined to
fail. That is our knowledge at the end of "East Coker."

In "The Dry Salvages," there is nothing to alleviate the pain; Eliot's
landscape here is the Massachusetts coast at Cape Ann, of the sea which
he so handsomely evokes. He tells us again, with hints of alleviation to
come, however, of the soul's struggle.

Not fare well,
But fare forward, voyagers.

Hints appear of "Little Gidding" and of some kind of peace as we reach
the end of the section, perceiving now Eliot's orchestration of the entire
work; it is intellectual, spiritual, and sensuous, remarkably controlled
and varied throughout. "Little Gidding" is a coda to the preceding three
poems, just as the whole poem is a coda to the poet's entire work. The
vision of suffering is sustained and enlarged by knowledge of a new war,
"the fire." The seasons lead us into the recapitulation, back through the
journey of the soul, back to the children in the garden of the first poem,
back to the waves of the sea, to Eliot's typical despairing expression of
hope, to

Quick now, here, now, always—
A condition of complete simplicity
(Costing not less than everything)
And all shall be well and
All manner of thing shall be well
When the tongues of flame are in-folded
Into the crowned knot of fire
And the fire and the rose are one.

We know the rose of this prayer, too, from "Burnt Norton"; it is Dante's
rose become Eliot's through spiritual autobiography.

It is an extraordinary performance. *Four Quartets* is the most lucid mystical poem in our language, a product of technical ease in the medium of poetry, of honest perception, and of spiritual bravery. No other terms will serve. Eliot's mysticism did not cause him to be loved, nor did his style of life. His style has left our world: his profoundly religious attitude, his conservatism to the point of black reaction in politics, his gentlemanly dress and bearing. He never suffered in public. He shunned publicity and kept his own counsel. Americans found his acquired British nationality wounding, and many of the English found his excessive Englishness American. He is to poetry in English as Rilke is to poetry in German and Valéry to poetry in French. He did for criticism in his time, as will be noted in Chapter 9, what Dryden, Samuel Johnson, and Arnold did for their times. The accomplishment was so far-reaching, so stunning, indeed, that in these years after his death we are in danger of taking for granted the poems and essays which nurtured us, of reeling away from a figure who makes us uncomfortable, like a loved but difficult parent.

Like Hemingway, Eliot did not need to wait for decades to pass or for death to overtake him before his authority and influence were clearly apparent. From the time of his essays, *The Sacred Wood* (1920), and of *The Waste Land* (1922), neither his poetry nor his literary theories could be ignored. Hart Crane (1899–1932) immediately comes to mind as a poet who accepted Eliot's patterns in most interesting ways. We may see Crane learning from Eliot, imitating him and his models, particularly Laforgue, then moving beyond Eliot to regions which he made uniquely his own. Again, a lurid life intrudes upon one's reading of the verse. The tale of Crane's alcoholism and homosexuality has been told too frequently, and too often by an idiot. Crane is the Edgar Allen Poe of our day, the writer as carouser, but more satisfactory than Poe because Crane committed suicide. It is well to dispose of the attacks upon Crane's life and work at the outset, since they appear with such frequency that it would be a most innocent reader who had not previously encountered them.

Most people encounter hostility from their enemies. It was Crane's distinction, if that is the word, to evoke it in his friends. Allen Tate, Crane's exact contemporary, began it with his markedly ambiguous introduction to Crane's first book, *White Buildings: Poems* (1926). Tate continued his odd campaign in a distinguished essay, "Hart Crane," in *Reactionary Essays on Poetry and Ideas* (1936). His words on the "failure" of *The Bridge* (Crane's second book, published in 1930) established a critical cliché. His attack was mild compared to that of another of Crane's friends, Yvor Winters, in his famous essay, "The Significance of *The Bridge* by Hart Crane, or What Are We to Think of Professor X?" (1947). This essay displays the brand of moral outrage that Crane elicited from a wide range of readers. Winters, who with his morality-mongering was the American F. R. Leavis, adopted the polemical device of calling Crane a genius and then proceeding to destroy him as uneducated, un-philosophical, demonic, naïve, a shocking example to the young, and worst of all, romantic.

Winters thrust at Crane through Whitman and Emerson, two of his favorite villains. According to Winters, most of Crane's "thought" derived from Whitman, and Whitman's "thought" derived from Emerson. Emerson had no vestige of originality, however; he simply mirrored romantic notions that go back to the third Earl of Shaftesbury. Emerson's emphases are interesting, however, and important in the American context. He asserted the pantheistic doctrine that God and His creation are inseparable; God is Good, and so, therefore, are man and nature. Reason is the enemy because it acts as a check upon impulse, which is always good because it is natural. Women, idiots, and savages are good because they are closer to impulse and remoter from reason. Emerson was particularly guilty of ignorance of evil; Winters quotes the passage in "Self-Reliance" in which Emerson answered the criticism that his impulse might be from "below," not "above": "They do not seem to me to be such; but if I am the Devil's child, I will live then from the Devil." Emerson further glorifies change for its own sake; he must do so, for that is his answer to the criticism, which he dimly apprehended, that he had concluded that all things are equal; that in the words of the essay "Circles," "No facts are to me sacred; none are profane; I simply experiment, an endless seeker, with no Past at my back."[23]

More alarming for poetry, according to Winters, are Emerson's remarks about composition, his argument in favor of spontaneity un-checked by reason. Apply all of Emerson's fallacies to Whitman, back them up with the contemptible modern school of Verlaine, Mallarmé, Rimbaud "and the lesser Symbolists to such Americans as Pound, Eliot, and Stevens,"[24] and of course you produce a Hart Crane—drink, sailors, suicide and all. Crane's vices, given his heritage, are virtues. If proof is

[23] Yvor Winters, "The Significance of *The Bridge* . . . in *Modern Poetry: Essays in Criticism*, (ed.) John Hollander (New York, 1968), pp. 219–224.

[24] Winters, p. 226. See also the amusing remarks about Yeats, p. 228.

required, Winters offers the fact that Crane interpreted Harry Crosby's suicide as Crosby's part in a "great adventure."[25] Winters, who knew good verse, then proceeds to an excellent analysis of *The Bridge*, to a part of his thesis that Crane was indeed a genius even though he wrote much bad verse, and that Professor X, Winter's version of Bouvard or Pecuchet, is a fool for believing that literature is not important.

I linger over Winters' essay because it represents a classic objection by many people after World War I, not only to Hart Crane's poetry, but also to much of the fiction, the philosophy, the very basis of American and European culture in the period. It is not hard for anyone who knows Emerson, Whitman, and Crane to dispose of Winters' arguments. What is remarkable is the elegant venom with which the arguments are produced. Winters' central fallacy is his partial reading of Emerson, together with his deliberate mis-readings of tone in Emerson, Whitman, and Crane. All were capable of an irony that Winters refuses to acknowledge. As for romanticism, one can only point out, in response to the new humanists and to Winters, that it did and does exist; it continues to inspire writing of merit, and it will not be disposed of by underhanded debating tricks. Part of Emerson's distinction and continuing interest for us was his lifelong attempt to combine traditional Christian morality with romantic spontaneity. Further, Crane's "thought" did not derive only from Whitman; the sources of his poetry were varied and far-ranging. In any event, Crane did not "think" in the sense that Winters sought to impose; he was neither a Goethe nor an Emerson.

Fortunately, Tate's and Winters' ambiguous assessments have been substantially negated in a critical biography that makes further mis-readings of Crane unnecessary. R. W. B. Lewis' *The Poetry of Hart Crane* is refreshing in its insistence that Crane's life was *not* "tragic, wasted, and bedevilled."[26] The work offers interpretations of the verse which are the

---

[25] Winters, p. 231. Crosby and his wife, Caresse, published *The Bridge* in their Black Sun Press, Paris, in February, 1930. The New York edition of Liverwright appeared in April. The Crosbys were glamorous American inhabitants of Paris throughout the twenties, until Harry Crosby's glamorous suicide in New York, 1929.

[26] R. W. B. Lewis, *The Poetry of Hart Crane: A Critical Study* (Princeton, 1967), p. 46. I criticize only Lewis' willingness to give Crane the benefit of all doubt and to find virtue in passages of verse where other competent readers find confusion. A corollary of that sympathy, as noted by a hostile reviewer (Denis Donoghue, "Moidores for Hart Crane," *New York Review of Books*, IX, no. 8 (November 9,

product of deep sympathy for Crane and a meticulous understanding of his life in relation to the intellectual background of the period. Hart Crane was that familiar figure, the self-educated American, who despite that circumstance challenges in his work the art of the ages and semi-consciously turns his self-education into a lifelong encounter with sources for his art. In this respect Crane was the opposite of Eliot, from whose example (and perhaps Pound's) he nevertheless came to Laforgue, and whose re-introduction of the metaphysical poets assuredly served to support Crane's own superb poetry in that vein. It is also essential to note that Crane would have written as he did—and I refer here to his highly individual diction and rhythms—had Eliot never existed.[27]

From his earliest verse, Crane showed a remarkable authority in diction, together with a precocious command of rhythm and variation. He was of two minds about Eliot and, to a lesser degree, about Laforgue from early in his career. He acknowledged having read Eliot's early verse repeatedly and having been disappointed by *The Waste Land*, but he added that he read it numerous times. By 1922, when he wrote "For the Marriage of Faustus and Helen," he had shifted his allegiance from Eliot to Blake, a logical shift (according to Lewis) since he was temperamentally opposed to Eliot's "perfection of death" as he called it, and far more taken with "praise." It should be noted that Crane never referred to Eliot's specifically Christian poetry. Crane's long poem, *The Bridge*, begun as early as February, 1923, was in part an answer to *The Waste Land*, although it is possible to over-emphasize that aspect of the poem. Certainly the poet of the "Voyages" sequence was a good distance from the ironies of the early Eliot and from the Hulme "cinders" aspect of much contemporary work. Crane was unique among the true poets of the American 1920's in his celebration of life, in the vibrant joy that pervades much of his verse.

The notorious difficulty of Crane's work distressed him as well as his readers. Its causes take us directly to his position in the history of the modern movement. The nature of the difficulty may be seen in one of his finest short lyrics, "At Melville's Tomb," and in Harriet Monroe's

---

1967), 16–19), is Lewis' conclusion, without argument, that Crane was a poet of the highest order. I agree with the conclusion, but I regret that Lewis did not argue it.

[27] One has to agree with Lewis that Crane "in part intuited an existing tradition. . . ." The tradition is that of Donne, Blake, Vaughan, whom Crane specified, and Keats, Shelley, Melville, and Whitman, whom Lewis adds (p. 98).

response to it; after raising objections, she published it in *Poetry* for October, 1926. The poem begins:

> Often beneath the wave, wide from this ledge
> The dice of drowned men's bones he saw bequeath
> An embassy. . . .

And in the second stanza we read:

> And wrecks passed without sound of bells,
> The calyx of death's bounty giving back
> A scattered chapter, livid hieroglyph,
> The portent wound in corridors of shells.

Miss Monroe asked Crane how "*dice* can *bequeath an embassy* (Or anything else)" and how, in the second stanza, "a calyx (*of death's bounty* or anything else) can give back a *scattered chapter, livid hieroglyph;* and how, if it does, such a *portent* can be *wound in corridors* (of shells or anything else)." Crane's answer constitutes his theory of what poetry is and how it functions. The poet constructs metaphors which do not depend for their effect upon a rational, denotative use of words. Rather, the "logic of metaphor" is to exploit the connotative, to work within and even beyond the surprising and illogical associations that words may set up. Such illogicality and beyond brings about a morticing of words into fresh metaphors and results in "increased perceptions." Crane had confidence that the perceptive reader of poetry was prepared to make the necessary logical jumps, to be "a reasonable connective agent toward fresh concepts, more inclusive evaluations." "At Melville's Tomb," then, refers first to Melville's own awareness of death by drowning and of knowledge gained by the drowned in their experience that could only be passed on by their bones, rendered by the sea into dice-like fragments and cast up on a beach. Such dice, messages from the dead, remind us of the transitoriness of human life. "Dice as a symbol of chance and circumstance," Crane noted, is also involved. To the query about his second stanza, Crane wrote:

> This calyx refers in a double ironic sense both to a cornucopia and vortex made by a sinking vessel. As soon as the water has closed over a ship this whirlpool sends up broken spars, wreckage, etc., which can be alluded to as a *livid hieroglyph* making a scattered chapter, so far as any complete record of the recent ship and her crew is concerned.[28]

---

[28] Quoted in Lewis, pp. 204–207.

Crane's theory and practice of the "logic of metaphor" is at once familiar from English, Italian, and Spanish Renaissance poetry, and new. It is new in the urgency with which Crane held it and in his view of its place in the current history and fate of poetry; Crane wrote:

> If the poet is to be held completely to the already evolved and exploited sequences of imagery and logic—what fields of added consciousness and increased perceptions (the actual province of poetry, if not of lullabyes) can be expected when one has to relatively return to the alphabet every breath or so.[29]

Without the poetry to back it up, such a statement would amount to so much wind. But when we can pursue the enunciated theory in the poetry, and when we recall Crane's affinity for William Blake, we know that we are in the presence of another mystic, another poet whose entire career as a writer was given over to the creation, or re-creation of the mystic's attempt, through language and imagery, to reach the godhead. A visionary poet, "*He is describing a visionary act.*"[30] Poetry for Crane is a process, not a recording of sentences fully formed and endowed with fullest meaning in the poet's mind beforehand. The process is a clarification for both the poet and the reader. The reader cannot be passive, for he must bring to the poet's words a state of receptivity and apprehension exceeded only by the poet's.

Most important and most difficult is to identify the exact nature of Crane's mysticism, to describe the character of his religious disposition. For religious it finally is, although the outlines of his religion are more difficult to see than, say, those of Hemingway or Eliot. And it is in this area that Crane is vulnerable to the charge that he is all fire and no heat, that he is a poet who uses language to find his subject for him. This brings us to *The Bridge*, in which language, particularly in Part II, "Ave Maria," is most overtly religious, and about which part no two readers commonly agree.

The Bridge fascinates if only for the fact that it ranges through at least a century of the American literary record. It interestingly questions the relationship of American experience to classical and modern European experience, it serves as either test or vindication (depending upon the reader) of Crane's ideas about the nature of poetry. Not least, it explores

---

[29] Quoted in Lewis, pp. 205–206.

[30] Lewis, p. 208, concerning "At Melville's Tomb" and "The Wine Menagerie." Lewis' italics.

in a serious and challenging manner the relationship between religion and poetry in an irreligious time. Much has been written about the alleged failure of *The Bridge*. If the poem is a failure, then let us have more such failures. There is a context within which the poem fails, just as Pound's *Cantos* fail or *Measure for Measure* fails. It has to do with the form of the work, with the poet's ambitions for it, and with the expectations he sets up within us, his readers. In Crane's case, the accusation of failure attaches, as well it might, to the theory that he was writing an American epic. Crane was partly guilty, for he was not averse to mentioning Vergil as he described his work. The idea of epic by definition involves a narrative of American history. Moving from Columbus in the section "Ave Maria" to "Powhatan's Daughter" (Pocahontas), Crane indeed appears to be creating a version of American history. The appearance was good enough for critics like Winters, who then noted that Crane lacked sufficient historical knowledge to sustain his epic ambition, and that in place of epic we get a drunken romantic confusion, neither accurate about the past nor wise in its vision of the future.

Crane's flirtation with the idea of epic, together with his critics' disappointment in his epic performance, is curiously of the period and curiously American. It is paralleled by the notion of the Great American Novel—Sinclair Lewis' G.A.N.—and what he hoped he was writing in *Main Street*. That flirtation is a provincial residue of the nineteenth century and its many appeals for native performance as opposed to imitations of European writers. Whatever his intention, Crane manifestly did not write epic. His use of history is closer to Ezra Pound's than to Vergil's or Milton's. In form, *The Bridge* resembles nothing so much as Pound's *Cantos*, although there is no question of influence at work. That is, despite both poets' conscious, even desperate, attempts to weave together the various sections of their work, the main organizational principle is juxtaposition. And juxtaposition is vindicated in the romantic principle of association, in which unity is achieved by the poet's authority of person and voice within his life and work. Pound's critics, too, allude to Dante and to epic, yet his attempts to superimpose pattern through historical allusion, repetition, thematic variation, and polyglot echoes hardly constitute the strategies of epic.

So Hart Crane. *The Bridge* is a sequence of lyrics of varying length and varying degrees of success. Their average of success as lyrics is remarkably high, however. Few lyrics since Keats' are as good as the "Proem," parts of "Ave Maria," "The River," "The Dance," and much of "Atlantis." *As epic*, of course, the poem as a whole fails. Crane simply was not an epic poet, as his theory of verse makes clear. He was a poet who moved in terms of images, not in terms of narrative or of epic idea. He went from image to idea, as lyric poets always have done. His "logic of metaphor" is the "logic" of lyric, not of epic. The entire argument to epic is misplaced in the case of both Crane and Pound, but both poets were partially guilty for having glanced, however fleetingly, at a form foreign to them and probably foreign to the entire modern movement.

The idea of epic involves not only history, but also, of course, religion. I return to the question raised earlier of Crane's problematic view of religion. His frequent liturgical diction, his borrowing of figures— Elohim, Magdalene, Mary, Lazarus—from the Bible, call our special attention to his efforts somehow to construct a transcendental range of meaning in *The Bridge*. Yet the attempt is intermittent, eclectic, and so casual that one must question its seriousness. The method of juxtaposition is nowhere more clear than in Crane's allusions to religion, and nowhere more unsatisfactory. Although the main source of the religious vocabulary is Christian and even Catholic, it is clear that Crane's theology, or quasi-theological attitude, is not Christian. Where Eliot is the agonized penitent, Crane is some manner of pre- or post-Christian reveller, unencumbered by sin or by the discipline of the sacraments. We may recognize at once the romantic pantheism on the pattern of Whitman's. But Crane's version of Whitman is more interesting for its complexity and for its greater precision of language and image.

Crane associates religion, however defined, with celebration, praise, and exaltation. What is celebrated, praised, and exalted varies greatly within the poem, but we may identify that "what" as vision itself, as the entire process of nature, including industrialism, which Crane would revere rather than, like Eliot, deplore. That vision is personal and extremely romantic, projected in fragments written over a period of years, to encompass within a single frame the mythical American past, literary history in the persons of Whitman and Poe, and in echoes from Milton and Blake; it evokes most terribly a modern present dominated by money and vulgar materialism; it is always and paradoxically an effort to realize the mystic's only purpose: transcendental union. The "what" is finally about Crane and about poetry, but never directly, and it is never confessional. "Religion," then, is a misnomer, for the word sets up expectations that Crane's kind of mysticism cannot satisfy. He is the most mystical of American poets, but the least religious. His mysticism is like Hölderlin's or Rilke's, not Eliot's, in spite of his use, or abuse, of the diction of Christianity and Judaism.

Wallace Stevens (1879–1955) was twenty years older than Hart Crane, yet his first book of verse, *Harmonium* (1923), preceded Crane's first by a mere three years. Stevens was thus far from precocious, yet his poetry retains a purity and freshness that makes the work of many of his contemporaries and juniors seem quaint and dated. Stevens' air of contemporaneity is not necessarily a virtue, yet posterity may forgive us if we find it so. Where Crane's work is all of a piece, given the complexity of his poetic mode and the brevity of his life, Stevens' work is of a piece because of the poet's steadfastness to his independent intuition of reality, belief in his own way of doing things, and fidelity to his belief in the absolute preeminence of art in the hierarchy of values. His work shows evolution but not fundamental change, as in the case of Yeats. Crane fulfilled the popular notion of the poet as damned and doomed, as romantic alcoholic who contrives to leave fine work both because of his disorders and in spite of them. Stevens, in total contrast, had a wife, a child, employment as an executive in a life insurance company; if he drank he has spared us record of it; he died in bed of natural causes; he was not glamorous.

Stevens' poetry, however, is glamorous, so much so that criticism and history fourteen years after his death are only beginning to arrive at a settled and more than approximately accurate account of his career. The first readers of *Harmonium* half accused, half praised his derivation from Laforgue and *symbolisme*. To the chauvinist, impressionist mind of Paul Rosenfeld, *Harmonium* was pretty music, "one of the jewel-boxes" of contemporary poetry, but not direct or strongly American. It was, in fact, one more inheritance from the verse of 1890:

> Little reveals the movement which has occurred in the American mind of late more simply than the fact that we should willingly feel its qualities of evasiveness, of archness and comic pudicity as slightly timed. (*Sic*. Rosenfeld had to mean "dated.")[31]

Later criticism has reversed its verdict, and on the basis of Stevens' having mentioned Walt Whitman in a poem of 1935, "Like Decorations in a Nigger Cemetery," has cooked ingenious sauces to give Stevens' verse

[31] Paul Rosenfeld, *Men Seen: Twenty-four Modern Authors* (New York, 1925), pp. 160–161.

a proper American savor.[32] Stevens was eclectic; he owed a good deal, in manner and attack, to Laforgue and the symbolists. He was not so much American, in the way of Whitman, as american, lower case, in the way of Marianne Moore and E. E. Cummings. He was remarkably original. His firm intellectual grasp, from the outset, of what he was doing was neither American nor american. Although he exemplified in his verse and was a lucid proponent in his prose of the romantic imagination, he appears, alongside Crane, almost neo-classical in his ease and control. In "The Plot Against the Giant," he wrote:

> I shall whisper
> Heavenly labials in a world of gutturals

and he proceeded to do just that. But he never lost sight of the "world of gutturals" or denied its existence. To the contrary, his life-long effort was to devise a strategy for evoking "a world of gutturals" by means of "Heavenly labials." Some of the titles from *Harmonium* demonstrate that clearly: "The Ordinary Women," "Ploughing on Sunday," "The Worms at Heaven's Gate," "Floral Decorations for Bananas," "Banal Sojourn," notably in "Thirteen Ways of Looking at a Blackbird," and in one of the great titles in the English language, "Frogs Eat Butterflies. Snakes Eat Frogs. Hogs Eat Snakes. Men Eat Hogs."

It is both Stevens' distinction and his limitation that he carried on after Valéry the widespread modern practice of writing poems about poetry.[33] It was his distinction to perceive very early that the logic of the predominant modern aesthetic—that mixture of "objectivity" and an alleged return to some manner of classicism—must lead to high, and with luck the productive self-consciousness in the poet of the very name and nature of poetry. Without a commonly accepted system of belief, without resorting to myth in the manner of Yeats or Hart Crane, and without the romantics' assumption of the primacy of the imagination, it became

---

[32] In particular Roy Harvey Pearce, *The Continuity of American Poetry* (Princeton 1961), pp. 379–380.

[33] The English romantics, of course, notably Wordsworth and Keats, had written about the *processes* through which poetry comes into being, but allusively and as a part of their confessional, merely personal approach. Yeats had done something similar. Stevens went directly to the poem as object, and when the self is included, it is an ironic self, heavily disguised as "Crispin" ("The Comedian as the Letter C") or as "Peter Quince" ("Peter Quince at the Clavier"), or later as "The Man with the Blue Guitar."

necessary for a poet of Stevens' nice intellectuality to establish, through example and poetic argument, the validity of the theory of the primacy of imagination. It was Stevens' limitation that in writing his poems about poetry, about the necessity for imagination, his fineness of perception and imaginative inventiveness often led him quite away from the "world of gutturals" to an area of preciosity, even fanciness, where some readers refuse to go. Thus the often-quoted "Bantams in Pine-Woods":

> Chieftain Iffucan of Azcan in caftan
> Of tan with henna hackles, halt!

But with his encompassing intelligence, Stevens was aware of his fanciness; he anticipated and wrote objections to it, as in Part IV of "The Comedian as the Letter C":

> Portentous enunciation, syllable
> To blessed syllable affined, and sound
> Bubbling felicity in cantilene,
> Prolific and tormenting tenderness
> Of music, as it comes to unison,
> Foregather and bell boldly Crispin's last
> Deduction. Thrum with a proud douceur
> His grand pronunciamento and devise.

It is all there—the symbolist noises, archaic diction, arch French words and the commanding intelligence that orders and informs the whole— while the poem itself is a tour-de-force. It is what Edith Sitwell attempted, but she succeeded only in reproducing the surfaces and the noises, not the undercurrent of self-parody and total seriousness.[34] That kind of medita-tive intellectual lyric on poetry itself, on the nature of the imagination, makes up a large segment of *Harmonium*, as of Stevens' later work.

His other major subject is related in technique, yet quite different in substance. It is Stevens' firm rejection of religion, all religion; unlike Eliot, he would find no point or spark in Christianity. Unlike Crane, he would not invent his own mystical vision, and unlike Pound and most other poets of the day, he did not choose to omit the subject from his view. Perhaps Stevens' finest poetry is his anti-religious poetry. Some-times the tone is the comic, playful tone of the poems about poetry:

---

[34] Cf. F. R. Leavis' only epigram: "But the Sitwells belong to the history of publicity rather than of poetry." "The Situation at the End of World War I," in *Modern Poetry: Essays in Criticism*, p. 80.

Hi! the Creator too is blind

    ★   ★   ★   ★

Incapable master of all force ("Negation")

Or this from "A High-Toned Old Christian Woman":

Poetry is the supreme fiction, madame.
Take the moral law and make a nave of it
And from the nave build haunted heaven

Or this from "Death of a Soldier," although the tone gives way here to something else than play:

The Soldier falls.
He does not become a three-days personage,
Imposing his separation,
Calling for pomp.
Death is absolute and without memorial. . . .

That tone is the tone of Stevens' finest single poem, the deservedly famous "Sunday Morning." The poem's fineness derives from subtly interrelated elements: technical perfection, economy, one's surprise and pleasure at the calmness of tone on a subject that conventionally brings forth argument and fervor. Stevens is no metaphysical making love to Christ as to a woman. Rather, his view of his central figure, a woman at her coffee and oranges of a Sunday morning, the day of masses and other religious observances, is to

. . . dissipate
The holy hush of ancient sacrifice.

We may feel surprise that Stevens disposes of conventional, formal religions, of informal paganism; that he affirms the sweetness of nature in their stead, yet does not lapse into romantic pantheism. Nature is not sacred, it is simply there, and although it is sweet and good, it contains and confirms death. Jesus, in the eighth and final stanza, is a man, not a god, and "We live in an old chaos of the sun," in nature, "unsponsored, free." But the deer, the quail, the sweet berries, give way to the appropriate and brave final image of death: the pigeons that make

Ambiguous undulations as they sink,
Downward to darkness, on extended wings.

The bravery—or the blasphemy, depending upon the reader's religious disposition—lies in the word "extended" to describe the pigeons' wings. They do not dive to death like airplanes, or flutter away from it. Death is there, like all nature. In its serenity, the poem makes exegesis unimportant, if not impertinent, a quality that many great poems possess. But it must be noted that such control, independence of mind, and serenity are unique in American poetry and rare at any point in Western literature since Vergil's death.

William Carlos Williams (1883–1963), poet and physician, had a good deal in common with Stevens, including hostility to religion. Williams gave special point to his view, and possibly to Stevens', too, when he made it specifically anti-T. S. Eliot. He devised a sketch in a letter of 1945, the point of which he had often made from the time of *The Waste Land* forward:

Christ: In my house there are many mansions.
Eliot: I'll take the corner room on the second floor overlooking the lawns and the river.
        And WHO is this rabble that follows you about?
Christ: Oh, some of the men I've met in my travels.
Eliot: Well, if I am to follow you I'd like to know something more of your sleeping arrangements.
Christ: Yes sir.[35]

Williams' main objection was not to Eliot's snobbish Christianity, but to his cosmopolitanism, his turning back to tradition for support, and his expatriation—especially syntactical and verbal expatriation. Five years older than Eliot, two years older than Pound, Williams' first book of verse, *Poems*, had appeared in 1909.[36] Early identified as an Imagist, Williams was never more than approximately a member of that group. He was formally allied to the Imagists for a time. His printed verse appeared to be imagistic, and he wrote a kind of prose-poetry in *Kora in Hell* reminiscent of Amy Lowell's *Can Grande's Castle*. From the beginning, however, Williams and the Imagists did not run along the same

[35] William Carlos Williams, *Selected Letters* (New York, 1957), p. 240.
[36] Williams' other publications to 1932: *The Tempers*, 1913; *A Book of Poems*, 1917; *Al Que Quiere!*, 1917; *Kora in Hell: Improvisations*, 1920; *Sour Grapes: A Book of Poems*, 1921; *Spring and All*, 1923; *Go Go*, 1923; *The Great American Novel*, 1923; *In the American Grain*, 1925; *A Voyage to Pagany*, 1928.

track. Like the Imagists, Williams at first was willing to confine his aesthetic to the visual, to break with the past, and to purify through simplification. He diverged from them, however, in his rejection of Europe and his corresponding emphasis upon America; in his view of the self as a source of poetry; and above all, in his humor, the quality that I have called craziness.

If the nature of Williams' American-ness is not understood, the result can be a complete misinterpretation of the poet and the poetry. Patriotic critics in the United States usually see Williams as a latter-day Walt Whitman, in part for certain characteristics of his verse, in part because Williams discussed Whitman more or less sympathetically in his prose from time to time.[37] There is no more reason to see Williams as deriving from Whitman than to see Stevens in that line of descent. The flavor of Williams' "American" outbursts can best be tasted in his essays on pre- and post-Columbian history, *In the American Grain* (1925). The book is not history as we usually understand it, but a series of impassioned meditations on the violence and bloodshed done to the men of the New World by the men of the Old World; a series of editorials on episodes in North American history from the Revolution to the Civil War; and an excellent literary essay on Poe. Much of the historical matter has the tone of the beginning of the essay on Ponce de Leon, "The Fountain of Eternal Youth." The essay shows an unusual point of view for belonging in time to the Presidency of Harding:

> History, history! We fools, what do we know or care? History begins for us with murder and enslavement, not with discovery. No, we are not Indians but we are men of their world. The blood means nothing; the spirit, the ghost of the land moves in the blood, moves the blood. It is we who ran to the shore naked, we who cried, "Heavenly Man!" These are the inhabitants of our souls, our murdered souls that lie . . . agh. Listen! I tell you that it was lucky for Spain the first ship put its men ashore where it did. If the Italian had landed in Florida, one twist of the helm north, or among the

---

[37] Pearce, *The Continuity of American Poetry*, pp. 288–289 and pp. 335–348. Pearce's thesis of "continuity" urges him to a mis-reading of texts he himself cites. He quotes Williams' surely ambiguous tribute to Whitman:
. . . from Whitman, we draw out—what we have to do today. We don't have to discover it from Whitman but we may discover it from Whitman if we want to. It is, not to impose the structures, the forms of the past which speak against us in their own right but to discover, first, by headlong composition perhaps, what we can do. (p. 288).
There is no evidence that Pearce is aware of any ambiguity.

islands a hair more to the south; among the Yamasses with their sharpened
bones and fishspines, or among the Caribs with their poisoned darts—it might
have begun differently.[38]

The careful construction of the illusion of spontaneity, the personal
note, by turns formal, colloquial, and slangy, the indignation and the
sense of a voice in our ear, are a gauge of Williams' intensity of feeling
for his country and a good introduction to his poetry as well. But he
has none of Whitman's mysticism about America, and none of his damp
pantheism. Both wrote about physical suffering, but Whitman's Civil
War poetry is diffuse and constantly on the edge of sentimentality.
Williams, who made his living as a general practitioner and later as a
gynecologist, writes of illness and pain with humanity but also with
humor and toughness, qualities foreign to Whitman.

The other side of Williams' feeling for America, his hostility to
Europe, is evident in his remarks on six weeks in Paris. After reviewing
the people whom he had met—everybody—he remarks:

> I was during that time, with antennae fully extended, but nothing came
> of it save an awakened realization within myself of that resistant core of
> nature upon which I had so long been driven for support. I felt myself with
> ardors not released but beaten back, in this center of old-world culture where
> everyone was tearing his own meat, *warily* conscious of a newcomer, but
> wholly without inquisitiveness—No wish to know; they were served.[39]

Williams lacked Whitman's all too easy universality, yet his American-
ness was not constructed out of hostility or fear of Europe, or out of
self-indulgent chauvinism. He wanted, rather, to use American history,
to use the resonance that history gave to English words, transforming
them into American ones, for poetry. In essay after essay and in poem
after poem, he remarked and annotated the individual turn and print of
phenomena. His poetics, limited until late in his life to the word and
the line, forced him to an extraordinary degree of control over diction
and to his individual, blurting rhythms.

Williams was less in the tradition of Whitman than in quite another
tradition that he knew through his Spanish-Puerto Rican mother and
through his own knowledge of Spanish poetry: I refer to the long Spanish
tradition of the easy, conversational, relaxed lyric, which is in total
contrast to the Spanish grand manner that English-speaking people

---

[38] William Carlos Williams, *In the American Grain* (New York, 1956), p. 39.
[39] *In the American Grain*, pp. 105–106.

commonly associate with Spanish poetry. The tradition goes back at least to the medieval period, as Williams was aware. By the time of Baltasar del Alcazar (1530–1606) the easy, colloquial note had been so perfected that in light love lyrics and epigrams, we may read verses without a precise parallel in English. That particular note has never gone out of Spanish verse, as Williams well knew.[40] One suspects that it was Williams' Spanish background, at least in part, that contributed to his hostility to Eliot.

Eliot was the enemy. Williams wrote in his *Autobiography* that *The Waste Land* came upon him suddenly,

> . . . and all our hilarity ended. It wiped out our world. . . .
> To me especially it struck like a sardonic bullet. I felt at once that it had set me back twenty years, and I'm sure it did. Critically Eliot returned us to the classroom just at the moment when I felt that we were on the point of an escape to matters much closer to the essence of a new art form itself—rooted in the locality which should give it fruit. I knew at once that in certain ways I was most defeated.[41]

---

[40] See Williams' careless but passionate article, "Federico García Lorca," *Kenyon Review* (I, no. 2, Spring, 1939), 148–158. In English, the nearest we have to the tone of the Spanish is in the poetry of Herrick, or in some of the witty verse of the Restoration. But such verse differs in being more formal and in verging on satire. The quality does not translate. Here is Alcazar's "A Inés":

> *Oyeme, así Dios te guarde,*
> *que te quiero, Inés, contar*
> *un cuento bien singular*
> *que me sucedió esta tarde.*

> *Has de saber que un francés*
> *pasó vendiendo calderas . . .*
> *Estáme atenta: no quieras*
> *que lo cuente en balde, Inés.*

> *Llamélo, desque me vido— – –*
> *Escúchame con reposo,*
> *que es el cuento más donoso*
> *de cuantos habrás oído.*

> *Díjele: "Amigo, a contento,*
> *¿cuanto por esta caldera? . . ."*
> *¿No me escuchas? . . . Pues yo muera*
> *sin óleo si te lo cuento.*

[41] William Carlos Williams, *Autobiography* (New York, 1951), p. 174.

We may recognize, from Williams' complaint, that he had trapped himself in the romantic insistence that art be forever new and individual, while he failed to take advantage of the romantic's respect for myth or to share the romantic quest for a structure of belief. "I felt that we were on the point of an escape to matters much closer to the essence of a new art form itself" is an extraordinary confession of belief in the ability of the individual poet to subsist on his own flesh alone. It is not only opposed to Eliot's kind of myth, religion, and ritual; it is also anti-historical and anti-intellectual. Willing to give up so much, Williams of necessity placed his emphasis on prosody; every word and every line had to be tested for stress and examined microscopically for hair-line cracks. Until the 1940's, Williams' poetry seemed, like much of Wallace Stevens', to be concerned with trivia, while Pound and Eliot were taking on the philosophical burden of the ages. Williams did not bother to argue his position against religion, as Stevens did in "Sunday Morning," nor did he have the advantage of Stevens' comic mask or his neo-symbolist elegance. Williams' poems are rarely narratives or conventional dramatic monologues. They are more often stated in the second person or the imperative:

> Beat hell out of it (*Paterson:* Episode 17)
> My townspeople. . . . ("Gulls")
> For heaven's sake though see to the driver!
>   ("Tract")

They are polemics by the poet often addressed to the poet, or to the community, or to the grass. As such they are comic, sometimes genuinely trivial, but more often surprising, disturbing, and delightful.

In a time of programmatic poetry, Williams even more than Pound was a programmatic poet whose programs may have got in the way of his poetry. He spent a great deal of time explaining himself and his programs in garrulous essays, an activity which may have been necessary to keep up his morale before the onslaughts of the Christian enemy. Although Williams was not at his best in prose, the essays are worth reading for their humanity, their humor, their occasional bawdiness, and for Williams' essential seriousness. In his lifelong search for the separateness, the *Ding an sich*-ness of each human action and each fact in nature, Williams produced some of the finest verse of the modern period. At his worst, he could be soft, sentimental, and trivial indeed. His independence of vision and his poetic integrity were unusual; it is still too early to assess his influence upon a number of younger poets. Suffice to note that it is considerable, and that without Williams' work, American literature of the post-World War I period would be thinner than it is.

Marianne Moore (born 1887) may best be described as a major-minor poet, with no condescension implied. She is like a conductor who can conduct a single symphony better than any other conductor in the world but who is not interested in trying his hand at any other composition. She was born in Kirkwood, a suburb of St. Louis, Missouri, a few months after T. S. Eliot was born in that city. Eliot, appropriately, was to write in the introduction to her *Selected Poems* (1935) that she was one of the few poets in English likely to endure. In her life and work, she was to continue to cross paths with a rich variety of people, from Jim Thorpe, the great Indian athlete who was her student for a time, to Hilda Doolittle, whom she knew at Bryn Mawr, to Ezra Pound and William Carlos Williams, who were at the University of Pennsylvania when she was at Bryn Mawr. As editor of *The Dial* from 1925 to its final issue in 1929, Miss Moore necessarily knew or corresponded with a large number of writers. Perhaps the only poet to follow baseball, she was for years an enthusiast of the Brooklyn Dodgers. Her verses, "Hometown Piece for Messrs. Alston and Reese," are cherished by athletes and other enthusiasts.[42] Her work as a whole has been praised, even overpraised, by critics so diverse as Pound, Eliot, Yvor Winters, R. P. Blackmur, Kenneth Burke, and by William Carlos Williams and Wallace Stevens as well.

Marianne Moore was never prolific. Her first book, *Poems*, was brought out by the Egoist Press, London, in 1921 without her knowledge, through the efforts of H. D. and Winifred Ellerman. In part because of her work on the *Dial*, she published only one other book in the twenties, *Observations* (1924). From 1924, when she received the *Dial* award, her reputation was assured among poets and critics. She was not to attain wide popularity until 1951, however.

It is Miss Moore's limitation rather than the historian's that one is

---

[42] Miss Moore's note identifying Walter Alston as manager of the Dodgers and Harold (Peewee) Reese as captain should perhaps have added the fact that Reese was one of the finest shortstops the game ever turned out. Baseball enthusiasts also prize Miss Moore's poem, "Baseball and Writing," a tribute to the New York Yankees.

driven inevitably to her brilliant but by now worn-out statement that poets should invent "imaginary gardens with real toads in them." That paradoxical joke at once defines what she has been doing since the beginning in her own verse, it leads us to her philosophical conception of reality, it may imply something of her moral concern, while it assuredly provides an example of her whimsicality. Miss Moore herself may have become weary of her toads. The original version of "Poetry" in which the phrase was written contained twenty-nine lines. The version in *Complete Poems* (1967) contains just three lines:

> I, too, dislike it,
>   Reading it, however, with a perfect
>   contempt for it, one discovers in
> it, after all, a place for the genuine.

The preliminary note to *Complete Poems*, "Omissions are not accidents," is also to the point. Few poets have written a body of work so slightly varied from the beginning over a period of decades. Miss Moore was, to be sure, claimed by the Objectivists, as were Wallace Stevens and William Carlos Williams.[43] She was obviously too independent to be claimed by the Imagists. Her method is her own, and it is inimitable· "In the Days of Prismatic Color," which dates from the period of her first book, may be taken as typical of that method early and late. The handsome title, as is so often the case, forms the first line, introducing a syntactically involved, apparently prosaic sentence, the subject of which we meet only in the sixth line: "obliqueness." The poem must be quoted in full, for paraphrase or partial quotation of Miss Moore is more than usually a violation.

---

[43] Louis Zukofsky, its leading figure, refused to call Objectivism a "movement." He did, however, put together *An "Objectivists" Anthology* (1932), in which he defined the "objective" as that which the poet aims for, and Objective poetry as "objectively perfect," adding, mysteriously, "inextricably the direction of historical and contemporary particulars." Miss Moore's "An Egyptian Pulled-glass Bottle in the Shape of a Fish" was offered as an example. The "philosophy" of Objectivism seems to be based on the psychology of association: the poet focusses upon an object or thing in the belief that reality inheres in the sensations and ideas it generates. Williams, and to some degree Stevens, were closer to this notion than was Miss Moore. See Bernard F. Engle, *Marianne Moore* (New York, 1964), pp. 17–19 for "Objectivism" and for some of the wisest criticism of Miss Moore's work that we have.

In the Days of Prismatic Color

not in the days of Adam and Eve, but when Adam
    was alone; when there was no smoke and color was
fine, not with the refinement
    of early civilization art, but because
of its originality; with nothing to modify it but the

mist that went up, obliqueness was a variation
    of the perpendicular, plain to see and
to account for: it is no
    longer that; nor did the blue-red-yellow band
of incandescence that was color keep its stripe: it also is one of

those things into which much that is peculiar can be
    read; complexity is not a crime,` but carry
it to the point of murkiness
    and nothing is plain. Complexity,
moreover, that has been committed to darkness, instead of

granting itself to be the pestilence that it is, moves all
    about as if to bewilder us with the dismal
fallacy that insistence
    is the measure of achievement and that all
truth must be dark. Principally throat, sophistication is as it al-

ways has been—at the antipodes from the init-
    ial great truths. "Part of it was crawling, part of it
was about to crawl, the rest
    was torpid in its lair." In the short-legged, fit-
ful advance, the gurgling and all the minutiae—we have the classic
multitude of feet. To what purpose! Truth is no Apollo
    Belvedere, nor formal thing. The wave may go over it if it likes.
Know that it will be there when it says,
    "I shall be there when the wave has gone by."

The technique of composition by syllable and line only teasingly conceals
the use of alliteration, a diction so controlled as to be finicky, and a
rhythm that departs sufficiently from normal English prose rhythm to
mock it in its deceptive resemblance. A most serious poem about the
nature of truth and the dangers of obscurity, in theme it is like Keats'
ode "On a Grecian Urn." The tone is nevertheless witty, the statement
moral, and the whole somehow more than the sum of its nameable parts.
Characteristically again, lines 23 to 25 contain an obscure quotation that

is solemnly identified in a note: " 'Part of it was crawling,' etc. Nestor. *Greek Anthology* (Loeb Classical Library), Vol. III, p. 129." Miss Moore's notes in all her poems, like Eliot's to *The Waste Land*, are often solemn jests extending her attack upon sophistication ("Principally throat"). The placement of each line on the page is important, more so than E. E. Cummings' flamboyant compositional effects. For Miss Moore, such placements are a form of exposition of an intellectual plot. Her poems, however lyrical they finally are, contain intellectual plots and moral or ethical narratives. She begins with detail or setting ("not in the days of Adam and Eve"), more or less scholarly, and builds to a climax, usually of an abstract nature which reinforces her moral. She is able to combine downright stuffiness with a drama that is both rhetorical and a product of her imagery. As such, she is unique among modern poets, absolutely independent, and old-fashioned in the most new-fashioned manner conceivable. Her affinity for La Fontaine was to lead her to translate him; it may also account for her animal poems. But where his animals were pretty much of the barnyard, hers are wide-ranging. Among them are the jerboa, swan, the frigate pelican, fish, monkeys, snakes, mongooses, an octopus, snail, whale, wood-weasel, elephants, ermine, a dragon, giraffe, and a tiger. Like her list of animals, her verse appears long-winded; she seems to be prolix, but she is not. She makes epigrammatic, cutting, elaborate statements with elaborate brevity.

The contrasts between Marianne Moore and E. E. Cummings (1894–1962) are so great as to be melodramatic. He was flashily public where she is private and secretive; he romantic and she classical; he self-indulgent and she self-critical; he knowing-innocent and she innocent-knowing; he physical and she intellectual. Cummings' early verse hardly merits consideration. His main claim to historical attention in the 1920's is probably his play, *Him* (1927), rather than his verse of those years.[44] His best verse was to be written in the 1930's and 1940's. Cummings is useful to the historian of the earlier period, however, in that his posturings and flamboyant "experiments" in verse were as much of the period as Sinclair Lewis or H. L. Mencken in their very different dimensions of activity. Because of both contemporary and later reaction to Cummings, he helps to define the period for us, much as Oscar Wilde helps to define the English 1890's.

[44] Cummings' poetry of the period is *Tulips and Chimneys*, 1923; *&* [And], 1925; *XLI Poems*, 1925; *is 5*, 1926; *W* (ViVa), 1931.

Cummings' small bagful of tricks—his experiments—successfully disguised for a decade or so the fact that he is one of the most Wordsworthian of poets, deeply embedded in that noble tradition of the poetry of nature and the self, with intermittent intimations of theology and mortality. Even when Cummings' subject matter was not exactly Wordsworthian, his impulse was. The indiscriminate, smothering flow of language was disguised, or so he must have hoped, by his typographical trickiness: the almost undeviating use of lower-case type, his breaking up of words into syllables or separate letters on the page, as in the title "poor But TerFLY" from *W;* his neglect of punctuation; and more interestingly, his amusing play with parts of speech in which adverbs, adjectives, and pronouns are used as concrete nouns (although only hints of that usage were present before *no thanks* of 1935).

One must assume that Cummings needed to disguise the profoundly traditional and indeed sentimental subjects that obsessed him exclusively in his first book and intermittently throughout his life: love, happy springtime love in a world of flowers, children playing outside the lovers' bedroom, a sunny world of lyrical, lovely, sensual play. Before Henry Miller and the sillier prose of D. H. Lawrence, Cummings is the most anatomically sexual of writers, his page trailing in thighs, genitals, pantings and heavings, all lower case and roiling with shy lubricity, as in

> her belly arched through me as
> one army. From her nostrils to her feet
> she smelled of silence. . . .
>
> [*·&*]

The steam rising from such matter may obscure the fact that Cummings' apprehension of nature is, to repeat, traditionally romantic, just as his lovers are in and of a natural world that came into being with Chateaubriand, Wordsworth, Byron, and Shelley:

> I will wade out
>   till my thighs are steeped in burning flowers
> I will take the sun in my mouth
> And leap into the ripe air
>   [*XLI Poems*, xi]

Only the manner, the explicitness, have changed. But Cummings' physical romanticism is very much of the post-World War I period. In his leering imitators such as Maxwell Bodenheim and worse, it became the necessary mark of the true bohemian, the Greenwich Village *épater* everyone north of 23rd Street and west of the Hudson. A few of Cummings' love lyrics have charm and authority, although his occasional classy Elizabethanisms may set the teeth on edge.

Cummings' enduring popularity among readers over age sixteen derives from his witty, comic verse more than from his love lyrics. Much of that verse is anti-political and what for lack of a better term one might call sociological. Unlike most of his contemporaries, who simply ignored politics, Cummings hated politics and gave eloquent voice to his hatred:

> a politician is an arse upon
> which everyone has sat except a man
>
> [1 x 1]

His poem on the death of Harding says more in twelve lines than all of Sinclair Lewis' burlesque novel, *The Man Who Knew Coolidge:*

> the first president to be loved by his
> bitterest enemies" is dead
>
> the only man woman or child who wrote
> a simple declarative sentence with seven grammatical
> errors "is" dead
> he's
> "dead"
> if he wouldn't have eaten them Yapanese Craps
>
> somebody might hardly never not have been
> unsorry, perhaps
>
> [*W*, verse XXVII]

American politics, if not American poetry, had moved some distance from "When Lilacs Last in the Dooryard Bloom'd." The next verse in *W*, also political but not so succinct, ends with the marvelous line, "Awake, chaos: we have napped." Good and funny as the political-sociological verse sometimes is, too often it is marred by Cummings' cast of sentimental whores and by his use, or mis-use, of 1920's slang, as in the title, "buncha hardboil guys from duh A.C. fulla" (*W*, verse XXIII), a practice revealing a certain unease that Cummings seems to have felt about himself as poet vis-à-vis "the people." On the one hand, he despises ordinary folk as stupid and unfeeling. On the other hand, he is obviously uneasy about his own lack of participation in their lives and preoccupations. In his attitude is something of gown versus town, of the professor's and clergyman's son, brought up in Cambridge and a summa cum laude at Harvard in Greek, a man who remains uneasy about what he regards as the "real" world of men who work with their hands for an hourly wage. Dos Passos, as noted, had the same attitude to excess, that of the aesthete who wants to be one of the boys. It is an undercurrent in much of the literature of the day.

Cummings' roughneck diction, together with his other experimental tricks, belongs to his strategy of surprise. His poems virtually always evoke surprise, but not resonance. They do not benefit from re-reading, for once the first surprise has been worked, we may feel tricked or simply bored. Once we have figured out that a collection of type such as

ST

u

mBl

Ing

is nothing more than "stumbling," we cannot be very much interested in reviewing the effect. At his best, however—and in most of the *Collected Poems* there are not many examples—the tricks transcend trickery, and all comes together into true poetry. Poem XLIII of *W*, "if there are any heavens my mother will (all by herself) have/one . . .' is such a poem, anticipating Cummings' famous elegy, "my father moved through dooms of love" (*50 Poems* [1940]). In the comparatively early period we are here concerned with, Cummings wrote no better poem than "i sing of Olaf glad and big" (XXX of *W*). In this poem about a conscientious objector, all Cummings' gifts are present: his lyricism, his gift for satire, his scatological inclination—if that is a gift—and his admirable scorn. Here are the final lines (Olaf has refused to retract, even when tortured):

> our president, being of which
> assertions duly notified
> threw the yellowsonofabitch
> into a dungeon, where he died
>
> Christ (of His mercy infinite)
> i pray to see; and Olaf, too
>
> preponderatingly because
> unless statistics lie he was
> more brave than me: more blond than you.

Cummings must have a lower-case footnote in history for inspiring by his earlier example a fair amount of the post-Korean War anti-war, anti-political, anti-society, anti-poetry verse. And he should have our admiration for having written such verse far better than his epigones.

With the emergence into fame after World War II of poets such as Stevens, Crane, Marianne Moore, and Cummings, it is easy to forget that with the exception of Eliot, and to a certain degree, Pound, none of the poets treated in this chapter was particularly well-known or even particularly admired in the years 1919 to 1932. Popular poets tended to be those who combined new-looking mannerisms with traditional, neo-romantic impulses, in particular the numerous women who wrote voluminously. A poet of the 1960's, Carolyn Kizer, has written cruelly but accurately of them:

> I will speak about women of letters,
>   for I'm in the racket.
>
>   ★   ★   ★   ★
> . . . the sad sonneteers, toast-and-teasdales
>   we loved at thirteen;
> Middle-aged virgins seducing the puerile
>   anthologists
> Through lust-of-the-mind. . . .
>   [*Knock upon Silence*]

The implication of elegance, bloodlessness, and staginess is borne out in much of the work not only of Sara Teasdale but also of Elinor Wylie, and above all in the unusually popular Edna St. Vincent Millay. Unlike her sister poets, Edna Millay remains popular among people who read no other poetry. Still others of the time, such as Hilda Doolittle, Conrad Aiken, John Gould Fletcher, Robinson Jeffers, and Archibald MacLeish, wrote verse of considerable distinction, yet their work never managed to sound its own unmistakable note. Fletcher, like Aldington in England and Hilda Doolittle, was perhaps unduly limited by the strictures of Imagism. Conrad Aiken, on the contrary, was widely eclectic and insufficiently self-critical. Like Cummings, he seemed to publish all that he produced. Jeffers had his partisans, but his matter and often his manner lie somewhere beyond identifiable human experience.

As we look back through the many slim volumes that have gone discreetly out of print, we may reflect, as many readers have done, that the poetic "revolution" was little more than the confecting of wedding cakes for marriages which time and events have brought to the divorce courts. The finest work would have been done anyway, according to this view, without all the marching and counter-marching in short-lived, esoteric magazines. But such a view is both ungenerous and inaccurate. The literary *ambiente* of the United States, England, and the Continent, in part created by the journeymen of poetry, was a factor in the lives and minds of those poets who promise to survive. The historian cannot produce scientific evidence for such a remark. He can only rely upon his interpretation of contexts to guide him—the contexts of poems, essays, personal relationships, of letters, of enunciated beliefs and unenunciated skepticisms about personas and things—all the detritus of the time, encountered in experience that not even he can accurately reconstruct. Literature, least of all poetry, does not yield itself to the unduly rigid mind.

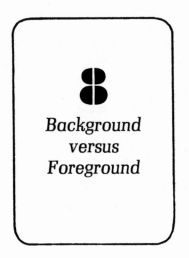

Background
versus
Foreground

The decline and fall of fixed and widespread forms of belief, whether in Caesar or in God, which gave shape to much of the poetry just examined, did not lead after World War I to a renewed faith in rationality. It led, rather, to the illusion of rationality in society, and with that illusion, to a renewed belief in facts, in all the phenomena of everyday life. In the United States, swifter transportation and the development of radio meant that all the concerns of the foreground of society became more prominent than ever, and by the end of the 1920's the life-denying processes of mass society began in earnest. Europe was soon to follow. Writers who pandered to the new rationality became rich: Sinclair Lewis in the United States, Lytton Strachey in England. John Dewey prospered at the expense of Plato. Biography, which claimed to deal with fact and foreground, tended to push original literature into the background. Emil Ludwig, the biographer of Kaiser Wilhelm and Bonaparte, sold better than any twenty poets combined. Literary history has always tended to confuse the two orders of experience: foreground, or transitory phenomena, with background, or imaginative work, and by confusing them, to explain the background in terms of the foreground.

In the following discussion of non-fictional and non-poetic modes of writing, one is not assuming causal relationships, then, but contingent ones. However pure, literature does not exist in a vacuum, but neither is it determined by the behavior of the stock market or the last lurid rape. The First World War, on the other hand, was not an occurrence of the foreground, but an event of such dimension that it penetrated into the viscera, becoming a fundamental condition of life and art, foreground and background, for years to come. Europe is included in the discussion not as evidence of direct transatlantic influence, although some such evidence there was, but because the period saw the beginning of men's doubts about the wisdom of the nationalism that had predominated since 1800, and because however nationalistic or isolationist a specific country remained, neither politics, science, religion, education, nor least of all literature, was conceived as it might have been a generation or more before World War I.

To the liberal mind of easy good will, the political face of the United States and Western Europe from 1920 to 1932 was deceptive, if observed from the standpoint of the literary arts; the liberal expects liberalism to produce good art and reaction to repress art altogether. That period in which such a variety of splendid work was accomplished by writers so various as Rilke and Valéry, García Lorca, Jimenez, and Thomas Mann; by Yeats, Eliot, and Broch; by Faulkner, Hemingway, Joyce, and Unamuno—the list itself oppresses—was a period in which politics varied from extremely conservative to Fascist. Russia was of course the exception, but even there, where the Modernist movement looked as though it might flourish, oppressive politics as early as 1925 enforced social realism in its place. "Conservative" is too generous a term to describe the administrations of Harding, Coolidge, and Hoover in the United States. Their style of government and of life was such that writers not so much ignored politics as snubbed them.

The war left Britain in chronic economic depression, and while the two Labour governments of Ramsay McDonald (1924 and 1929–1932) varied the basic Conservative pattern, the burden of that pattern, the inheritance of the war, and unemployment was too much for Labour to accomplish anything more than a holding action. Writers, upper middle class almost to a man (D. H. Lawrence, W. W. Jacobs, and J. B. Priestley were among the very few exceptions), conspicuously ignored politics. There were, however, occasional references in novels to the general strike of 1926, and there was Aldous Huxley's would-be comic depiction of a British Fascist movement on the order of Oswald Moseley's in *Point Counter Point.*

France, even more than Britain, had been depleted and exhausted by the war. Prime Ministers flashed in and out of office like dolphins in the wake of a leaky ship. Between Clemenceau in 1919–1920 and Laval in 1931–32, the office changed hands twenty-three times, although often the hands belonged to the same man: Aristide Briand was Prime Minister eleven times between 1925 and 1932. The shakiness of the French system, together with the ultimate move in the direction of the unsavory Laval, was all too symptomatic of what was going on in Germany, Italy, and Spain. Germany drifted from near-anarchy at the end of the war to the prolonged misery of the doomed Weimar coalition, which under a succession of men too weak to cope with the defeat, inflation, the effects of the Versailles treaty, and the economic depression, pointed like an arrow to the emergence of Hitler as Chancellor in 1933.

Mussolini needed less time in Italy. Neither Orlando, Nitti, Giolitti, Bonomi, nor Facta, the Prime Ministers from 1919 to July, 1922, could govern effectively. Mussolini needed only the months from July, 1922, to the end of October to consolidate his position. In Spain, Primo de Rivera became dictator under the minimally intelligent Alphonso XIII, following the assassination of Eduardo Dato in 1921 and the brief premierships of Mauro and Sánchez Guerra. Upon the forced abdication of Alphonso in 1931, Azaña was elected the first President of the Republic, that Republic which was slowly to be put to death by the rebellion of the military in 1936.

The depressing political outline was accompanied by three broad manifestations in literature. In Italy, Russia, and to a lesser degree Spain, imaginative literature was curtailed virtually to the point of extinction. In Germany, politics may have contributed to the renewed post-war vitality of expressionism, to the vogue for Kafka's work, which was published after his death in 1924; and to the conscious, desperate confrontation with history that we find in Thomas Mann's *The Magic Mountain* and Hermann Broch's trilogy, *The Sleepwalkers*. The third manifestation, by far the most productive for imaginative literature, was that of the United States, France, and England. There for perhaps the last time in modern history, writers either ignored or satirized politics. In France, Dada and surrealism were vigorous, and even André Malraux, the most egregiously political writer of the 1930's, in his first novel, *The Royal Way* (1927), wrote politically only at second or third remove. Huxley's burlesque of Fascism in *Point Counter Point* is balanced by the political aspect of E. M. Forster's masterpiece, *A Passage to India*, but even there the center is less political than it is an example of Forster's charming philosophical humanism. He uses and alludes to politics, but he does not address politics.

Despite presidential dullness, there was a good deal of political activity in the United States, but little of it got into literature. American society was in an interesting stage of rapid transition immediately after World War I. The majority of the population had moved from the farm to the city, but farm life and small town life still strongly marked men's minds and behavior. Radio, car and air travel had not yet homogenized the population; semi-literacy, *Kitsch* and camp were waiting in the wings but had not yet appeared. The continuing force of provincial attitudes is best seen in some of the scruffier political attitudes of the time: John Dos Passos, in his brilliant memoir of the period, writes of "the violence of revulsion against foreigners and radicals that went through the United States after the first world war."[1] Such revulsion seems to have been compounded of national regret at having become involved in the war, even after Wilson's campaign promise of 1916 to keep the country out of it; fear at the example of the revolution in Russia; and the virulent xenophobia that only large numbers of recent immigrants can generate. The results were hysteria against "anarchists," fed by bombings in the financial district of New York City and the bombing of the Attorney General's residence in Washington; the rounding up of "reds" and their wholesale deportation; the genuinely tragic political symbol of the decade, the trial of Sacco and Vanzetti, their execution, and the aftermath. The violence of symbols and events made for the adoption of easy, extreme attitudes on both the Right and the Left, it made for the total separation of the two groups, and paradoxically for literature, for the illusion that politics were futile and therefore not worth one's interest or energy. Together with that conclusion went an apparent openness, a sense of personal freedom that was as heady as it was short-lived. That ease and freedom from social concern are obvious in the casual anti-Semitism of Fitzgerald, Hemingway, and Faulkner, an attitude so casual, so traditional, that it is not even conscious, and therefore perhaps all the more wounding. The attitude toward Negroes—see Faulkner's Negroes in *Sartoris* or Wallace Stevens' title, unthinkable at a later date, "Like Decorations in a Nigger Cemetery"—is even more casual, traditional, and un-thought out. Again, for perhaps the last time in history, men had the pleasant illusion that events did not require them to take a

[1] John Dos Passos, *The Best of Times* (New York, 1966), p. 166.

stand, that they could go their way in pleasant skepticism without having to be engaged by public events.

We therefore find widespread iconoclasm, but not the corrosive (and fashionable) alienation from society of the thirties. Lytton Strachey's *Eminent Victorians* (1918), the bible of iconoclasm, was widely popular in the United States, as it was in England. Waldo Frank's *Our America* (1919), which had little of Strachey's brittle literary finish, was nevertheless written from a similar point of view. Harold Stearn's anthology, *Civilization in the United States* (1922), including thirty-three writers and covering just as many facets of American life, may be seen as a closer parallel than Frank's book to Lytton Strachey's attitude. The contributors agreed almost unanimously that whatever the United States was, it was in the process of destroying whatever civilization it might once have possessed. The enthusiasm with which a huge public bought and read the burlesques of Sinclair Lewis has been already noted; the satires of Ring Lardner should also be mentioned, together with the intermittent dipping into satire of writers so various as Hemingway, Cummings, Dos Passos, and Thomas Wolfe. No single writer, however, personified in his life and work a certain cynical, burlesque attitude of the period more fully than did H. L. Mencken. His career is instructive for its representative nature, and for his influence. In addition, it is necessary to put straight a record that is in danger of being falsified by ignorance and sentimentality.[2]

Mencken (1880–1956) was a provincial Baltimore, Maryland, newspaperman who became involved in book-reviewing through the *Smart Set*, beginning in 1909. Although book-reviewing was a diversion from his basic interest in politics and civic affairs, he nevertheless achieved a certain fame as a literary critic which his admirers continue to propagate. Energetic and profilic, he affected a tough-mandarin style partially borrowed from G. B. Shaw, partially his own, and partially a product of his mis-reading of Nietzsche, about whom he wrote a book in 1908. Mencken's style, which varied between a kind of eighteenth-century clarity and directness at its best and the barkings of a cur in an alley at its worst, was refreshing in its day. His mannerisms have had an effect, for better or worse, upon American newspaper writing and upon such magazines as *Time* and *The New Yorker*. His most enduring achievement is not literary but philological: *The American Language* of 1919 and its

[2] See the peculiar study by William H. Nolte, *H. L. Mencken, Literary Critic* (Middletown, Conn., 1966).

many supplements. Affecting to loathe pedants and pedantry, Mencken himself was a fair pedant, as his home-made scholarship on American speech and usage makes evident. He achieved his highest fame between 1923 and 1930 as co-editor with George Jean Nathan of *The American Mercury* (Nathan left in 1925, and Mencken became sole editor). Mencken's formal preparation for his career as literary dictator was limited to completion of work in a technical high school in Baltimore. His ignorance of literature stood him in good stead, for only so ignorant a man could have been so noisily convincing to readers whose literary taste was as imperfect as his.

Mencken was first in the modern line of radical reactionaries that leads to the John Birch Society. He affected to admire Germany and Germans, although his actual knowledge of the country and its culture was faint. One result was a reverse chauvinism, according to which he idolized Kaiser Wilhelm but defined American democracy as "the worship of jackals by jackasses." From Nietzsche he drew an imperfect portrait of a beleaguered aristocracy of superior men, like him, surrounded by a mob of Bible-reading, puritanical, ignorant, superstitious scoundrels, hoggish and sentimental, determined to bring down the aristocrats to their own inferior level. He hated Wilson, Harding, Coolidge, Hoover of course, and Franklin Roosevelt. Although he opposed the Palmer raids (round-ups for deportation of alleged anarchists, 1920), he was anti-Communist and had only contempt for Socialism. Crudely materialistic and atheistic, he reserved a particular brand of venom for Christianity and its many American sects. He opposed literary censorship and congressmen—"the gaudy cock of some small and usually far from appetizing barnyard"—and fought the fundamentalist viewpoint that brought about the Scopes trial in Dayton, Tennessee, in 1925.[3] He did not attack racist politics, the notorious immigration acts of 1921 and 1924, or come to terms with the fact that by 1924 the Ku Klux Klan had a membership of about 4,500,000. He was, in short, a flogger of dead horses or an adept rider of the living ones which afforded self-publicity. He thought of himself as a wit and was given to jests like "Never trust a man who parts his hair in the middle."

Mencken's sociological views played an important part in his literary

[3] John Thomas Scopes was a young teacher of biology who lectured deliberately on evolution, the teaching of which was forbidden by state law, in order to test that law. Despite national press coverage and perhaps because of Mencken's presence in Dayton, Scopes lost and was fined $100.

judgments. As a reviewer—it is hard to agree that he was a literary critic—he was interested only in content. In what is perhaps his best literary essay, "The National Letters," he wrote that "superior fiction" represented the conflict between "a salient individual and the harsh and meaningless fiats of destiny," and a hero who struggles and fails rather than one who yields and wins.[4] Mencken admired Theodore Dreiser and helped materially to bring Dreiser to public attention. He ranked James Branch Cabell and Joseph Hergesheimer only slightly below Dreiser and again pounded the drum for those very special men. He had kind words for Willa Cather, Edith Wharton, Sherwood Anderson, and Ring Lardner. Among poets he singled out Lizette Woodward Reese, Edgar Lee Masters, Sara Teasdale, and John McClure. He preferred H. G. Wells to Dickens, and in biography he preferred Frank Harris on Oscar Wilde to Henry Adams on Henry Adams in *The Education*. One of his biographers notes that he had never read *Alice in Wonderland, Moby Dick, Pilgrim's Progress*, or the great English Victorian or Russian novelists.[5] He either did not know or did not care for either ancient or European classical literature. He knew well only the naturalists, only those whose views were an extension of his own. Conspicuously missing from his reading are Eliot, Pound, Frost, Tate, Ransom, I. A. Richards, or any of the really interesting novelists of the day. He saw Henry James not in literary terms, but in terms of his own hatred of England:

> . . . we have Henry James, a deserter made by despair; one so depressed by the tacky company at the American first table that he preferred to sit at the second table of the English.[6]

So equipped, it is not surprising that Mencken confined his literary warfare to attacks upon his weakest enemies. American life was intellectually thin, he maintained at boring length, because American professors were timid, stupid, and narrow. He carried on quarrels with the new humanists—William Crary Brownell, Paul Elmer More, and Irving Babbitt—and some of their less impressive followers, Stuart Pratt Sherman foremost. He attacked weakly romantic popular fiction, con-

---

[4] F. Scott Fitzgerald reviewed for *The Bookman* (March, 1921) Mencken's *Prejudices: Second Series* (1920) in which the essay appeared. He may well have been influenced by Mencken's ideas in his subsequent work, as Perosa maintains in *The Art of F. Scott Fitzgerald*, p. 47. Fitzgerald was one of the few really good American writers to be impressed by Mencken.

[5] Edgar Kemler, *The Irreverent Mr. Mencken* (Boston, 1950), p. 123.

[6] "The National Letters," *Prejudices: Second Series* (New York, 1920), p. 97.

sidered all playwrights and actors mountebanks, and raved and roared to the applause of the impressionable. Increasingly toward the end of the twenties, this *Lumpenintellektuelle* turned his attention from literary matters to politics, although he remained a cultural demagogue to the end of his days, and he remained provincial at a time when American writing was no longer so.

No word came off Mencken's typewriter more frequently than "puritan," further evidence that, like all good publicists, he at once followed and led public opinion. He indicated in his essay, "Puritanism as a Literary Force" (1917), that he had an adequate historical understanding of American puritanism, sufficient to underline his cynicism in mis-using the term in his subsequent writings. No single term was more widely abused in the period. Puritanism came to define exclusively the cast of character of those who favored literary censorship of sexual matter, prohibition of drink, and repression of animal spirits while fostering a churchy, holier-than-thou withholding of the self from carnal indulgence. By easy extension, in Mencken's usage, puritanism defined everything that was wrong with American life and letters, from gentility in fiction to defects in education to the soft-minded acceptance of southern Baptist theology. It was what made the difference between American and European life. It is amusing that Mencken, who pretended to barroom bawdry and candor, shared the American small-town notion that Europe, and particularly France, was somehow sexier than puritanical America, and that until American women became as promiscuous as they thought the French were, civilization in America would be impossible.[7] As for drink, Mencken prided himself on his capacity to pour a liter of beer down his throat without swallowing. When he became seriously involved in presidential politics, he advised his candidate, Ritchie of Maryland, that the most urgent national issue was repeal of prohibition; this in 1932 in the abyss of the Depression.

With the day of the asterisk well and truly over, it may be hard to sympathize with the uproar about "puritanism" in the 1920's. Mencken and his crew were culpable in insisting upon puritanism as a peculiar disorder of the United States rather than a virtually universal and recurring phenomenon. Mencken, the flayer of the academy, might have been aware, for example, of John Stuart Mill's anti-puritanical tract, *On*

[7] It might be noted that when Mencken and Nathan took over the editorship of *Smart Set* in 1914, they also took over the editorship of *Parisienne* and *Snappy Stories*, which paid the bills of the respectable magazine of the trio.

Liberty. Puritanism as Mencken chose to interpret it not only existed in England and Europe but exerted powerful influence. English literary censorship, to say nothing of censorship of the theater, was harsher than it was in the United States.[8] In Mencken's own *American Mercury* of May, 1924, is an account of the fact that a translation of Sherwood Anderson's story "Hands" caused the suppression of the issue of *Figaro* in which it appeared, together with the suppression of other stories from *Winesburg, Ohio* which were planned for publication.[9] In an article published in 1931, Cesare Pavese wrote that Americans received Joyce and Freud hospitably because of puritanism; Americans saw such writings as a species of sex, whereas "when we [Italians, Europeans] speak of sexual problems, it is to return to Boccaccio and to Rabelais."[10] Pavese implied that puritanism was not all evil if it resulted in the favorable reception of Joyce and Freud, a view that few Americans of the day, certainly not Mencken, would have held. On the other hand, T. S. Eliot, a genuine puritan, was ignored in Mencken's discussions of the subject.

Along with the naïveté and crudity of conception in the popular view of puritanism, a view that makes much of the minor writing of the period look distant and sophomoric, was the separate issue of literary censorship. Here Mencken's crusade was salutary, and we owe him gratitude for it. The efforts of the Reverend T. Frank Chase, secretary of the Boston Watch and Ward Society, and of other quasi-official bodies in various American cities were vicious. Mencken's having provoked his own arrest in Boston in 1926 was a paragraph in the long American narrative of anti-censorship. What was, and remains, uncomfortable about the discussion of literary censorship is the emphasis upon content, which carried over into the literary aesthetic of the time. It produced an exaltation of naturalism over any other mode in fiction, the kind of fiction that Mencken professed to admire. The censorship controversy led to long, autobiographical narratives, to the vogue for confession, for "reality" at the expense of the wide-ranging imagination. That emphasis upon a narrowly conceived idea of truth is responsible

---

[8] Nothing in the United States during the twenties equalled the police raid on the Warren Gallery, London, July, 1929, when the police seized thirteen of D. H. Lawrence's pictures and threatened to burn them. Lytton Strachey's account of the affair is amusing. *Lytton Strachey,* II, pp. 642–643.

[9] Lewis Galantière, "American Books in France," *The American Mercury* (II, May, 1924), 100.

[10] Cesare Pavese, "Sherwood Anderson," *La Revue des lettres modernes* (X, 1963), 42.

for the omission from the bulk of American writing of the time of the kind of speculation, both formal and philosophical, that we find in European writing. An entire range of activity, natural and essential to all writers, was recessive or entirely missing, and was to remain so for at least another decade. Preoccupation with "puritanism" was largely responsible.

As was remarked, for Mencken organized religion in the United States was a function of puritanism. His jibes against southern fundamentalist sects are too crude to merit review. His popularity, however, served to force the subject into prominence, while his jubilant venom helped cause Sinclair Lewis to deal with the subject in *Elmer Gantry*. What was not so obvious then as it since has become was that after the First World War, Protestantism and Judaism were at a point of crisis in their historical development which, decades later, is still unresolved. Catholicism, too, was in trouble, although the nature of its trouble was not so apparent as it was to become after the Second World War. World War I brought into question certain of the churches' positions, first, the pacifist movement during the war, and second, because after the war, pacifists associated with the churches questioned a Christianity that could defend and participate in war. Simultaneously, the pre-war Protestant majority had been altered by immigration, while the movements of population from country to city further upset traditional church patterns of membership. Actual church membership either barely held its own with increases in population or declined.[11]

What the multitude of statistical analyses cannot indicate are the reasons for the decline. Among the most obvious was the continuing hostility of the churches to natural science at a time when scientists such as Jeans, Eddington, and Millikan were doing their utmost to reconcile science with religion. Second, by the 1920's a long, slow decline in the quality of men attracted to the clergy was apparent; this was particularly true of the Roman Catholic clergy. One obvious result was the alienation of a significant number of well-educated people from American churches, people who a century earlier had furnished the leadership among the laity. Third, the churches themselves, with the exception of the Roman Catholic, were in disarray because of the feud between the fundamentalists

[11] See Robert T. Handy, "The American Religious Depression, 1925–1935," *Church History* (XXIX, March, 1960), 3–16. One point here is that the decline in quantity and quality of worship began at the end of the war; also, during the Depression, worship fell off even more rapidly than did material wealth.

(Orthodox in the case of Judaism) and the moderns, the latter insisting that dogma and doctrine be made liberal if the structure was to survive. Fourth and most prominent, although least specific, was the widespread sense in the country at large, including even portions of the clergy, that religion had become irrelevant to contemporary life, and that if the church had a place, that place was simply to offer a center for social gatherings and to provide some manner of vaguely defined ethical influence upon the young and impressionable. Such anaemia was precisely wrong for a time of social change and widespread rebellion. At one end of the scale, sophisticated people found it increasingly difficult or impossible to believe any traditional religion, Christianity least of all. Frazer had made his impact, to say nothing of Freud. At the other end of the scale, excessive zeal too often turned into membership in the Ku Klux Klan, which always appealed, however cynically, to white fundamentalists. Otherwise, religion became an observation of forms as a measure of conformity or as part of an effort to promote business. One way or another, the supremacy of the white Anglo-Saxon Protestant in America was over, although the fact was not to become vivid until World War II had been fought.

The tenor of religious revolt in the United States after 1919 is in lively contrast to what we may observe in Europe. That contrast is valuable in defining a basic difference in the two orders of society. In Europe, theological crises affecting the whole social order were well in the past, with the result that each country had worked out its way of navigating the ripples upon the surface. It was understood in predominantly Catholic countries that one might believe in God but loathe His clergy; the Church of England remained the established church, and that very structure made possible individual latitude in belief, in observation or non-observation of religious forms. The result for literature was that writers could allude to and use religious attitudes or their absence within the mode of manners. The only clergyman in Proust's *Remembrance of Things Past* is gently satirized in terms of manners. Gide was free to turn 180 degrees in his attitude toward religion. Virginia Woolf effectively ignored religion, while E. M. Forster, in *A Passage to India*, uses eastern religion to make social, historical, and even anthropological points, while keeping his main emphasis upon the unique human being. The European writer, that is to say, could take or leave religion as a subject. He did not tense up when he came to religion, in the manner of the American who wrote from the conviction of crisis.

T. S. Eliot's religious intensity is in this sense American, not English; it explains his scorn for the godless typist in *The Waste Land* and her casual lover.

In France, the intellectual was occasionally converted to Catholicism— Paul Reverdy, Jean Cocteau—but that was nothing very new. It did not indicate a wave of conversion, a post-war search for religious faith. The neo-Thomist philosophy of Jacques Maritain was taking form in those years, but it was not to attract a large number of followers either in France or in the United States, where Maritain was later to live. Against his beautifully eloquent writings must be placed the attitude of Montherlant, who believed that he could take what he needed of his native Catholicism and leave the rest; this attitude did not attract followers but did represent the attitude of many intellectuals. Europeans in the main saw the post-war crisis not in religious terms, but in historical, philosophical, and aesthetic terms. The United States produced the evangelism of Aimee Semple McPherson and the burlesques of Sinclair Lewis and H. L. Mencken; Europe produced Heidegger, Jaspers, Ludwig Wittgenstein, Robert Musil, James Joyce, and William Butler Yeats. Basically, the disparity is not one of intellectual quality. It is rather a disparity in sources of literary energy, together with the necessity to assert once again the secondary nature for literature of intellectual sources that so invitingly seem to solve all problems when we look at the past, even at the past in the middle distance.

Europe also produced Freud, but it was in America that he found his first broadly popular and continuing welcome. Although Freud's first book, *The Interpretation of Dreams*, was published in 1900, the English translation did not appear until 1913, while the impact of that book and of his later works was not felt in the United States (or in England) until the 1920's.[12] Half a century after their publication, Freud's theories do not need review here. His influence on literature, however, has been widely misinterpreted. In the United States in the twenties and later, Freud was widely regarded as an ally in the war on puritanism. It is ironic that both Marx and Freud, two grandfathers of the twentieth century, should have been more discussed than read. Hence Freud's ideas were promptly boiled down to a series of cultural noises: id, ego,

---

[12] Freud's *Three Contributions to a Theory of Sex*, 1905, was published in translation in 1910; *The Psychopathology of Everyday Life*, 1904, in English in 1914; *Totem and Taboo*, 1913, in English in 1918; *A General Introduction to Psychoanalysis*, 1920, 1927; *Beyond the Pleasure Principle*, in English 1924; *Civilization and Its Discontents*, 1930.

superego, Oedipus complex, infantile sexuality, repression, oral/anal, and so on, *ad nauseam*. But for the anti-puritan crusade, Freud's popularity had the immediate effect of making talk of sex not only respectable but chic, a dubious victory, perhaps, but a necessary stage in the removal of the nineteenth-century fig leaves from the arts. Discussion of sex at once elevated the subject to the respectability of science and liberated the sinner from his sin. Freud could be used to show the harm in repression, and, by logical extrapolation, to justify conduct which the nineteenth century would have condemned as libertine. Interestingly enough, the early Freud's view of art—and one is here discussing the early Freud— is in itself "puritanical." Freud saw art as hedonistic, self-indulgent, and devoted to illusion rather than to his conception of reality. Indeed, one may be tempted to think that Freud's early and continuing popularity in the United States may have been owing to his possession of the very qualities that he was supposed by post-war intellectuals to have liberated people from: puritanism, materialism, positivism verging on deter-minism.

Freud's actual influence on literature in the period is equivocal, to say the least. Extensive claims have been made for that influence. Lionel Trilling sees Freud's entire system as somehow an outgrowth of the romantics' fascination with the self—a most debatable idea—and he gives credit to Freud for surrealism, for Kafka's themes of guilt, punishment, fear of the father, and his use of dreams; for Thomas Mann's use of myth and magic; for Joyce's emphasis on the unconscious and his use of "familial" themes.[13] That the surrealists certified their credentials through Freud is undeniable. His alleged influence on Kafka, Mann, and Joyce is another matter altogether. I would argue that Kafka probably would have written as he did had Freud never lived, and Mann, too, despite his two essays on Freud. As for Joyce, Trilling mistakes an Irish pre-occupation with family bickering for something quite different. It assuredly is impossible, as Trilling notes, to write of the influence of a man such as Freud with precision. As with Marx, that influence is un-deniable yet diffuse, everywhere and nowhere.

In the United States, Freud's literary influence—where we can pin it down—was disastrous. I have noted how Sherwood Anderson's

[13] Lionel Trilling, "Freud and Literature," *The Liberal Imagination* (New York, 1950), pp. 34–40. Trilling further adduces "a whole Zeitgeist" and "a direction of thought" as accounting for Freud, but such abstractions serve mainly to center attention upon romantic egotism.

nodding acquaintance with Freud led him to his most embarrassing fiction in *Many Marriages* and *Dark Laughter*. Anderson's example is egregious, but in lesser degree Waldo Frank, Ludwig Lewisohn, and Conrad Aiken were also more hindered than helped by Freudian insight. As for Eugene O'Neill, the dark gravy that emerged from his mind as thought was made lumpy and more than usually indigestible by his exposure to Freud, as *Strange Interlude* (1928) and *Mourning Becomes Electra* (1931) testify. To say this is in no way to deny that Freud was a very great man indeed, and that his ultimate view was humane and ennobling. It is only to repeat that his theory before the diffusion of *Beyond the Pleasure Principle*— that is, before Freud attained his late, tragic grandeur of conception— was unfortunate for certain writers, particularly in the United States. It was so because his early thought seemed to reinforce and to sanction a native prejudice for mechanical naturalism in literature and positivism and materialism in philosophy. Freud's system seemed to liberate Americans, for the wrong reasons, at the very moment in their history when liberation was inevitable. Freud seemed the logical counterpart to women's suffrage, to the notion of equality between the sexes, to defiance of prohibition, and to the elimination of any form of conduct smacking of nineteenth-century moral orthodoxy. As Cesare Pavese's comment on sexual matter (p. 170) makes clear, Europeans had available to them a certain paradigm for dealing with sex in literature. For Americans, Freud was doubly blessed in that he seemed to be the vehicle by which great areas could be invaded and worked over.

Other psychoanalysts were of course at work, notably Jung, Adler, Ferenczi, Brill, Stekel, and Ernest Jones, but their influence on literature was hardly so prominent as Freud's. Hermann Hesse, who had been analyzed by Jung at the end of the war, wrote the unimpressive *Demian* (1919) under Jung's direct influence. Hesse's *Der Steppenwolf* (1927), one of the finest German novels of the time, also shows some Jungian influence, but it is far more a product of expressionism. In the United States, it has been argued that Jung's archetypes are present in Faulkner's *As I Lay Dying* (1930), but that, too, is debatable.

It is a measure of Freud's achievement that unscientific readers could find reflected in his work those qualities which most disturbed or absorbed them, as though his essays were poems or novels. A later generation was to find Freud reassuring for his reflections upon human isolation, alienation, and the probable inevitability of war. The generation of the twenties, however, found support in Freud for causes that seemed to need support—expression as against repression, an acceptable explanation for civil war within the family, an equally acceptable justification for relentless individualism detached from social considerations. Freud appeared to justify an attractive immorality that in turn would lead artists to utopias of aesthetic accomplishment. Such a reading of Freud is further testimony that awareness of fragmentation and alienation on the part of American society, as opposed to Europe, was only beginning. Such awareness is present in the prophetic voices of a few poets and novelists, but it was not to be widely disseminated until the Depression descended and another vast war loomed in the decade to follow.

The common view of the American 1920's as a period of political folly and corruption, of fundamentalist obscurantism or middle-class hypocrisy in religion, of universal disregard for legality, and of an encompassing and delightful mindlessness in manners and mores is a cliché, but like many clichés it has an uncomfortable core of truth. The state of philosophy just after the war is symptomatic. Although it had fared well in the generation before the war with the work of Charles Sanders Peirce, William James, Josiah Royce, and George Santayana, philosophy had never truly flourished in the United States. Men like Emerson had made brilliant comments and interpretations upon European philosophies, but the nearest thing to an original American philosophy, William James' pragmatism, had seemed to many Europeans an anti-philosophical philosophy, a rationale for the American sin of materialism. From 1919 to 1932, the contrast between the United States and Europe was vast. There were no American counterparts to Russell, Whitehead, Wittgenstein, or G. E. Moore in England; no one of the stature of Jaspers, Barth, Heidegger, Bergson, or Maritain on the Continent. Rather, the dominant American figure was John Dewey, whose *Democracy and Education* (1916) made its central impact after the war, together with *Reconstruction in Philosophy* (1920), *Human Nature and Conduct* (1922), *Experience and Nature* (1925), *The Quest for Certainty* (1929), *Individualism, Old and New* (1930), and *Philosophy and Civilization* (1931). Whatever the virtues of his "instrumentalism," a designation he preferred to "pragmatism," Dewey's main interest for literary history is his dismal effect upon educational theory and practice.

In books and essays which go back to the turn of the century with *The School and Society* (1899), Dewey laid the groundwork for eradicating from American public education the classical curriculum and substituting a positivistic hypothesis. This theory held that the purpose of education is not to produce what had been considered a civilized human being, but one who had learned "skills" of value to him for earning his living and for living at peace with his neighbors. Standards of evaluation were to be democratically relative, and the subject matter of education was often to be elected by the pupil rather than imposed by tradition or by any abstract ideal of culture or civilization. Dewey's ideas, usually vulgarized, were politically palatable because they were cheaper to put into force than was the traditional method. Their practical results were generations of schoolchildren who were semi-literate in English, ignorant of any foreign language, and impatient of any suggestion that their education had been less than excellent. Dewey himself wrote execrably.

Dewey might thus be seen as a kind of engineer, and the shift away from the abstract and the theoretical to the concrete marks the main impulse of American natural science in the period. Industry had discovered and was beginning to exploit the practical uses of the laboratory sciences, while academic scientists, often grossly underpaid, were learning the delights of the consultant's fee. Just as the most interesting philosophy of the post-war period was a product of Cambridge, England, in the work of Whitehead, Russell, and Wittgenstein, rather than of Dewey's Columbia in New York, so the most speculative work in science was done abroad by Einstein, Planck, and Bohr. The practice of medicine in the United States was widely regarded as a profitable business, and the leading form of psychology, behaviorism, was propounded by the same Watson who gave up psychology to go into the advertising business.

The writing of history, often a guide to the intellectual health of a period, flourished within the limits of American historians' tendency to domesticate Ranke's positivism. In reaction against romantic and idealistic history, Charles Beard and his wife, Mary, emphasized economic interpretations in *The Rise of American Civilization* (1927). Beard represented the last gasp of an American native radical tradition that was only tangentially Marxist, if at all. Carl Becker's writing, however, was less tendentious than the Beards', less *a thèse*, and beautifully lucid in the manner of Henry Adams rather than in the no-nonsense manner of the positivists. V. L. Parrington attempted intellectual history in *Main Currents of American Thought* (1927–1930) with varying success. Like Beard a representative of native radicalism, he stressed economic motivations at the expense of aesthetics. His literary judgments, as a result, are often strange, while his purely historical matter is often superficial. He wrote with an admirable passion, however, which was at odds with his efforts to be scientific and objective. Joseph Wood Krutch wrote a kind of intellectual history of literature in *The Modern Temper* (1929) and *Humanism in America* (1930). *The Modern Temper*, Krutch's best book, is marred by his excessive reliance on psychology and by a tendency to write down to the common reader. A. O. Lovejoy, who was to become the best of the American academic intellectual historians, was just beginning his work at the end of the period. *The Revolt against Dualism* (1930) was still devoted to technical philosophy, his first area of work.

These writers were all affiliated with universities; and some, like Beard and Becker, were outstanding teachers. Apart from them, it should be noted that American academic life, despite Mencken's attacks and despite some of the outbursts of the new humanists, was far from moribund. In each of the large state universities and in the better private universities and colleges of the east, mid-west and far west, there was at least a handful of notable men at work in the humanities, social sciences, and natural sciences. The unenviable reputation of American higher education in the period, however, is the result of many conflicting factors: the anti-intellectualism, whether active or passive, always present in American society; pure ignorance; the presence of too many indifferently trained, lazy, pseudo-gentleman scholars; political pressures upon state universities to educate all comers, irrespective of their qualifications; and the tendency in democracy, hardly confined to the United States, not only to deny the possibility of an educated élite but to eliminate as promptly as possible any élite other than one based on money. In some areas, higher education was still dozing in the nineteenth century. In others, it was being pulled and torn, bleeding, into the present by the demands of industrialized society. All these matters are obvious, but it is relevant to note their appearance immediately after the First World War.

Two things remain to be said about the foregrounds of literature between 1919 and 1932. First, we err if we consider only the United States. Just as literature was no longer local, indeed could not be if it tried, so all areas of intellectual life had become subject to cosmopolitan influences. In politics, historiography, philosophy, psychology, or physics, the writer or teacher ignored the world beyond his own borders only at his peril. In politics especially was this true, as we know to our sorrow, but it was no less true in virtually all areas. As a result, what had previously been considered "American" (or British or French or whatever) was in a process of chemical, qualitative change, and efforts to see the national product, above all in literature, with the vision of the past was necessarily to distort not only the present, but the past and the viewer, too. Second, in the 1920's, the parallel processes of disintegration and reconstruction of the traditional social structure resulted, for a few brief years, in that sense of openness, even irresponsibility and apparent freedom, that has been noted of some of the literature. It is imprecise to apply that characteristic too broadly, but it is equally imprecise to deny its existence. It is that striation of liberty in its outlook that makes the period seem enviable to us, that suggestion of a world open to live and move in without visas or identification tags that was so soon to change, to vanish from our vision and virtually from our memory.

Literary
Criticism

Literary criticism in the United States after World War I was in an interesting state of evolution. The movement which made the most noise, that of the new humanists, was the least significant, while all the time the prime mover, T. S. Eliot, worked quietly and forcefully to transform the subject. Among writers, we may note contradictory attitudes. Poets such as William Carlos Williams, Ezra Pound, and Yvor Winters wrote tendentious essays in defense of their own positions, while novelists such as John Dos Passos and Ernest Hemingway consciously cut themselves off from criticism, would not write it themselves, and held in contempt those who did. The universities, for the most part, confined themselves to literary scholarship in which philology came first. Occasional renegades such as Stuart P. Sherman, Henry Seidel Canby, and Carl Van Doren left teaching for literary journalism, where their work was tasteful, tame, and inflated. The cleft between those who create and those who criticize was unfortunate and uncivilized; the United States needed but never developed the Continental custom of the eminent man of letters who wrote for the literary *feuilletons*. That lack, in turn, reflects the rigidity of American journalism and the increasing institutionalization of all aspects of life during the twenties. At the same time, a certain amount of compartmentalization may have contributed to the increasing American and English emphasis upon method

in criticism and to the desirable movement away from the convention
of polite impressionism that dominated—Henry James excepted—until
at least 1918.

The humanist controversy had begun before the war in the writings
of W. C. Brownell, Irving Babbitt, and Paul Elmer More.[1] The humanists' position was hardly logical. They correctly analyzed modern
literary movements as romantic in origin, but their antipathy on moral
grounds to romanticism caused them to urge the substitution of their
own pallid version of classicism for neo-romantic work. Since writers
do not function quite as the new humanists would have them do, the
movement came to nothing. Before its death, however, it took on a
carnival air when Mencken singled out the humanists for particular
attention, thus bringing to wide public attention matters usually confined
to small literary sects. In this instance, it was unfortunate that they were
not so confined, for Mencken managed to convey to his gullible readers
the notion that all American professors were bigots, fools, and reactionaries. The humanist case was so weak that opposition to it created at
least two very peculiar bedfellows: Mencken and T. S. Eliot. Mencken
objected to humanism because he thought it puritanical; Eliot objected
because it was not puritanical enough—in the sense that puritanism was
religious—and More and Babbitt were irreligious.[2] In Eliot's two essays,
"The Humanism of Irving Babbitt" (1927) and "Second Thoughts about
Humanism" (1928), he centers his argument upon Babbitt's theory of
"inner" and "outer" moral checks, Babbitt's attack upon the refusal,
as he saw it, of the modern person to accept anything on authority beyond
the individual self. Eliot objects that Babbitt's analysis is correct, but that
only religion, more precisely Catholicism, can provide the necessary
authority for the inner check—in More's phrase, the *frein vital*. Without
Catholicism, for Eliot, there is nothing for the will to will; there must
be a force either "anterior, exterior, or superior" to the individual.[3]

---

[1] See Berthoff, *The Ferment of Realism*, pp. 211–215.

[2] Harry Levin's eloquent defense of Babbitt, "Irving Babbitt and the Teaching
of Literature," *Refractions*, pp. 321–347 should be read as a corrective to Mencken's
ravings about Babbitt and the humanist movement at large. I am dealing only with
the humanists' relationship to literature, of course.

[3] Eliot inadvertently shows us that the new humanists' efforts were not confined
to the United States. In "Second Thoughts about Humanism," he quotes the new
humanist, Norman Foerster: "the essential reality of experience is ethical." This,
Eliot remarks, puts the second generation of humanism back to Kant: Eliot means
obviously, back to Kant's conception of the categorical imperative. What is striking

Eliot's criticism is relevant to the humanists' attack on modern literature, and it tells us a good deal about Eliot's own later critical principles. The humanists' position was not subtle, nor, as the term had traditionally been understood, was it particularly humanistic. It asserted the necessity of recognizing that classical literature was classical because it honored timeless human qualities and virtues, virtues which depended upon restraint rather than indulgence, upon reason rather than imagination as defined by the romantics. Rousseau was the villain, as Babbitt revealed in his *Rousseau and Romanticism* (1919), for it was Rousseau who introduced the romantics to the exploitation of the self and to the corresponding indulgence in behaviour intolerable to the classical temperament. In an essay of 1930, Edmund Wilson pointed out the obvious fact that the humanists' reading of classical literature, Sophocles in particular, was at best dubious.[4] Their readings of modern fiction were even more so. More's notorious description of Dos Passos' *Manhattan Transfer*— "an explosion in a cesspool"—may stand for their view of Dreiser, all the naturalists, all neo-romanticism, in fact. Humanism had the negative virtue, however, of marshalling the opposition, giving it an obvious target to shoot at, and thus intensifying awareness of the value of critical method.

No one influenced critical method more fundamentally and more permanently than Eliot. Had Eliot never written a line of verse, he would still take a prominent place in literary history. From the time of his first book of criticism, *The Sacred Wood* (1920),[5] throughout the 1920's, and beyond that to the day of his death, Eliot exerted upon our language and literature an influence equalled only by that of Samuel Johnson. As in the case of Dryden and Johnson, part of Eliot's authority as a critic derived from his stature as a poet. (This was also true of the poet–critics of the Agrarian group, John Crowe Ransom and Allen Tate in particular.)[6]

---

is that Hermann Broch was working out just such a framework at the same time, departing similarly from Kant. The irony of Kant's service to romanticism and to the new humanism hardly needs underlining. See T. S. Eliot, *Selected Essays* (New York, 1960), p. 432.

    4 Edmund Wilson, "Notes on Babbitt and More," *A Literary Chronicle*, pp. 146–148.

    5 Eliot's other collections of criticism in the period: *Homage to John Dryden*, 1924; *Shakespeare and the Stoicism of Seneca*, 1927; *For Lancelot Andrewes: Essays on Style and Order*, 1928; *Dante*, 1929; *Charles Whibley: A Memoir*, 1931; *Thoughts after Lambeth*, 1931; *John Dryden the Poet, the Dramatist, the Critic*, 1932.

    6 The reader is again reminded that the Agrarians are omitted from this volume because they are treated in Vol. VII of the History.

Unlike Matthew Arnold, Eliot refused to insist upon the common distinction between criticism and creation. In "The Function of Criticism" (1923) he wrote that criticism is both "the elucidation of works of art and the correction of taste" and a necessary function of the creative writer's work, an activity that goes on prior to or alongside the "frightful toil" of "sifting, combining, constructing, expunging, correcting, testing." Implicit in such rhetoric is an Arnoldian high seriousness that opposed the dilettantism of much American and English reviewing of the day, a denial of romantic inspiration, together with an affirmation of the critic's need for the highest credentials. This is made clear in Eliot's remark, in the same essay, that he had changed from his earlier insistence that *only* critics who wrote imaginative work were worth reading, but had expanded his view that only those were worth reading who brought to their criticism "a sense of fact." This may be read as a denial of impressionism, an emphasis upon the text of a work, and an indignant refusal of what Eliot calls "acrostic" interpretation, or any other manner of self-indulgent, irrelevant remarks about a work.

These are not matters of detail. They are central to Eliot's position, together with his elucidation, in the most important essay, "Tradition and the Individual Talent" (1919), of his "institutional" view of literature.[7] Eliot conceived of literature past and present, regardless of national origin, as an organic, living and breathing whole and of the writer as owing his allegiance to that whole. He did not see the writer as a romantic, piratical, or anarchistic figure who started from scratch and worked through divine or terrestrial frenzy. With Pound, he emphasized the need for broad acquaintance with the past, and he deplored in "Modern Education and the Classics" (1932) the omission of Greek and Latin from modern school curricula. Eliot's institutional view necessarily included society, and his predictable, consistent social views were to become an embarrassment to many of his admirers, although never to him. We have already noted the influence of T. E. Hulme upon Eliot's thought; his conversion to Anglo-Catholicism in the mid-twenties; his defense of monarchy and other un-Americanisms in the famous Preface to *For Lancelot Andrewes:*

[7] In its contemporary usage, the term "institutional" is Harry Levin's, not Eliot's. See Levin's important essay, "Literature as an Institution" (1946), now most readily available in his book, *The Gates of Horn* (New York, 1963), pp. 16–23. Although Levin discusses in his essay attempts from Taine on to relate literature to society and to use the idea of the "institution" as a way of discussing the novel, his term defines very nicely Eliot's own view of the western literary tradition and may ultimately derive from Eliot.

". . . classicist in literature, royalist in politics, Anglo-Catholic in religion" was never forgiven. That in spite of his high seriousness Eliot could also tease and give vent to a pawkish humor was ignored, although the most bitter political attacks upon him were to come much later in his career and even years after his death. It is true, but not particularly relevant, that he appeared to share the casual anti-Semitism of his day, and he gave no second thought to the plight of the Negro or the colonial peoples. His courage in maintaining a position not only unpopular but in total opposition to the political climate of his time cannot be denied.

Eliot's most permanent literary contribution may have been to put to work with originality and incisiveness in his criticism, as in his poetry, his Vico-like view of literary history, a correlative of his encompassing view of tradition. Thus Seneca and Dante, the Elizabethans and the metaphysicals, Dryden and Arnold, Baudelaire and F. H. Bradley could all mingle in his mind and contribute to his finely reasoned evaluations and re-valuations. With I. A. Richards, he was the first and the best of the new critics. He disdained biography, writing in *Dante* that the less he knew about the poet, the better. His textual criticism, based on a sound knowledge of classical and modern European languages and an inspired sense of historical and contemporary English diction, is a model. His essays on Elizabethan drama and on the metaphysical poets alone constituted a revolution in English literary scholarship. Beyond that, however, they influenced the standards and practice of a generation of younger poets.

Of equal importance, although perhaps not so obvious, was Eliot's editorship of *The Criterion* (also known as *The New Criterion*, *The Monthly Criterion*, and finally *The Criterion* again) from 1923 to 1940. Without any question, Eliot's *Criterion* was the most distinguished literary magazine in English of the period on either side of the Atlantic. Its only rival in the United States was *The Dial*, which was good, but hardly as good as *The Criterion*. On the Continent, *La Nouvelle revue française* under the editorship of Jacques Rivière (to his death in 1925) came closest to equality with Eliot's magazine. For a time, Eliot was the English correspondent for the NRF, a fact that underlines his comparative view of literature, his conviction that literature is one entity rather than a collection of national entities. Eliot and Rivière between them performed the important and rarely acknowledged service of helping to heal the wounds of the war by their cosmopolitan views and by their hospitality to good work, no matter what its origin.

Apart from Rivière's fine essays, his accomplishment as editor, in the brief years left to him after the war, was remarkable.[8] He published translations of Gorki, Tolstoy, Chekhov, Dostoevsky, Gogol, Tagore, Ambrose Bierce, Samuel Butler, Conrad, Browning, Shakespeare, Blake, Donne, and Meredith. He published articles or reviews of Joyce, Stevenson, Shaw, Kipling, Hardy, Galsworthy, Vachel Lindsay, Jack London, Poe, Pirandello, Ferenc Molnar, Gerhart Hauptmann, and of course, Eliot. His French contributors are a catalogue of the finest work then being produced in France. The list of Eliot's contributors is remarkably similar; among them one might single out both Hermann Broch and Thomas Mann. Eliot's influence through *The Criterion* upon modern letters is incalculable. He not only broadened and extended contemporary taste, he also educated the generation of poets and critics that were to dominate the next two decades in both England and the United States. That influence was further extended by Eliot's association with Faber and Gwyer, publishers (Faber and Faber from 1929), as editor and later as a director.

Fine a critic as Eliot was, it is not to undercut him to remember

[8] Rivière's peace-making and his cosmopolitan editorship supported the efforts of many French intellectuals to put aside the hatreds of the past and to come to terms with the new Europe. Not the least of those efforts were the "Entretiens de Pontigny." Pontigny had been a Cistercian abbey from which the order was ejected by state decree in 1880. In 1906 Paul Desjardins bought it as a sort of French Unitarian center; he wanted to found "a moral and religious association with neither dogma nor cult nor hostility to any established church." By 1920, under the direction of Charles Du Bos, Pontigny had lost its religious overtones and become a center for wide-ranging intellectual discussions. The French who attended the three-week summer sessions included André Mauriac, Roger Martin du Gard, André Malraux, Léon Brunschwicg, André Maurois, Jacques Madaule, André Gide, Paul Valéry, Jean Schlumberger, Ramon Fernandez, Raymond Aron, and René Lalou. Among foreigners were the German, Ernst Robert Curtius; the Englishman, Lytton Strachey; and the American, Francis Fergusson. I am indebted to Mr. Fergusson for information about Pontigny. See also Abel Moreau, *Pontigny* (Paris, 1950); and Anne Heurgon-Desjardins, *Paul Desjardins et les décades de Pontigny* (Paris, 1964).

Other magazines besides *La Nouvelle revue française* that had similar international concerns were *Europe* and *Revue Européene*, both founded in 1923 and the quarterly *Commerce*, 1924–1932, which published translations from half a dozen languages and was edited by Paul Valéry, Léon-Paul Forgue, and Valery Larbaud. Articles on Franco-German relations, of which there were many, included André Gide, "Les Rapports intellectuels entre la France et l'Allemagne," *NRF* (XVII, 1921), 513–521; Jean Maxe, "Les Relations intellectuelles franco-allemandes," *Mercure de France* (Vol. 174, 1924) 686–706; and Regina Zabloudovsky, "La Crise de la culture intellectuelle en Allemagne," *Mercure de France* (vol. 173, 1924), 289–306.

that he was not infallible. His few essays on novelists are not remotely of the same quality as his essays on poetry or drama; he gave the impression that fiction either bored him or that he actively disliked it. His generosity to friends led him into errors of judgment. Like most reviewers of the time, he praised the work of Virginia Woolf highly, comparing her to Conrad; her reputation in England was as bloated as Sinclair Lewis' in America. Eliot somewhat redeemed himself in the eyes of one branch of modern opinion, however, by his dislike of D. H. Lawrence and by his perception of the slightness of Aldous Huxley's fiction.[9] He thought, mysteriously, that his friend Wyndham Lewis had a better prose style than anyone else writing in English. In Eliot's criticism of poetry and drama, he was capable of special pleading and of Anglo-Jesuitical casuistry, as in his essay on Seneca, the attack on *Hamlet* of 1919, his attack on Tennyson, and his view that Yeats was outside the English tradition; these were views of 1922 that he was to reverse in the thirties. Eliot's relationship to T. E. Hulme should also be remembered in this context. Hulme was not a literary critic as such, but as was mentioned, Eliot took what he needed and could use from Hulme's thought, expressed it better than Hulme had done, and went on very much his own man, always more than generous in acknowledging his friend's influence and stature. Both Hulme and Pound may serve to remind us that Eliot remained severely at odds with one entire range of thought and feeling of the post-war period in America. He of course opposed on principle the hedonistic, no-tomorrow school of behavior exemplified by Carl Van Vechten's fiction and some of Edna Millay's verse. Eliot would have been uncomfortable in a speakeasy full of drunks. In a time that prided itself on reading Spengler and wore its despair on its sleeve, so acute a critic as Edmund Wilson could "deplore" Eliot's "fatigued and despondent mood" of the mid-twenties, a reaction that tells us more about America than it does about Eliot.[10]

One further aspect of Eliot's critical work, I think, is that his methodological advances on poetic criticism of the past were of such compelling interest that criticism of poetry advanced well beyond the criticism of prose. Neither he nor anyone else of his school did for prose what he did for poetry; it was to be decades before criticism of fiction began to

[9] T. S. Eliot, "Les Lettres anglaises: le roman anglais contemporain, *NRF* (XXVIII, 1927), 670–675.
[10] Edmund Wilson, "The All-Star Literary Vaudeville" (an essay of 1926), in *A Literary Chronicle*, p. 89.

approach the sophistication of Eliot's treatment of poetry and poetic drama. However that may be, Eliot's performance in the 1920's was remarkable. Proof may be seen in the fact that he was almost alone in being acceptable to both practicing writers and specialists in the universities, and his influence was equally felt in both areas. He thus spanned a gap that few, anywhere, have been able to span in their lifetime. Hostility to his theology, his sociology, and to his aloof personality has never been able to negate his overwhelming importance, not just for the United States and England, but for the entire audience he addressed: that of modern western civilization.

Eliot's power as a critic tended to overwhelm both his mentors and his followers. This is particularly true of Ezra Pound. Pound's critical insight was considerable, but partially because Eliot was so much more eloquent and reasonable, to say nothing of readable, Pound's influence was exerted mainly upon individuals, in the form of letters, through the force of his personality, or through his bludgeoning of editors. His principles were a welcome corrective to the easy aesthetic of poetry in force at the time, but his critical essays, too often written in back-country talk or some other lingo, become tiresome. They do not wear well. There is about them something of Mencken's semi-serious hatred for his own countrymen, and something of Mencken's specious rhetoric. We have already seen Pound's critical principles in his poetry, and apart from the letters, his poetry remains his best criticism. Eliot's introduction and editing of Pound's essays is an example of his generosity and of certain breaches he could make in his wall of principle on behalf of a friend. There remains, nevertheless, a certain chill when it becomes obvious that Pound does not share the master's social and moral views.

In England in the period a great deal of critical, or pseudo-critical, activity took place, but not much of it survives in literary history. Most of that activity was in the form of reviewing at a fairly high level, yet not high enough to merit the description "criticism." The habit of intelligent reviewing had not been lost during the war, and the *Times Literary Supplement*, with its tradition of anonymous contributions, injected a welcome note of asperity that otherwise would not have been heard. But the bulk of the work, whether by Frank Swinnerton of the older generation or Virginia Woolf of the younger, was elegant, amateurish, and insular. Novelists and poets took in one another's washing, while D. H. Lawrence stood aside from the crowd, he thought, snarling away about class, snobbery, and sexlessness, pausing in his jeremiads to produce that polemical comic book, *Studies in Classic American Literature* (1923). Lawrence does not yield to analysis; he has to be quoted. (That is a quality he shares with a latter-day American descendant, Norman Mailer.) In his essay on Hawthorne, Lawrence moves from Adam and Eve to Hester Prynne and Arthur Dimmesdale:

> No wonder the Lord kicked [Adam and Eve] out of the Garden. Dirty hypocrites.
> The sin was the self-watching, self-consciousness. The sin, and the doom. Dirty understanding.
> Nowadays men do hate the idea of dualism. It's no good, dual we are. . . .
> And on the other hand, the mind and the spiritual consciousness of man simply *hates* the dark potency of blood-acts: hates the genuine dark sensual orgasms, which do, for the time being, actually obliterate the mind and the spiritual consciousness, plunge them in a suffocating darkness.
> You can't get away from this.[11]

Nor can you get away with this, one might add. During the twenties, Lawrence was read more widely in the United States than in England, the country he wanted most to outrage. For some Americans, he was interesting as an English exhibitionist; for others, welcome as a critic because he looked "experimental," and experiment at once made virtually any manner of intellectual effusion acceptable. In his role as critic, Lawrence was a type of Nottinghamshire Mencken, with sex instead of beer on his mind.

Of much greater importance for any permanent record was the work of Eliot's friend and occasional mentor, I. A. Richards (born 1893). Cambridge, where he worked, is notable for its excellence in natural science and philosophy. Richards is famous for his efforts to work outward from science and philosophy to a new aesthetic for poetry. In a series of books in the period, particularly in *The Meaning of Meaning: A Study of the Influence of Language upon Thought and of the Science of Symbolism* (with C. K. Ogden, 1923), *Science and Poetry* (1926), and *Principles of Literary Criticism* (1929), Richards brought together his own fine literary sensibility, his erudition, certain views of the Cambridge school of philosophy, particularly those of Wittgenstein, and the results of his own experiments in what might be called the psychology of literary response. Richards' results were not precisely what he had first aimed at, but they constituted a central chapter in the development of

[11] D. H. Lawrence, *Studies in Classic American Literature* (New York, 1966), p. 85.

the new criticism, as well as the nucleus of a brilliant group of students, most prominent among whom was William Empson.

Richards began by questioning whether traditional views of poetry were any more correct than traditional views of the behavior of natural phenomena. Thus, at the outset, his approach was poles apart from Eliot's. In spite of that fact, their views became complementary. Eliot and Pound were concerned with the writing of poetry, Richards with the reading of poetry. He concluded that "official" views of poetry were assuredly wrong, and he set about determining through rational methods what poetry is and how we may recognize it. Within the context of the traditional debate about the importance of poetry—high to Matthew Arnold, nil to the modern scientist—Richards proposed, in *Science and Poetry*, to use the new "science" of psychology to define poetry, then proceed to question its value. By psychology Richards did not mean psychoanalysis, although he was fully aware of developments in that area. He meant, rather, experimental psychology, the efforts of psychologists to measure and perhaps to predict responses of organisms to stimuli. While such a method as applied to poetry may appear naïve after the fact, and while Richards was to admit that his high hopes for experimental psychology were disappointed, what was permanently valuable in his work were the things that he turned up along the route: his way of asking questions, the questions themselves, his care in scrutinizing traditional attitudes and judgments with open eyes.

Richards questioned the various attitudes of both writer and reader; he asked what is meant by form and content in verse, and he reviewed the separability or inseparability of those entities. He looked closely at how language functions in poetry as opposed to its use in logic or science, and he asserted the unimportance of thought in poetry. The poet, he said, is not a scientist. He disposed of traditional answers to the questions of the "use" of poetry, to value, to the ideas of good and evil. The only test, he wrote in *Science and Poetry*, is

. . . that only genuine poetry will give to the reader who approaches it in the proper manner a response which is as passionate, noble and serene as the experience of the poet, the master of speech because he is the master of experience itself.[12]

Richards' own diction in this statement is evidence of the nobility of his own search and of the generous sympathy with which he approached

[12] I. A. Richards, *Science and Poetry* (New York, 1926), p. 51.

the entire art of poetry. The essence of his teaching lies in such a statement, and in his further remarking that the poet's work is to give freedom to a body of experience by the very process of giving it order and coherence. Like Eliot, Richards had the "institutional" view of literature, and he used Eliot's own poem, *The Waste Land*, for evidence of our social response to the educated man's realization that traditional sources of belief had disappeared. He saw Eliot's own apparent despair as healthy, because inevitable, and he remarked that it would be temporary if Eliot and all of us could simply have the courage to accept that our entire system of belief must be reassessed. Poetry was an important vehicle for that reassessment.

Brief as it is, *Science and Poetry* is nevertheless one of the most central critical documents of the time. It mainly asks questions, while the answers were forthcoming in *Principles of Literary Criticism* and *Practical Criticism*. The latter was addressed to what Richards saw as the main difficulties under which critics labor. His list of those difficulties is valuable for its indication of his own preoccupations and for its evidence of the direction that criticism was to take in succeeding years. His ten points are virtually a manifesto of the new criticism to follow. Richards notes: (1) people do not read poetry in the sense of properly construing what is there; criticism cannot begin until the poem has been read; (2) the difficulties of a sensuous apprehension of poetry, and variation in that apprehension, increase the difficulties of actually reading; (3) the problems of imagery and of variations among critics in their responses to imagery; (4) the tendency of readers to introduce into their reading irrelevant associations derived from their private experiences: Richards calls these "mnemonic irrelevances"; (5) the traps of stock responses; (6) the sentimental response, and its opposite; (7) the inhibited response; (8) erratic judgments induced by "doctrinal adhesions," or the freight brought to the poem by exterior doctrine, as may be the case of the religious poem for the believer; (9) the presupposition that a given technique, once successful, will ways be so, and the reverse: prejudice against a technique for having in one instance failed; (10) "general critical preconceptions" which are likely to get between the reader and the poem.[13] It is necessary to note that Richards discusses poetry, not prose fiction or drama, and lyric poetry exclusively. Considerations of genre were not so much cast aside as ignored in the school of new criticism, the assumption being that the

[13] I. A. Richards, "Introductory," *Practical Criticism* (1st ed. 1929; London, 1960), pp. 13–17.

only poetry worth detailed attention was lyric poetry. Conspicuous by its absence from Richards' list is any mention of the poet, which is to say that considerations of biography are cast aside, any considerations of history and any discussion of milieu, the old stand-bys of pre-war history and criticism.

The fact that Richards himself wrote well, even gaily and with panache, and that he might have been directing his theories against the prevailing Virginia Woolf sort of intellectual snobbery, her Bloomsbury impressionism, might logically have insured him a wide audience in his own country. Such was not the case. Richards remained an academic figure in England, but he was read by a wider spectrum of people in the United States. This is not to suggest that criticism in the United States was in better condition than in England; far from it. Indeed, it may have been because of its greater desperation, its more imperious need for change, that America gave hospitality to Richards' methods.

There were other exceptions to the pleasant barrenness of the English critical landscape. Middleton Murry thought that he was creating an exception when he took over the editorship of the *Athenaeum* in 1919, but he lacked the critical originality, to say nothing of the necessary administrative ability, and was removed from the post two years later. Ford Madox Ford (formerly Heuffer, 1873–1939) would have been the logical person to carry on the needed reforms, but his main efforts in the 1920's went into the composition of his splendid tetralogy of war novels: *Some Do Not* (1924), *No More Parades* (1925), *A Man Could Stand Up* (1926), and *Last Post* (1928). Robert Graves, perhaps the finest single poet of the period in England, very definitely was an exception, although he only began his critical writing with scattered essays, many with Laura Riding, and with *A Survey of Modernist Poetry* (1927), also in collaboration with Laura Riding. The main force of Graves' poetry and criticism would not be felt until the thirties and after.

For perspective, it is necessary to glance at the journeyman work in reviewing and criticism done in the United States in the period. What sociologists refer to as the openness of American society was more apparent in the literary world in the United States just after World War I than in the society at large. People with an itch for the literary life found it comparatively easy to set up shop as literary critics, if not as writers. Economic prosperity led to the founding of several publishing houses and to a philosophy of literary risk-taking on the part of editors. Newspapers were prosperous; literary pages or supplements grew in size; books were sold rather as other commodities, not only in advertisements but also in reviews. Reviewers who could sell books found ready employment for their talents. Other literary folk set up magazines of their own, and some set up publishing houses abroad, like the Black Sun Press of Harry and Caresse Crosby, and the Contact Publishing Company of Robert McAlmon, in Paris. The profusion of small literary magazines, both in the United States and those supported by Americans abroad, created markets of a sort for still other critics, while the existence of such magazines also supported the argument that in order for there to be a few good writers, there must be many average or frankly incompetent ones.

The influence of the small, unpopular review upon poetry has already been remarked. Its influence upon criticism was almost as profound, even though if we regard sheer bulk, it may have been a negative influence. At its worst, the magazine named *Thither* or *the green thorax* and printed entirely in lower case was self-indulgent, often silly, and uncritical, while announcing itself as discriminating and disinterested. At its best, it was invaluable for providing an outlet for genuinely good but uncommercial work, for giving poets, critics, and occasionally writers of fiction a place in which to stretch their muscles and try out their hunches about what they could or could not do. In the welter of writers who came and went, only a few need be recorded here: some for their typicality, others for their exceptional qualities, and still others to put straight a record written by loyal friends or sentimental historians.

Among newspaper critics, the change in emphasis from literary considerations, however mistaken, to selling books may be seen in the editorship of the New York *Herald Tribune* literary supplement. Stuart P. Sherman, ertswhile new humanist, literary chauvinist, and disastrous editor of the disastrous *Cambridge History of American Literature*, was editor from 1924 to his death in 1926. He was succeeded by Burton Rascoe, a competent literary journalist with no pretensions to high seriousness. Heywood Broun (1888–1939), a charming and unusually literate newspaperman, occasionally wrote book reviews, in addition to reviews of plays and two novels. His political liberalism sounded a rare note in the period, while his personality as expressed in his writings forms a permanent part of the social history of the twenties. On the political left was a handful of men who similarly influenced our view of the social, if not the literary, history of the period: V. F. Calverton, Max Eastman, and Mike Gold, all associated with the Marxist *New Masses*, and all only on the fringes of literature.

In quite another category, from the standpoint of literary quality, were the two weekly journals, *The Nation* and *The New Republic*. Of the left but not on it, liberal in the nineteenth-century sense but not Marxist, the two weeklies were particularly active in the arts between the war and the Depression. The literary editors of *The Nation* included Carl and Mark Van Doren, John Macy, and Ludwig Lewisohn; Joseph Wood Krutch was theater critic. *The New Republic*, founded as recently as 1914, was from a literary point of view the better magazine, if only for the work of Edmund Wilson, who was associated with it from 1926 until it virtually eliminated literature from its pages in the Depression. Stark Young wrote southern baroque theater criticism for *The New Republic*, and almost every writer interested in reviewing wrote for either of the two magazines in the years before the Depression. The magazines' literary influence was greatly out of proportion to their modest circulation.

From 1920 to 1929, the American review devoted to the arts of greatest distinction was *The Dial*. It was the only magazine to attempt to mine the same ore as Eliot's *Criterion* and the *NRF* in Paris. *The Dial*, supported by private wealth, died the moment that Scofield Thayer withdrew his support. Where the *Criterion* and the *NRF* were edited by men of the stature of Eliot and Rivière, *The Dial* was edited by Gilbert Seldes and Marianne Moore. Seldes, a man of many virtues, was more interested in the popular arts of vaudeville, comic strips, and films, three of what he called *The Seven Lively Arts* in his book of 1924, than he was in the unlively art of literature. If Miss Moore erred, it was in the opposite direction: see Hart Crane's account of her confusing editorial work of his poem "The Wine Menagerie"[14]; as an editor she was not, at any rate, a Jacques Rivière. No quibble about relative merit should be allowed to obscure the fact that *The Dial* was a most valuable source of knowledge of contemporary European life and literature, a place in which good American work could find an outlet, established writers earn their bread, and young writers begin their careers. John Peale Bishop, Edmund Wilson, Paul Rosenfeld, Kenneth Burke, and Glenway Wescott are only a few names on the long and distinguished list. Toward the end of its life, *The Dial* spawned, if that is the word, a rival in *Hound*

[14] Summarized in Lewis, *The Poetry of Hart Crane*, p. 192.

and Horn (" 'Tis the white stag, Fame, we're a-hunting, / Bid the world's hounds come to horn." Ezra Pound, "The White Stag"). Founded at Harvard in 1927 and edited in 1929 by Richard Blackmur, *Hound and Horn* moved to New York in 1930 to be edited by Lincoln Kirstein. Allen Tate, Katherine Ann Porter, Francis Fergusson, and many more young writers and critics got their start, or gained further energy to keep going, in the magazine before it died of the Depression in 1934.

Not only the profusion of small literary magazines but also their tolerance of a variety of points of view was characteristic of the period, a quality of its openness. Such tolerance was not without its dangers, however. Only in the 1920's and only in the United States would so unprofessional a writer as Paul Rosenfeld (1890–1946) have been encouraged to flourish. At any other point or place he would have been edited out of existence, as indeed substantially happened when *The Dial*, whose darling he was, went under, and the harsh years and harsher editors of the Depression took over. Rosenfeld was a peculiar mixture of good and atrocious taste. What he says is interesting, but his prose is indigestible. He wrote like a man who had been brought up in Budapest on Hungarian, German, and possibly Finnish, learning English in his maturity. He had actually been brought up in New York City and attended Yale. He was first a music critic, although his reputation as a literary critic has outlived his nineteenth-century program notes for music; he admired the specious James Huneker and tried to imitate him. Rosenfeld had a flair for digging out excellence, but his own prose style was so flawed that his essays are almost unreadable and probably always were, although his kindness and generosity were allowed to compensate for his prose. His most interesting collection, *Men Seen* (1925), contains twenty-four brief essays on American and European writers. Among the Americans are some of the earliest and most interesting estimates of Scott Fitzgerald, E. E. Cummings, Wallace Stevens, and Marianne Moore; the catch is that he is equally enthusiastic and breathless about Alfred Kreymborg, Waldo Frank, Jean Toomer, and Herbert J. Seligmann (". . . the increasing frequency and consequentiality of his spark-like relationship with things, and the increasing freshness and freedom of his phrase, promise a proximate emergence"). Rosenfeld's Europeans include Joyce, D. H. Lawrence, Apollinaire, Proust, Rostand, and Verhaeren. His flagrant good taste, his posturings, his prose, and his enthusiasms belong to a period which felt it could afford such an indulgence or which did not feel the need to count up its resources and conserve them.

Rosenfeld's friend and fellow contributor to *The Dial*, Edmund Wilson (born 1895), stands in complete contrast to him for his professionalism, his level-headedness, the solidity of his judgment, and the eighteenth-century excellence of his prose. A product of Princeton, where he was a student of Christian Gauss and a friend of Scott Fitzgerald and John Peale Bishop, Wilson seems to have enlarged his appetite for French literature through army service in France. His taste for American writing seems to have been with him since the outset. He is remarkable in the period and since for combining great sympathy for his own country with a knowledge both broad and deep of European, particularly French, literature. No critic wrote more in bulk and no critic wrote essays of higher literary quality. Wilson is invaluable not only for what he said about his contemporaries, but for having represented qualities lacking in an impressionist like Rosenfeld or in a scholarly and self-limiting critic like Eliot. Wilson shared many qualities with Eliot. He had something of Eliot's range of interest; he shared his prejudice for French; he was able, like Eliot, to be both popular and scholarly, to bridge that large gap in the American audience in particular. With one part of his mind and character, Wilson too is an aristocrat who distrusts democracy, dislikes democratic levelling at the expense of the classics, and disdains some of the more egregious democratic vulgarities. His views differ from Eliot's in at least one fundamental—religion—and in many points of emphasis in essays that appear in outline to be similar to Eliot's.

Wilson's differences from Eliot are also instructive. Where Eliot wrote as a poet and from the standpoint of one who had abandoned his native country as uninteresting if not hopeless, Wilson writes as a critic first and as a very minor poet and fiction writer a remote second. His combination of a cosmopolitan outlook with an unchauvinistic literary patriotism is unique. He is a man of his time in his criticism of Eliot's *For Lancelot Andrewes*.[15] To Eliot's doubt that civilization can endure without Christianity, Wilson responded, "We have got to make it endure." He honors the churches for their work in the past, but he points out that they can no longer persuade "educated people to accept their fundamental doctrines." The two men also differ in their kinds of literary

[15] In "T. S. Eliot and the Church of England" (1929), reprinted in *A Literary Chronicle*, pp. 133–138.

strength. Eliot wrote best of poetry but slighted prose. Wilson writes best of prose but is shaky on poetry. He wrote admiringly of the verse of Edna St. Vincent Millay and Elinor Wylie, and remarked that Carl Sandburg "writes well." Some readers would take exception to his judgment that Robert Frost "certainly writes very poor verse."[16] Wilson's essays on prose are another matter. He was generous in his praise and imperious in his dispraise. He was among the first, if not the first, critic to recognize and to single out Ernest Hemingway's qualities; if later his enthusiasm for Hemingway the man chilled, his judgment of his literary qualities continued to be accurate and impartial. He was early and remarkably impartial about his friend Scott Fitzgerald, and about Dos Passos. As a reviewer who made his living by writing, he was necessarily in touch with the contemporary. What is unusual was the sureness of his taste for the contemporary and the quality of permanence about his early reviews and essays, written under editorial pressure to deadlines. Wilson did not ignore Europe. He wrote the first American essay on André Malraux, and a fine one; he also wrote on Lytton Strachey, Joyce, Dostoevsky, and many others. His range of reference distinguishes him from Carl Van Doren. Van Doren also wrote a great deal about American subjects, but his writing is dull, in part because he was narrowly nationalistic in outlook. Wilson's prose, compact, witty, yet basically serious, was capable of a wide range of effect, from parody to epigram. One of his sentences on Theodore Dreiser suffices for the historian of the period:

> Dreiser commands our respect; but the truth is he writes so badly that it is almost impossible to read him, and, for this reason, I find it hard to believe in his literary permanence.[17]

If a part of Wilson's strength derived from his ability to read American writing with a native's affection, yet criticize it like the most skeptical foreigner, his weakness was also typical of America. It is quite simply his bored lack of interest in formal aesthetics or philosophy. It is remarkable that a critic so widely informed should never have mentioned Croce's *Aesthetics* (1922), or that his single references in *Axel's Castle* to Herbert Read and to I. A. Richards are grudging and disparaging. Until *Axel's Castle* (1931), Wilson resembled most of the American critics of his time where questions of aesthetics were concerned. His interest in such

16 *A Literary Chronicle*, p. 86.
17 *A Literary Chronicle*, p. 78.

questions came out in disguised and devious forms, in discussions of a given writer's immediate tactics, of influence, or more commonly in the form of a sort of sociology. At least since the time of Poe in the United States, serious questions of literary meaning have tended to degenerate into metabolism tests of the entire culture: partaking of the cultural hypochondria, critics have turned to political speculation, estimates of the Gross National Product, or arguments about the future of movies or radio or television. However admirable and necessary such speculations may be, they cannot take the place of aesthetic speculation. The fault lay in the willingness of Wilson and others to slight problems of method and tacitly to accept the principle of the separability of form and content. It had also to do, one suspects, with the equally tacit assumption that prose is closer to "life" than poetry is, and that the critic therefore had to approach prose in quite a different frame of mind from that in which he approached poetry. Wilson's preference for material, for life, accordingly, meant that his best pieces were those that let him discuss the background of a work rather than those in which formal questions were posed first. He is excellent on biography, good on fiction, and weak on poetry, He carried to a high point the common assumptions of reviewing in his time, no mean achievement, and in *Axel's Castle* he produced one of the finest critical books of the post-war period. But he remained closer to Ste. Beuve than to Dryden, or Arnold, or even Poe; closer to Georg Lukács than to Curtius or Ortega y Gasset.

The radical American dissociation between poetry and prose, between the pragmatic, day-to-day reviewing of books that passed for criticism and the tendency to see any other approach as esoteric, may be even clearer when we note that it was the poets who engaged in aesthetic speculation to support their own work, and who, in so doing, extended the boundaries of criticism. The process is quite clear in Eliot, but it is even more so in William Carlos Williams, a poet who went specifically to the problem of the differences between poetry and prose. Some of Williams' work is historically important because it diverges radically from Eliot's, while it demonstrates early and well the duty that American poets have taken on in the ensuing decades: the explication of their own work and their contemporaries'. In the prose sections of *Spring and All* (1923), Williams displayed his valuable capacity for going to the essence of certain matters which had nagged him in the writing of verse. He developed a theory of diction regarding the writer's relationship to nature and to the imagination, without reference to the past. What he provides us with, therefore, is a practical aesthetic, and by implication, an apology for his own work. He rejects the notion of poetry as imitation, not in terms of Aristotle or the classic-romantic polarity, but in terms of writing: "Writing is not a searching about in the daily experience for apt similes and pretty thoughts and images."[18] The nature of the writer's mind, however, sends him to external nature, not because nature is a blotter image of human experience in which to admire the self but because it is independent of us, and by its independence is valuable, a reality. Williams next uses the differences between prose and poetry to construct his theory of imagination. Prose, in brief, has to do with fact, with statement about emotion. Its form is "the accuracy of its subject matter. . . ." Poetry makes emotion dynamic in quite another, separate form; with Coleridge, whom Williams does not mention, he affirms that poetry is a new form having its own reality with which the poet must deal. The intelligence itself is involved in the "leap" from prose to the processes of imagination in poetry.

> Imagination is not to avoid reality, nor is it description nor an evocation of objects or situations, it is to say that poetry does not tamper with the world but moves it—It affirms reality most powerfully and therefore, since reality needs no personal support but exists free from human action, as proven by science in the indestructability of matter and of force, it creates a new object, a play, a dance which is not a mirror up to nature. . . .[19]

This is the Williams of whom in 1965 Yvor Winters made the following extraordinary statement:

> To say that Williams was anti-intellectual would be almost an exaggeration: he did not know what the intellect was. He was a foolish and ignorant man, but at moments a fine stylist.[20]

Williams' words are useful as explication and for indicating how he diverged from Imagism. They are even more useful to the present context for their ability to indicate to us the public intensity with which poets of the period went about their work, their sense of almost missionary fervor, their conviction that readers must understand why they were

---

[18] Reprinted from *Spring and All* in *William Carlos Williams: A Collection of Critical Essays*, (ed.) J. Hillis Miller (Englewood Cliffs, N.J., 1966), pp. 23–26.

[19] *William Carlos Williams*, (ed.) Miller, p. 25.

[20] Yvor Winters, "Poetry of Feeling," in *William Carlos Williams*, (ed.) Miller, p. 69.

turning away from the past, and some intimation of what they were moving towards. Some of the most valuable new criticism to follow was written out of just those motives. Although in America and to a degree in England, Eliot dominated, he was not completely dominant, as Williams', Stevens', Marianne Moore's, Hart Crane's, or John Peale Bishop's essays and letters of the time make clear. Eliot's public, however, was far wider than that of the others combined.

American criticism between 1919 and 1932 ranged fairly widely and showed an interesting texture. It did not, however, produce figures remotely equivalent to Richards in England, Valéry in France, Ortega y Gasset in Spain, Lukács in central Europe, or Curtius in Germany. This is only to say that the United States was not Europe, but flatly to do so would be an error. For the brief moment, Americans were spared the Europeans' preoccupation with civilization as a whole, their efforts to think through the results of the war, to come to terms with the abyss by looking down into it. America had no Entretiens de Pontigny, no need quite yet to meet the revolt of the masses, in the words of Ortega's title; not yet to try to merge aesthetics with politics, like Lukács, nor to negotiate an intellectual Versailles Treaty, as Rivière, Gide, and Curtius in a sense tried to do. Yet Americans did not need to repeat or to duplicate what the Europeans were doing, both because of the increasing process of cosmopolitanization and because of the American illusion of separateness within its consciousness of Europe. And not least because the final, faded, very old illusion still at work in the minds of men so various as Edmund Wilson, Paul Rosenfeld, and Van Wyck Brooks that America was a greener, grander, somehow finer place whose way in literature was necessarily different from that of Europe. The criticism of the period does not, finally, present a neat, formal pattern. But what pattern there was did not really survive the economic collapse of November, 1929, that exterior event which had a great deal to do with aligning Americans and Europeans as they had not been aligned since the American Revolution.

10

Summary

Der Rationalismus ist etwas Begrenzendes, Begrenztes—HERMANN BROCH [Rationalism is limiting and limited] The period from 1919 to 1932 in the United States has come down to us in terms of two contradictory sets of ideas. According to one, the "twenties" is a proper noun always preceded by "roaring," as though the decade were a spoiled, naughty, but somehow endearing child whom we look back upon fondly because the children who followed were not endearing, and any manner of fondness for them is ruled out. We have all read something like the following many times:

> The skepticism, the iconoclasm, the Rabelaisian humor, the brilliant Mencken style—those qualities were catnip to the Roaring Twenties, when all wars had been fought, and in vain; when there were no more tomorrows, only the gay, and infinitely sad, today; when America took its dizzy ride slam-bang into the desolate thirties.[1]

Here the decade is not a spoiled child but a cat indulged in the catnip of skepticism and iconoclasm, but the point is equally vague and sentimental. The special reputation of the period as a time when writers lurched about wearing funny hats and drinking bad liquor is the result of two things: 1) self-conscious self-congratulation on the part of certain writers, summed up in the title of Edmund Wilson's plays, *This Room and This*

---

[1] Nolte, *H. L. Mencken, Literary Critic*, Preface, p. x.

Gin and These Sandwiches, which, although published in 1937, belongs in sensibility to the earlier decade, and 2) envy, often economic, on the part of a younger generation burdened by the Depression and the threat of war. The post-atomic envy of the years since 1945 may have a more serious base, but the special jocularity of the terms in which it is expressed still does violence, although rather harmless violence, to the variety and complexity of the literature of the time, while it also falsifies the genuinely responsible outlook of many of the best writers then at work.

The second set of ideas is contained in the attack upon post-World War I writers that was mounted during World War II by Archibald MacLeish and Bernard DeVoto. MacLeish's essay, *The Irresponsibles* (1940) may have been intended as an American counterpart to Julien Benda's *La Trahison des clercs* (1927) in which the terms were reversed; if so, it failed on all counts. MacLeish accused the writers of the twenties of having, in effect, falsified the meaning of their experience in the First World War by having stopped short with experience itself. When they seemed to say, with Hemingway's Frederick Henry, farewell to arms, when they rejected war and politics, they failed democracy, and they failed to prepare society for the new test of arms only then begun. Four years later, DeVoto brought out one of the most unpleasant books ever published, actually a collection of lectures, entitled *The Literary Fallacy*. Literature is fallacious, according to DeVoto, when it loses touch with the common life of the common people, when aesthetics or some other esoteric doctrine gets in the way of the writer's perception of the solidity, decency, and correctness of the ordinary man's life and being in ordinary society: ". . . literature's repudiation of American life during the Twenties shut it away from the realities of that life, the evils as well as the good."[2] One result was the falsification of the form of American society by writers, a falsification which Hitler carried over into *Mein Kampf* and which served the Nazi enemy well: "Clearly the master race accepted in good faith the description of America which American writers had provided, and made their plans in accordance with it." (p. 20.) Warming to his work, DeVoto went on:

> Never in any country or any age had writers so misrepresented their culture, never had they been so unanimously wrong. Never had writers been so completely separated from the experiences that alone give life and validity to literature. And therefore because separation from the sources of life makes

[2] Bernard DeVoto, *The Literary Fallacy* (Boston, 1944), p. 18.

despair, never had literature been so despairing, and because false writing makes trivial writing, never had literature been so trivial.[3]

DeVoto's criticism, in itself, would not be worth reviewing were it not for the fact that it is one more demonstration of an attitude we have seen before, one always just below the American surface: that attitude which naïvely misunderstands what literature is and how writers work, and which as a result insists upon identifying work of the imagination with social and political truth. It is an attitude which denies both life and art their complexity and much of their interest. Something like DeVoto's quarrel about the shape of art had gone on in France almost a century before, in the banning of Flaubert's *Madame Bovary*, but DeVoto's populism, his insistence that writing reflect the commonplace, everyday democratic fact, is peculiarly American. It is another aspect of American drunkenness on naturalism and of the insistence that art be useful, like a course in motor mechanics. And it further reflects the deep American desire that good artists be good men, that they have good thoughts and be good influences; that art, again, be useful. Arguments about the artist's "responsibility" are as futile as they are ancient. They are futile, first, because they reveal a misunderstanding about the definition of art, and second, because as they are developed, they inevitably turn into totalitarian threats that art serve the state. If art is the projection of the artist's conception of one or more of the facets of reality, then the artist cannot be "irresponsible." The moment that he is false to his own vision, which is also a vision of truth, he ceases to be an artist.

Needless to say, the nostalgic definition by which the twenties were forever "roaring" is inadequate to define the period. On the other hand, the wartime patriotic axis of MacLeish and DeVoto indicates that they themselves were the true irresponsibles. Unquestionably the period was one in which the literary face of America and Europe was fundamentally changed. It is now time to bring together the various qualities of that change, to account, insofar as history ever can do so, for that grand outburst of literary energy. History as the record of events in and among political societies will not give an answer; it was a part of MacLeish's

---

[3] *The Literary Fallacy*, pp. 167–168. Among the writers whom DeVoto attacked, namely all American writers of any reputation whatsoever, only Sinclair Lewis bothered to respond. Lewis' "Fools, Liars, and Mr. DeVoto," *Saturday Review of Literature* (XXVII, April 15, 1944), 9–12, is a nasty piece of work, but given the provocation, satisfying and appropriate.

error that he came to equate poetry with messianic prophecy. History in the form of the First World War and the flawed peace merely said to the artist, "There is the abyss. It probably contains monsters."

Thus conceived, history posed for writers, with an intensity previously unknown, the question of their relationship to literary tradition. It forced them to decide very consciously which traditional elements they could use, which discard, or whether tradition had any place whatsoever in their new, post-war world. One of the most attractive aspects of the period, however, is that awareness of the abyss and its monsters did not terrorize writers into solemnity, as it was to do after 1929. Their awareness, rather, served as *banderillas* to the bull, waking him up and reminding him of his still unused power. The question of one's relationship to the past became a discussion of the hoary antagonism between classic and romantic, as in the case of Eliot, or it became on the part of less intellectual (or less educated) writers an acting out in their work of the implications of the classic–romantic antagonism. We have seen that the most outspoken advocates of classicism in America, the new humanists, were the least interesting and the least effectual pleaders of their cause. No imaginative writers were convinced of their justice, and the humanists remained a negative force, raining ineffective blows upon the body of contemporary writing.

Eliot believed that he represented the classic in opposition to his version of the romantic. In "The Function of Criticism" (1923), he elaborated his institutional view of writing, saying that literatures of the world, of Europe, of separate countries constitute "organic wholes," that artists form a community, consciously or unconsciously, and that ideally the individual would work in a sort of collaboration with others in that community. The second-rate artist, however, "cannot afford to surrender himself to any common action." His insistence upon his "trifling differences," Eliot implies, is a function of romanticism and a betrayal of the ideal of community. The difference between classic and romantic, he wrote in the same essay, is "the difference between the complete and the fragmentary, the adult and the immature, the orderly and the chaotic."[4] T. E. Hulme's essay "Romanticism and Classicism," which Eliot often appears to have in mind, discussed our having been "debauched" by romanticism and predicts a classical revival. Eliot's views carry weight not only for his eminence as a critic but also because of his own experimentation in poetry. Experimentation, we have seen,

[4] T. S. Eliot, *Selected Essays* (New York, 1960), pp. 13–15.

covered a multitude of sins, while axiomatically the presuppositions of experiment lead to the question of the writer's attitude toward tradition. Despite Eliot's unambiguous theoretical preference for classicism and his denigration of romanticism in general and romantic poets in particular, his own position is not beyond reproach. Francis Fergusson wrote in *The Idea of a Theater* (1949):

> Eliot . . . probably the most accomplished poet alive, does not seem to find the Aristotelian formula (of imitation) useful or valid. Thus he suggests that the aim of the poet is to find objective equivalents for his feeling. The phrase "objective equivalent" seems to support Eliot's announced classicism. Yet it refers, not to the vision of the poet, but to the poem he is making; and it implies that it is only a *feeling* that the poet has to convey. Thus the formula is closer to the romantic notion of art as the expression of feeling or passion than to the doctrine of imitation.[5]

The impersonality that Hulme, Pound, Eliot, the Imagists and their successors, in their sometimes contradictory ways, were looking for was doubtless impossible in the twentieth century. The poetry of impersonality of the past, classical poetry, was possible only in homogeneous cultures in which the illusion, if not the reality, of belief was available to all. But the efforts in the skeptical twentieth century to achieve something resembling classicism paradoxically centered the reader's attention more fully than ever upon the poet's idiosyncrasies, in fact, upon his personality.

A parallel process was at work in prose fiction, although the lack of an ancient tradition allowed the writer of prose to be less self-conscious, less Eliot-like, with respect to the past. The lack of a highly developed body of criticism probably also supported that position. The attainment of objectivity served prose as the classical ideal served poetry. Along with objectivity went efforts to escape from the confines of traditional narrative by manipulation of time schemes, and to give fiction the objective validity of science by borrowing some of the insights of psychology and psychoanalysis. Again, the results were paradoxical. Wherever one turns in fiction in English, whether to Gertrude Stein's verbal play or Joyce's far more important technical accomplishment in *Ulysses*, whether to Hemingway's attempts at simplification of diction, dialogue, and character or Faulkner's reverse effects of elaboration and magnification, the various experiments serve to fasten attention upon the writer and upon the very efforts designed to disguise the writer and his individuality. Writers such as E. M. Forster, Scott Fitzgerald, or Katherine Ann Porter seem to intrude less

[5] Francis Fergusson, *The Idea of a Theater* (Princeton, 1949), p. 254.

upon their narratives than Theodore Dreiser with his naturalistic theories, or John Dos Passos writing in the mode of Joyce. Extreme consciousness on the part of the writer makes for extreme consciousness on the part of the reader and for the enhancement of his sense of the writer's unique sensibility.

All of this is not to say that post-war writers were romantics, but rather that the shape of their world was the same familiar shape the romantics had sketched, and that they could not escape from certain essential romantic traits until a philosophy other than romantic philosophy was found to be valid for the definition of modern experience. It is hard not to agree with Cyril Connolly, who wrote, ". . . it is what an artist does with his romanticism that constitutes modern literature."[6] The two philosophers to whom post-war writers frequently turned, Nietzsche and Bergson, did nothing to distort the romantic pattern. Although, in radically different ways, both were irrational; irrationality was far more the order of the day than rationality. Bergson's notions of creative evolution, time, memory, and his insistence upon the primacy of instinct and intuition were all useful in liberating writers from an all but worn-out theory of knowledge. His ideas at second or third remove also served the writer who was so obsessed that he had no choice but to be carried along by his own intensity. Bergson's influence is at work in Proust's *A la Recherche du temps perdu*, where time and memory are structural, not loosely schematic, and deeply essential to the novel as a whole. In Virginia Woolf's novels of the period, particularly *To the Lighthouse* (1927) and *The Waves* (1931), the intention to achieve a Bergsonian framework is more obvious if only because of the disparity between the impulse and the achievement. One's impression of obsession in Faulkner derives from a similar focus upon time which may or may not be a matter of philosophical influence. The lack of evidence seems to indicate that Faulkner achieved all the liberation he needed by having been born when he was and by having been sensitive, as we know he was, to the literary and social climate of his day. Whether Faulkner ever laid eyes on his work or not, Bergson served literature well; his kind of irrationality was humane and innocent, never intended to serve man's diabolical underside. His theory of time was valuable, marking as it did one of the few absolute advances in narration in the history of prose fiction. That it reinforced the romantic ego accounts, at least in part, for its hospitable reception by writers.

[6] Cyril Connolly, "Alain-Fournier," in *Previous Convictions* (London, 1963), p. 214.

Although Nietzsche's influence (in English) was as pernicious as Bergson's was benevolent, Nietzsche appeared only in the work of minor writers of fiction, and on the sociological fringes of literature inhabited by thinkers of the stature of H. L. Mencken and Wyndham Lewis. It should be remarked that the Nietzsche of Mencken, Ben Hecht, or Floyd Dell was the theatrical, semi-crazed Nietzsche of legend, but never Nietzsche the classical philologist or the Nietzsche who anticipated Freud in his apprehension of the unconscious. In two of Ben Hecht's novels, *Erik Dorn* (1921) and *Humpty Dumpty* (1924), a shallow and vicious anarchism is given a veil of respectability by allusion to Nietzsche and by suggestions that the central figures are acting out sequences proposed by the German master. In Floyd Dell's *The Moon-Calf* (1920), Nietzsche is referred to as an authority for rebellion and for holding the self above and apart from the mob. Both novelists are unintentionally comic in their pretensions to philosophic meaning. Nietzsche probably influenced only a handful of writers in the United States and England because his aphorisms, as translated and as usually understood in English, are even more absurd than in German.

On the other hand, Nietzsche as perceived by Mencken in the United States and by Clive Bell and Norman Douglas in England was quite different from the Nietzsche of the callow, half-educated novelists. Mencken used his own peculiar interpretation of Nietzsche as a base from which to attack Christianity and to support his own loathing for American political forms. We have already seen the lengths to which his anti-democratic posturings could take him. He relied on Nietzsche for his vision of a German aristocratic ideal; for approbation of his personal sense of superiority, he looked to the "booboisie"—his word. Mencken could be ignored if it were not for his popular influence. Clive Bell's *Civilization* (1928), Norman Douglas' *Goodbye to Western Culture* (1930), and some of the maunderings of Wyndham Lewis represent rather more fundamental attacks upon a Christian, humanistic concept of society than Mencken's attacks in America. Clive Bell spoke for one aspect of Bloomsbury culture: it assumed the superiority of the artist to any other form of life, and took heavy satisfaction in the thought that civilization was doomed now that the inferior classes no longer knew their place. Douglas' view is roughly similar, and similarly Nietzschean, with a larding of Spengler. Again, such views supported cynicism about politics and served to rationalize what philistines referred to as the irresponsibility of artists. Nietzsche, whether partially or wholly understood, gave England and the

United States powerful support for glorification of the romantic self and for a romantic exile of that self from the concerns of society.

On the Continent, however, where Nietzsche had been read more carefully than in the English-speaking countries, his influence was more diffuse; it emerged often in pleasantly ironic contexts. In the twenties, Musil was working out his delightful satire upon the Nietzschean strain, both individual and social, in *The Man Without Qualities*. Montherlant could write a fairly straightforward Nietzschean character like Alban into *Le Songe*, followed by satire upon certain Nietzschean attitudes in *Les Jeunes filles*. In Spain, Nietzsche was a profound influence upon the entire modernist movement that reached a high point in the 1920's.[7] Wherever he was read, Nietzsche served the purpose of indicating the innate duality of romanticism, its ability to evoke both work of great emotional power and work so trivial and suspect that one must doubt the evidence of the senses upon reading it. Nietzsche's irrationality was largely responsible for his attraction, as was his apparent bravery in deriding the sanctions of traditional Christianity and traditional social forms. He seemed to support the American and English movement toward liberalism in all forms of art and society, to be a force not for repression but for freedom, an ally in the war upon puritanism.

The main difficulty with questions of philosophical influence on literature is that philosophy presents a more solid façade than does any mere work of art; therefore, the importance of its influence is easily and often exaggerated. More often than not, it is as vague as the influence of psychology or natural science, and just as difficult to establish with precision. A more rewarding line of inquiry may be that of genre: whether in the period one genre predominates, and whether the pursuit of genre by nationality may turn up conclusions that might otherwise remain hidden or only partially revealed. On the one hand, we find during the twenties an acceleration in the breakdown of traditional genres, a process that had begun long before the war in the aesthetic of symbolism, and before that in the romantic impulse to synaesthesia.

In the work of Proust and Joyce, José Ortega y Gasset complained in "Notes on the Novel" that the genre of the novel was being run into a dead end. By that he meant that it was not possible for other writers to work in the manner of Proust or Joyce; further, they paradoxically

---

[7] The extent and complexity of Nietzschean influence may be seen in Udo Rukser, *Nietzsche in der Hispania* (Bern and Munich, 1962); and in Gonzalo Sobejano, *Nietzsche en España* (Madrid, 1967).

cast suspicion on the vitality of the genre by their superb but definitive use of it. For the United States, something of Ortega's analysis could be applied to Faulkner's and Dos Passos' work. Writers who have tried to imitate Faulkner, no matter how gifted—as in the case of William Styron—or Dos Passos—as in the case of Norman Mailer—have found themselves very definitely at the dead end that Ortega describes. The same is true for Hemingway, although his style and mannerisms appeared to be more available than they in fact were. Nor is the question of genre in this context simply a matter of imitation. The question is: are whole areas blanked off by the relentless superiority of a few writers of genius in treating them? It is not, fortunately, a question that must be answered here; to do so properly would require another book. It seems likely, however, that Ortega confused the genre of the novel with the over-powering strategies and mannerisms of a few remarkable writers.

One crucial difference between the rather soft, romantic impulse to synaesthesia and the formal experiments of post-war writers came about through the appearance of obsession. Obsession is the intermittent but unmistakable sense one has in reading writers so various as Proust, Hermann Broch, Faulkner, Céline, or Thomas Wolfe that the material rather than the man is in charge—the man is in the grip of a compulsion so intense that he has no alternative but to write as he does. There was little or nothing of that quality of obsession in the traditional plotted novel, no matter how gothic, nothing of it in Joyce or Thomas Mann, whose every word seems dictated by a superior intelligence. Joyce, however, made possible the registering of obsession, however, by his technical advances in narration. And writers' awareness of a world adrift after the First World War, as has been previously noted, offered reasons in abundance to support their temperamental predisposition to obsession.

At this point, a peculiarity of American fiction and criticism arises. It is one of the few points at which we may see exterior events and aesthetic events in causal relationship. I refer to the tentativeness of outline in the creation of character and narrative techniques that is obvious when we place the best of American fiction alongside the best of European. If, for example, we put Jay Gatsby alongside Joachim von Pasenow, the central character of Hermann Broch's *Die Romantik* (*The Romantic*, volume I of the trilogy *The Sleepwalkers*), that tentativeness becomes fully apparent. Both novels have a common theme, the difference between romantic illusion and harsh reality. Joachim, eldest son of a *Junker*, believes that he believes all the legends of *Junkerdom*—the militaristic tradition, the paternalism on the family estate, the feudal outlook—and he does his best to live in accordance with the unbending code passed on to him by his family. But the time, 1888, is indeed out of joint, and Joachim's efforts to live up to an impossible ideal—impossible to him because of temperament and even more so because falsified by history—are by turns amusing, touching, and close to tragic. Hence, while Broch's character is tenuous and tentative, there is nothing tentative about the form of the novel, about the writer's intention, or about his remarkable achievement. Through parody of the traditional German romantic novel and through the use of a technique in which naturalism and surrealism are mixed, Broch registers the degree of Joachim's dissociation from the army, his fiancée, his friends, and from the entire society. The novel is finally a brief, beautifully realized statement about one entire range of causes of the world war to come. In it are blended, with absolute authority, imaginative and historical reality.

The Great Gatsby, too, as we have seen, is directed to history, but Fitzgerald's techniques are very different from Broch's. Fitzgerald's use of a narrator and of flashbacks is standard and straightforward, as opposed to Broch's explorations of the peculiar geography of Joachim von Pasenow's mind. Gatsby, the central character, is withheld for the first third of the narrative, and when he makes his appearance, it is a ghostly one. The plot involves the gradual revelation of Gatsby's true self, while his meaning within the novel, together with the setting and many of the incidents, take us to a misty, real-unreal area where outline must be inferred through metaphor and symbol. This is not to imply that Fitzgerald's novel is inferior, simply that it is different.

The symbolic nature of *The Great Gatsby*, its relative opaqueness and hesitancy, are qualities that many American novels have had from the time of Brockden Brown on. It is those qualities which have urged the fashionable notion that the characteristic American novel is not a novel at all, but a romance. That suggestion is in line with the formula that Hawthorne began and Henry James carried on: that life in the United States is too thin, too lacking in social convention and picturesque artifact, too un-historical, in fact, to provide material sufficiently rich for the novelist's imagination. American novelists, therefore, according to the "romance" school, have been forced to use allegory and symbol in order to say anything whatsoever about American experience. The period 1919–1932 would seem to point up the falsehood of the "romance" point of view.

To return to the differences between Broch and Fitzgerald: much of Broch's strength lies in his knowledge of his country's historical situation. There was no escaping that Germany and the Austro-Hungarian Empire had fought a major war and had been defeated on the battlefields of that war. One task for Hermann Broch, as novelist, was to go back in history and try to discover *as a novelist* what had gone wrong. That same order of strength, deriving from an unequivocal historical position, however depressing that position might be, is apparent in many post-war German writers, in poetry and in prose. It is there in Trakl and Heym, in Thomas Mann (more fully after World War II in *Doktor Faustus*), in Musil, and in Döblin. Americans, by contrast, did not quite know who or where they were, historically, after 1919. On the one hand, they sensed that they could never again be isolated from world events, that the United States, for better or worse, was now a world power with all the terrifying responsibilities attached to such a position. On the other hand, from the Presidency on down, Americans tried to retreat into isolationism and to deny that there had been a war. On the whole, writers ignored or denied politics, saying with Hemingway's character, Mr. Frazier, in "The Gambler, the Nun, and the Radio," "What you wanted was the minimum of government, always less government." And again, "Revolution, Mr. Frazier thought, is no opium. Revolution is a catharsis; an ecstasy which can only be prolonged by tyranny. The opiums are for before and for after."[8] Even the First World War itself became a legend. When Dos Passos published *Three Soldiers*, a novel less than enthusiastic about the war, Pershing, the former commander of the American forces in Europe, said that the book was an insult to the American Army. In other words, the relation in the United States between historical reality and society was itself equivocal. Therefore, writers were deprived of an important basis for fiction, but they were not deprived of manners or mores, as the fiction of the entire period makes clear.[9] The contrast between American and European

[8] These are notable for being Hemingway's only overtly political remarks in his fiction until the 1930's.

[9] Americans have resisted an historical identity for a long time. Perhaps the most persistent and false idea we have of ourselves is that we are a "young" nation, lacking in history. I have written elsewhere that "The United States has been interpreted as a country without a pre-history, a country which came into being at a given moment in recorded history. American society, according to this theory, did not develop like traditional communities, but is closer to a human artifact, manufactured to satisfy conscious, reasoned needs. Lacking the nourishment of

novelists is related, then, to history. It seems to be greater than it is because of Americans' preoccupation with process and material, that inheritance from the naturalists. Process in America appears even more fully than is in fact the case to take the place of analysis as we see it in the Europeans. As in *The Great Gatsby*, analysis is there and at work, but it is disguised in metaphor and symbol, and its conclusions are tentative when compared to a good European model.

We have seen in the period a good number of poets who produced work of merit and abundance. Thus, poetry in the United States, regarded from the special point of view of genre, may be said to have shown an admirable balance to prose. The sources of poetic energy are even more mysterious than the sources of prose fiction, but among the obvious sources are surely the elevation of American English to the purposes of poetry, reaction against the poverty in quality of the immediate pre-war group of American poets, and the special American relationship that one can sense between experiment and optimism. The openness and freedom, often more apparent than real, that many writers experienced after the war led to a sort of intoxication with the self and the world. We see it in much of the work of William Carlos Williams, in Hart Crane, in portions of Wallace Stevens' work, and it is present, however faintly, beneath the Christian despair of Eliot. For obvious historical reasons, European literature of the time lacks that openness and optimism altogether. The American 1920's may have been the last point in history at which even a limited belief in the idea of progress, that powerful force which extended from the Enlightenment to Darwin and beyond, was possible.

The central literary question one may ask about the period from 1919 to 1932 is beguiling in simplicity but laden with ambiguity: the question of which ideas or literary modes had value, and the related question of what kind of value. More than any other question, that of value defines whether a given span of time is an actual "period" or merely a chronological sequence more or less arbitrarily selected. And the answer, which by now should contain no surprise, is that the first and highest value attached to irrationality, whether instinctual and

pre-historical traditions, it paradoxically lacks a history: 'a society born in a certain moment of history comes to find itself outside history; . . . it lacks any deep-rooted consciousness of history'." John McCormick, *Catastrophe and Imagination* (London, 1957), p. 29, and footnote, F. G. Friedmann, "America: A Country Without Pre-History," *Partisan Review* (XIX, no. 2, March–April, 1952), 142.

inevitable, as in the case of Hart Crane and García Lorca, or irrationality as a conclusion to a rational process, as in the case of Yeats, Eliot, and Valéry. All the influences in what has here been called the foreground of literature conspired to irrationality in the post-war period. The war itself foremost, the influence of Nietzsche and Bergson, the apparent abstraction from human experience of the new mathematical logic and the new physics, the exaggeration of romantic impulses, psychoanalysis (often misunderstood, to be sure)—all led to the widespread and inescapable conclusion that traditional religious and social forces were not only invalid, but also deleterious. Gilbert Murray's famous description of literature in antiquity after the great classical writers applies after 1918: "There is an intensifying of certain spiritual emotions; an increase in sensitiveness, a failure of nerve."[10] The modern failure of nerve is clear in Paul Valéry, that most rational of men who spent decades in a denial of rationalism, turning to illuminism and theosophy, honoring Nietzsche over Pascal,[11] and shaping himself into a monster of rational irrationality. His service, apart from his splendid poetry, was to define for us "with classic brevity the theme of the decline of the West through an excess of the very rationalism whose discovery had been its greatest triumph."[12] The case of Rilke is similar. For English, however, Yeats is our grand irrationalist, the poet who not only ransacked theosophy and spiritualism, but who invented his own vast mystical cosmography in order to give his poetic vision a frame of reference, a basis which he could not find in Christian belief or in Irish politics. We have seen Eliot writing *The Waste Land* as his contribution to the irrational camp, then turning almost frantically to traditional religion, to monarchy, and to literary tradition out of horror at the abyss he had glimpsed and helped to colonize.

Fitzgerald and Faulkner created a myth of history, not so much out of irrationality as from an absence of rationality. Each writer in his different way represents a triumph of the intuitive, of the intelligence as a function of the senses. Hemingway, who resembled Eliot with a significant part of his apprehension, also indulged in myth-making on a modified scale in his first novel, then turned away from that kind of irrationality to the other, special American variety, the irrationality of

---

[10] Gilbert Murray, *Five Stages of Greek Religion* (New York, 1925), p. 155.

[11] The point is surely debatable, but the mere fact that it arises is significant.

[12] Joseph Frank, "Introduction," Paul Valéry, *Masters and Friends* (Bollingen Series XLV, Princeton, 1968), p. ix.

life in nature, of life enhanced and given point by the imminence of death. Again like Eliot, Hemingway possessed a religious concept of art, although he was suspicious of it and covered it with layers of mannerism. Dos Passos, by contrast, retained his loyalty to rationalism; fully aware of the ᴘocesses of irrationality, whether in Freud's system or in capitalism, his ᴘtionality is nevertheless limiting, and among his contemporaries, his fiction appears to a later decade to be the most naturalistic and provincial, if only for its efforts to catch and record the passing moment. It seems likely that the attraction of Europe for Americans after the First World War had a good deal to do with the wider recognition of irrationality in Europe. In America, the official rationality of politics and business life was palpably at odds with intuited truths about what had happened and what was about to happen to our civilization. Even the megalomaniacal prophecies of a Wyndham Lewis had more truth than Coolidge's remark that the business of America was business. Broch was only stating the obvious when he wrote so flatly, "Rationality is limiting and limited." The mere satires of writers like Sinclair Lewis or Mencken were local and thin in comparison with writers who had seen the apocalypse and who sensed another apocalypse to come. The concept of value thus comes down to a concept of truth to experience. America had yet to experience apocalypse at a time when Europeans were still burying their dead and trying to survey the contours of the present.

The differences between American and European writing of the period became inescapably clear after the American economic and social collapse of 1929. Europe, in effect, had experienced its collapse in 1914, or shortly thereafter; the American mood of optimism had persisted, giving a significant part of the literature a brightness too brilliant to be convincing. For Europe, the years from 1929 to 1932 were no more dreary or dramatic than the years preceding 1929. Economic stagnation was deeper, but not significantly deeper than it had been. The war and subsequent disasters had toughened Europeans in a way that Americans had yet to discover. Something of that toughness appears in Aldous Huxley's remarks about Dada:

> The work of the Sitwells and a few others in England, of Cocteau, Morand, Aragon, MacOrlan and the rest of them in France helps me to make that guess [that a new comic synthesis will come about]. The new synthesis that will reassemble in an artistic whole the shattered relics of the postwar world,

the synthesis that will reflect the disintegration in an artistic unity, will surely be a comic synthesis. The social tragedy of these last few years had gone too far and its nature and origin is too profoundly stupid to be represented tragically. And the same is true of the equally complicated and devastating mental tragedy of the breakup of old tradition and values. The only possible synthesis is the enormous farcical buffoonery of a Rabelais or an Aristophanes,—a buffoonery which, it is important to note, is capable of being as beautiful and as grandiose as tragedy.[13]

Although Huxley's statement is more valid as a defense of his own sort of fiction than as a prediction of things to come, it reflects a steely facing up to events and a resolution to cope with them that contrasts with American hysteria after 1929. In a book of 1932 entitled, significantly, *Fear and Trembling*, Glenway Wescott enunciated the vulnerable American sense of betrayal, the sense that one had been taken for a ride by life:

Loneliness is a very modern, especially a very American, feeling. (p. 3).

. . . we are being borne, oh, rapidly indeed, like a great mail coach, running on to an appointed accident—hastening or just sliding toward who cares what beliefs, who knows what downfalls, with a worse vision of sudden death, a worse dream fugue of collisions and confusions, ineffable wars and national bankruptcies, and, for what we call civilization, a great riotous funeral, at the end! (p. 8).

Literature has lagged pusillanimously behind life, and failed to develop even an accurate language, to say nothing of what is called a philosophy, by which changing society might at least classify its experience and govern some of its reflexes. (p. 11).[14]

One would like to have known Baudelaire's, Joyce's, Kafka's, Broch's, Mann's, or a dozen other Europeans' responses to the suggestion that loneliness is either particularly modern or American. What is to the point is that it required social collapse to make so good a writer as Wescott aware of the sensation. The latter two quotations suggest something of the DeVoto attack in the notion that literature and language had failed to keep up with events. But Wescott's own best work, to say nothing of other American writers', denies the accusation. That does not detract from his honestly expressed sensation of fright and despair,

[13] Quoted in W. C. Frierson, *The English Novel in Translation: 1885–1940* (Norman, Oklahoma, 1942), p. 240.

[14] Glenway Wescott, *Fear and Trembling* (New York, 1932).

a despair rather different from that of Kierkegaard, who furnished the title of the book, or from the mythically expressed despair of *The Waste Land* or *The Sun Also Rises*.

The collapse of 1929 in the United States might be compared to what happens to a rotten log in the forest when a bear comes along, claws off the surface, and so creates chaos in a colony of ants in its interior. Some are crushed, others eaten, and still others drop to the ground to run off any which way, until such time as the bear passes, when they re-orientate themselves and set about re-building their colony. Many writers were like the ants. Some careers came to an end; Hart Crane committed suicide, following the pattern of his publisher, Harry Crosby. Others scurried off to study coal mines and common people, like Sherwood Anderson or Edmund Wilson (see Wilson's *The American Jitters*, 1932). Or to change the figure, the writers of the 1920's self-consciously thought of themselves as a new *Sturm und Drang* movement, while in fact they represented only the *Drang*, for their *Sturm* was yet to come.

For Europe, the years 1919 to 1932 proved that the time of order was long over, and that the time of disorder unquestionably had arrived. For America, the time of order was assuredly over, but the time of disorder was still on its way. Each situation produced literature of abundance and beauty. History cannot, finally, provide a reason for either the abundance or the beauty; it can only point in admiration, and from the fascinating post-World War I period perhaps draw an irrational hope that civilization is tougher than we suspect in our latter-day, rational despair about its future.

11

A
Postscript on
Method

"*Le plus grand hommage que l'on puisse offrir à un artiste est l'attention.*" D'Annunzio . . . .
Et j'ai écrit, à propos de Malraux, que la plus grande qualité de l'artiste lui-même était l'attention.—
HENRY DE MONTHERLANT, *Va Jouer avec cette poussière: carnets, 1958–1964* A note of
explanation about the method of this book may be in order. Both the
professional and the non-professional reader for whom one really writes
may well ask, Why a comparative history, and what is comparative
history, anyway? I have undertaken *The Middle Distance* out of the
conviction that most literary history I knew was neither very literary
nor really historical. The matter that follows was my attempt at the
outset to clarify to myself what seemed out of joint in conventional
histories and to construct the lines along which another kind of literary
history might be written.[1]

An American literary historian has written that "the occupational
disease of American literary histories, however ostentatious their prefaces,
has been to have no point of view at all. . . ."[2] The pursuit of literary
history is everywhere recent, chaotic, and exemplary only in a negative
sense. American literary history has been more incapacitated than most
by an inadequate tradition and by a set of apparently willful miscon-

[1] A version of this essay, "Notes on a Comparative American Literary History,"
was published in *Comparative Literary Studies* (V, no. 2, June, 1968), 167–179.

[2] Howard Mumford Jones, *The Theory of American Literature* (Ithaca, N.Y.,
1948), p. 145.

ceptions about the nature of history and literature. Our difficulties
began in the past, for the legitimate grandfathers of American literary
history were not the Americans Samuel Knapp or Moses Coit Tyler, but
Leopold von Ranke,[3] the magisterial professor in Berlin, who by practice
and precept over a period of fifty years prepared the ground for the idea
that history is science, not art; that historical fact is ascertainable; and
that given objectivity and serenity, the historian need only go about the
job of ascertaining fact. Everyone knows his famous statement, "My
object is simply to find out how events actually occurred"; and elsewhere,
"I am first a historian, then a Christian." Ranke's influence on literary
history is not direct but devious. It is often intermingled in the historian's
mind with notions of rationality and order derived from the Enlightenment, together with late nineteenth-century positivism and pragmatism.
Thus we are told that

> Literary history conceives of literature as one aspect of organic evolution,
> limited by time and space for the purpose of study, and determined by
> forces and factors both within and without the individual and collective
> experience of the writers who lived in that time and place. Its primary concern
> is with relations rather than with absolute values, but it is dependent on
> criticism for appraisal of these values, and on other forms of history for the
> analysis of its causes.[4]

Or again, literary history is not literary criticism,

> . . . although it must depend upon the literary critic to identify and to evaluate
> the works of literature with which it is to deal, to eliminate from its con-
> sideration as literature those writings which are not literature, and to establish
> the necessary hierarchies and other relationships in terms of value of the
> literary works which it is to use as data in its historical account.[5]

---

[3] Knapp's *Lectures on American Literature* (1829) is generally regarded as the first
attempt at an historical view, although Knapp was preceded by John Neal, who
published a series of even more fatuous essays on American writing in *Blackwood's
Magazine* in 1824–25. Tyler (1835–1900) published his *History of American Literature,
1607–1765* in 1878. It is the first organized, full-scale treatment, and was followed in
1879 by his *Literary History of the American Revolution, 1763–1783*. Ranke (1795–1886):
an essential document in his theory was *Zur Kritik neuerer Geschichtschreiber*, which
was appended to his first book, *Geschichte der romanischen und germanischen Völker,
1444–1514* (Berlin, 1824).
[4] Robert E. Spiller, *The Third Dimension: Studies in Literary History* (New York,
1965), p. 15.
[5] *The Third Dimension*, pp. 222–223.

Or again,

> In order to do research and to write, the literary historian must first set up
> some sort of working hypothesis as to what a literary event is and how it
> may be related to other literary events, and he would probably not be too
> seriously challenged if he merely assumed that the literary event, the unit
> with which he is to deal, is any piece of formal writing which is generally
> accepted by the critics as a work of literary art.[6]

The diction derives from the vocabulary of natural science rather
than art—"organic evolution," "causes," "data," "necessary hierarchies,"
"working hypothesis"—just as the clotted syntax is that of a laboratory
technician, while the writer's emphasis upon determinism evokes the
generation of Taine and Joseph Texte rather than that of Eliot and
Blackmur. Still another standard literary historian defines literary history
as "an orderly record of those written works (and of pertinent facts
about them) mankind values or has valued in the past. . . ."[7] All such
statements have in common a pseudo-scientific bias, an attempt to exclude
criticism from history, and a begging of the question of value. "Written
works mankind values or has valued" not only begs the question of value,
but it also leads to the inclusion of all manner of marginalia, journals,
political polemic, letters, and laundry lists, matter which may be pertinent
to the history of culture but hardly to a history of literature rigorously
conceived. It is assumed that the record—the canon, in fact—is there in
history to be uncovered, and that the historian's job is simply to uncover
it. In the United States, we find reverence for a canon of great works,
together with the principle that anything goes. Ultimately, "anything"
becomes the stuff of cultural, as opposed to literary, history. The manner
in which an American canon of major and minor work has arisen may
best be defined in Auerbach's memorable phrase, "aesthetic historicism,"
with emphasis upon "historicism."

Two generations of political historians in Europe and the United
States have been far more critical of the positivistic tradition in historiography than the literary historians have been. History itself, after all,

---

[6] *The Third Dimension*, p. 225. Spiller writes elsewhere in his book that the
historian may also be a critic, but that when he writes history, he must, so to speak,
remove his critic's hat in the interests of "objectivity."

[7] Jones, *Theory of American Literature*, p. 9. Although Jones adds, "but such a
statement tells us nothing," he clearly believes that his statement is as close as he can
come to a definition.

has encouraged skepticism about the nature of "fact." Under the whiplash of figures so diverse as Croce, Dilthey, Jaspers, Collingwood, Becker, Beard, Lovejoy, and Popper, political history has returned to its great tradition as a subtle and indeed aesthetic art, as distinct from the intellectual poverty of the great majority of literary histories.

The other grandfather of American literary history is romanticism in its interesting American form. Its genes and chromosomes show a most complex pattern, and nothing like it has existed in Europe since Friedrich Schlegel, De Sanctis, or Taine. It is made up of two parts rhetoric, two parts mysticism, two parts unintentional nationalism, one part Whitman-like bicep expansion, and three parts provincialism. We may observe it in a recent book on American poetry:

> For the achievement of American poetry is a good measure of the achievement of American culture as a whole. The poet's particular relation to his culture—his self-imposed obligation to make the best possible use of the language he is given—is such as to put him at the center of the web of communications which gives his culture its characteristic style and spirit. The poet continually inquires into the genuineness and comprehensiveness of that style and spirit. He asks—above all, in the United States he has asked—how much it has cost to achieve them. And he measures that cost in terms of something as simple, and as difficult, as his sense of the dignity of man.[8]

The writer insists upon the uniqueness of American "experience," and by hauling in the dignity of man, he establishes an ungainly, heavy-breathing image of the American poet as someone beyond normal human life and expression. The emphasis upon experience is essentially romantic in origin and American in its continuing attraction for analysts. The appeal to uniqueness, together with an unspoken but clearly audible call to nationalism, is present in still another typical statement:

> English-speaking settlers arrive in North America, children of British intellectual and literary traditions. In the New World they and their descendants develop first a colonial, then a provincial, and finally a national culture.[9]

In itself, the statement is not romantic, but behind the necessity to insist upon a "national culture" lies an assumption about the relationship

[8] Roy Harvey Pearce, *The Continuity of American Poetry* (Princeton, 1961), pp. 3–4. Pearce calls his book cultural, not literary, history, unlike many who reverse the terms and procedure.

[9] Jones, *Theory of American Literature*, p. 18.

between literature and a people that is romantic in origin and implication.

In the first instance, the call for American Shakespeares and Miltons was a product of the political revolution against Britain, but the continuing clarity of that call—and it is present in some degree in every American literary history of any ambition—is the result of powerful romantic impulses that have outlasted the chronological limits of romanticism as assigned by literary history. Faced with heterogeneity, Americans have insisted upon homogeneity, and thus the literary historian asserts, without convincing proof, that we have in truth achieved a "national culture." What may be less obvious is that our national search for identity came into prominence at the high tide of the romantic movement: see the early volumes of George Bancroft's *History of the United States* (1834–1876), while musings about who we are, where we have been, and where we are going have provided a bulky literature in a variety of disciplines from 1776 to yesterday morning's newspaper. Such self-consciousness about our historical situation, again, is not in itself romantic, but it is closely allied to the kind of historical awareness so prominent in Emerson's work, to say nothing of William Faulkner's or Thomas Wolfe's.

American literary historians often discover rare beauties in the American landscape and a special sweetness in the American air (despite the pollution index). Behind that pastoral habit lies an entire complex of romantic clichés. Rousseau and Chateaubriand took Greek pastoral and turned it into the myth of the noble savage and the forest primeval. Native American writers, from Bryant and Cooper to Mark Twain and Hemingway, turned those myths to good account. But a myth that served American imaginative literature so well is of dubious merit when it infuses the work of literary historians. At its worst, it had led to the glorification of the provincial under the heading of "local color," and to a kind of rhetoric that rides along on inflated phrases, blandly neglecting disciplined scrutiny of meaning. More specifically, in the period 1919–1932, the pastoral prejudice led to the glorification of a versifier like Carl Sandburg and to applause for an entertainer like Vachel Lindsay, while Wallace Stevens went unread.

Semi-conscious or unconscious romantic nationalism has also led to many historians paying lip service to European influences and origins in favor of Freudian or Jungian explanations through myth and symbol. Valuable though some of that work is, at its pedestrian average it represents a single tool trying to do the work of a machine shop. The identification of myth and symbol is a technique, that is to say, not a method. In the hands of the less than competent, it is one more evasion of the true task of literary history.

What, then, is literary history, and even more difficult, *recent* literary history? Dilthey suggests the beginning of definition when he says that history is not separated from life or divided from the present by distance in time, a view with which Eliot would agree. By definition, literary history ought to be both literary and historical, within Dilthey's meaning of the term. By "literary" one does not mean that which was written, but only work of the imagination of a high order. Any other interpretation takes us back to the principle of anything goes, to positivism, and to the sociological jungle. Judgment, it follows, is essential, and without taste, impossible. Croce stated the ideal in his *Aesthetic* when he wrote that scholarship, taste, and historical comprehension are the essentials for the literary historian. His ideal rules out literary history as identical with the history of culture. That literary history has a certain place in the history of culture is another matter. It becomes the historian's job to distinguish between events that belong to "culture" in Max Weber's sense—events which are peripheral to his primary concern as literary historian—and events that belong to "culture" in Matthew Arnold's or T. S. Eliot's sense. It also follows that literary history should be critical. The moment that one rules out historical inevitability, objectivity, notions of progress in art (there is "development in art, but no progress"),[10] or any other convenient cultural formula, one has forced the historian to exercise his judgment in a critical manner. Any history worth reading, literary or political, is of necessity critical and subjective. The alternative assumes either a Platonic absolute with which the inspired historian is in mystical union or an "objectivity" which produces the familiar handbook of names, dates, instant powdered biographies, and assorted notes having to do with culture.

The historian's job is to ask questions about certain events in time past. But the historian's own time, all the influences of his own history, personal and public, will influence the questions that he asks. His own history will dictate a priority of values among those questions; it will eliminate, perhaps, certain traditional questions as irrelevant; and it will to a certain degree influence his vocabulary and syntax. For example, American literary historians of the 1920's and 1930's were professors on the defensive, much concerned with establishing American literature as

---

10 R. G. Collingwood, *Idea of History* (New York, 1956), p. 330.

a discipline in itself rather than as a branch of English literary study. They therefore assumed the most rigorous, Germanic objectivity in their approach, attempting to rival the natural sciences by creating not a branch of humane studies, but *Amerikanische Literaturwissenschaft.* Hence their suspicion of subjectivity, of literary criticism, and hence their diction and syntax. They would push back to Bacon, but after doing so, they emerged with a sentimental positivism.

Questions of the historian's relationship to his own time and his own awareness of that relationship are equally prominent in the writing of all history, literary or political. Where the literary historian diverges from the political historian is in aesthetics. An aesthetic fact differs qualitatively from a political fact, and the history of art differs qualitatively from the history of steamboats on the Mississippi. Collingwood, following and expanding upon Croce, has stated the problem lucidly:

> The artist's problem, in so far as he is an artist, is not the problem of doing what his predecessor has done and going on to do something further which his predecessor failed to do. There is development in art, but no progress: for though in the technical processes of art one man learns from another, . . . the problem of art itself consists not in mastering these technical processes but in using them to express the artist's experience and give it reflective form, and consequently every fresh work of art is the solution of a fresh problem which arises not out of a previous work of art but out of the artist's un- reflective experience. Artists do better or worse work in so far as they solve these problems well or ill, *but the relation between good and bad art is not an historical relation, because the problems arise out of the flow of unreflective experience, and that flow is not an historical process.*[11]

If one agrees with Collingwood about the nature of the artistic process, one might seem to agree that the very possibility of a history of art is ruled out. Collingwood partially resolves the dilemma when he says, "There is . . . a history of art, but no history of artistic problems, as there is a history of scientific or philosophical problems. There is only a history of artistic achievements."[12] But only partially. It seems to me that the literary historian can, and must, record in so far as he is capable the nature of the technical problems facing the artist in the past; he must indicate the dimensions of the problems, and more important, the nature of the artist's solutions. This is rather more than critical comment upon the achievement to which Collingwood would limit the historian.

[11] *Idea of History,* p. 330. My italics.
[12] *Idea of History,* p. 314.

Despite Collingwood, it is not really possible or desirable to separate the achievement from the techniques that brought it about. It is in the historian's awareness of the writer's technical task that cultural and literary history meet. For the writer, far more than the musician, the dancer, or the painter, engages society intellectually, simply because his medium is words, and words, however esoteric, take their contemporary meanings and nuances from contemporary social experience. Literature, finally, *is* in history.

Social experience, for the literary historian, is different from socio-logical experience. Social experience from the standpoint of literature defines what culture actually is, and at this point the need arises for the comparative approach. It is vaguely possible that in the past it might have been possible to write a good literary history from the national point of view; none comes to mind. At present, as in the American post-World War I period, it is impossible. Culture in the west since the fall of Rome—"high" culture, literary culture, social culture, in fact—is composed of a marvelously subtle and complex mixture of influences: religious, philosophical, linguistic, political, social, and sociological. American culture is a particular strain of the mixture, but unless our European antecedents and contemporary leanings are duly noted, any resulting history is predestined to provincialism and distortion. This is of course a truism, but it needs to be repeated with special reference to the composition of American literary history. Comparative literary history begins with that truism firmly in mind, then under the difficult heading of influence proceeds to refine, to define, and to judge.

Judgment, accordingly, becomes a process of weighing the canon inherited from one's predecessors, of seeing in the light of one's own experience how that canon came into being, and of determining its renewed validity or lack of validity. Comparative literary history is not concerned with listing all work in a given period, major, mediocre, and minor, but rather with identifying the major as fully as possible and relegating the mediocre and minor to their proper place as explanatory of social or sociological fact. Above all, the comparative historian's judgments of a national literature take into account the place of relevant foreign works. Contemporary culture, American culture certainly, is nothing if not cosmopolitan, and to account for that fact is not exclusively the task of criticism, as many historians have insisted, but central to the task of history. Again, any attempt to separate history from criticism creates a positivistic horror.

We may now perceive that the traditional, false division between history and criticism was the result of misapprehensions about the nature of literary influence. By and large, historians have taken for granted a crude, positivistic theory of influence in which the literary work is seen as the sum of a set of identifiable and provable influences. According to this theory, if we simply can learn enough about a writer, his tradition, and his time, we may fully account for his work by balancing out the literary-biographical ledger. Such ledger-balancing, in turn, assumes that movement and progression occur from epoch to epoch, nation to nation, movement to movement, and writer to writer. History in this way becomes the chronicle of movements and writers rather than of writing. To criticism is left the problem of the genesis of the work, as opposed to the worker, together with the entire complex of "unprovable," subjective insights about the work. Objections to the ledger-balancing idea of influence are obvious. Not only is it excessively positivistic, but also in practice, influences on the work tend to have equal weight with the work itself; in addition, it has been pointed out that confusion is likely to arise between influences and textual similarities.[13]

Textual similarities or parallels between two writers are legitimate subjects for history, and it is here that history and criticism legitimately divide. The historian needs such evidence for his grasp of a given period, while to criticism of a specific work, parallels more often than not mislead. The entire question of when an influence is an influence is a matter for aesthetics; it is here that comparative study, with its emphasis upon a disciplined pursuit of aesthetics, can support the historian. At the opposite end of the field from positivism is the aesthetic of creation in a void, or the notion of art as the product of a misty and transcendent inspiration. Influence plays no part. Rather, the artist, god-like, forms his work out of nothing that history or criticism can rationally apprehend. Happily, objection to that theory need not detain us. At mid-field, between the two extremes, is the aesthetic most commonly held in our generation: the theory that the work is a result of true influences, but that at the same time, the work is more than the sum of influences. If the theory is defensible for the literary historian, where does it lead him?

It leads, I suggest, to the necessity for the historian to have two sets

---

[13] Claudio Guillen, "The Aesthetics of Influence Studies in Comparative Literature," *Comparative Literature, Proceedings of the ICLA Congress in Chapel Hill, N.C.,* (ed.) W. P. Friedrich (Chapel Hill, N.C., 1959), 9. Guillen's essay is exemplary except for his heavy emphasis on psychology.

of eyes. With one set he identifies the specific work of the specific writer, a work which may be the product of the writer's psychological mood, his reading, major or minor events in his daily life and the life of his historical period. At the same time, the work, if genuine, will at once encompass and move beyond those biographical and intellectually tangible facts; in his recognition of the work's unprovable nature, the historian is identical with the "pure" critic. But with another set of eyes, the historian will set up parallels, establish intellectual patterns, note the prominence of themes common to a national group or to international groups of writers; he will look at many landscapes, at the other arts, at the politics, the philosophy, possibly even at the sociology of events which he believes to be relevant to his period. In his treatment, the "objective," provable matters will blend with the subjective and unprovable. Unless they do so, he is shirking.

Some examples. It is a provable literary fact that Thomas Mann published *Der Zauberberg* in 1924 and that it appeared in English translation (*The Magic Mountain*) in 1927. Katherine Ann Porter published the novella *Pale Horse, Pale Rider* in 1939. Although the historian may loathe the work of both Mann and Miss Porter, he cannot ignore it, for he knows that both writers have challenged the intelligence and sensibility of the best representatives of our civilization; in this respect, unlike the critic, the historian is slave to a canon. The historian might be able to "prove" that Miss Porter read *The Magic Mountain* and that it was on her desk as she wrote her novella. Such "proof" would not necessarily prove anything. What finally interests the historian, however, is the use of illness in Mann's work, together with the parallel use of illness in Miss Porter's work. Thematics, that is, suggests an insight into the manner in which two good writers in different countries and in different decades approach a common fact: the fact of social and spiritual disintegration before and during World War I. Mundane facts of publication, together with "influences" after the fact, such as sales and critical reception, remain tangential to the unprovable but far more interesting phenomenon of parallel theme. From such material, the historian, with the critic, may well conclude that had Mann not written *The Magic Mountain*, and indeed all his earlier work, it might not have been possible for Miss Porter to write *Pale Horse, Pale Rider* in the form we know it.

Or a more complex example. James Joyce's *Ulysses* appeared in 1922. Hermann Broch's *Die Schlafwandler* appeared in German between 1928 and 1931, but it was not published in the United States as *The Sleepwalkers* until 1947. John Dos Passos' *Manhattan Transfer* was published in 1925, and Thomas Wolfe's *Look Homeward, Angel* in 1929. We know from biography and from a published lecture that Broch was in the provable sense "influenced" by Joyce, and we know from biography and stylistic analysis that both Dos Passos and Wolfe were similarly influenced. Yet these provable influences remain of negligible import, while the unprovable influences are genuine. One might express it as the cosmopolitan need on the part of Broch, Dos Passos, Wolfe, and of course, Joyce himself, who led the way, to experiment in an area of human consciousness that had been closed off to earlier writers; to cope with social and political events that seemed to be out of hand when approached through traditional methods in the novel; to register, like Mann and Miss Porter, compelling convictions about World War I and its effect upon traditional mental attitudes in and apart from society. Any such conclusion does not particularly illuminate the specific work, yet it derives from the work and must be supported by the reader's security that the historian has first reacted to the work as work. The danger of the approach, of course, is that the historian may drift off into intellectual history and merely use literary insight to "prove" in quite another sense his notions about the chronology of ideas. A. O. Lovejoy's *The Great Chain of Being* is an example of a powerful work which suffers the defect of ignoring aesthetics in favor of the use of literature to support a non-literary pursuit.

The comparative historian, then, hopes to avoid literary chauvinism through his assumption that in the course of describing a given literary culture, he is not balancing a ledger of provable influences but using the best that a period has produced within the limits of a common language. Language, in this sense, does not mean *langue* or *Sprache*, but all that is accessible to the minds and sensibilities of literate people in a given period. While the historian interests himself in themes and movements, he does not assume that writers move in schools like herrings. He must take into account true movements, those which are identifiable in works of the literary imagination, those which have an identifiable aesthetic resulting in memorable work. But the American historian needs to be aware that the various groupings, manifestoes, collections, and collectives have yet to make up a true movement, in the sense that French symbolism or German expressionism were movements. That is not to say the writers in a given period may not share a common style. Imagism, briefly, identified a common style, but hardly a movement.

Sociological rather than literary analysis has given us Greenwich Village, the Chicago School, the southern renaissance, the Negro renaissance, and all the rest. Only in American literary history is it possible to have a *renaissance* without there having been a *naissance*. Such a turn of mind indicates the American tendency to treat literary history not as an intellectual problem, but as a social and institutional problem. And that tendency reflects our American disposition to justify both art and scholarship. Despite manifestations to the contrary, we are ill at ease with the notion that art does not *do* anything, is not good for anything. A romantic and visionary people at base, we distrust our own romance and visions, turning, for the public record, to mechanism and positivism and to the comforting thought that all questions have answers. The literary historian can give no answers. Perhaps all that he can do is to give aesthetic proportion to the past, but that is a most important task to accomplish. The world has shown us countries which, having failed to see their books in proper proportion, have burned them.

Bibliographical Notes

The basic bibliography for *The Middle Distance* is the works of the writers treated. The matter that follows is not a full bibliography, nor is it intended to be. For American writing, the *Bibliography and Supplement* of Thomas H. Johnson and Richard M. Ludwig, Volume III of the *Literary History of the United States* by Spiller, Thorp, Johnson, and Canby (New York, 1962) is fortunately available, and it is invaluable. It is hardly necessary to reprint information there assembled. My lists serve two purposes; to acknowledge works which I have found useful but have not cited directly, and to provide the professional student with a selective list of theoretical works which I have found particularly informative, to be argued with, or which otherwise serve the valuable purpose of goading or luring the mind into response. Works cited in footnotes in the book proper are not repeated here.

Books

Ansermoz-Dubois, Félix. *L'Interpretation française de la litterature americaine d'entre-deux-guerres* (*1919–1939*). Lausanne, 1944. Valuable for bibliography.

Arbó, Sebastian Juan. *Pío Baroja y su tiempo*. Barcelona, 1963.

Arnavon, Cyrille. *Histoire littéraire des Etats-unis*. Paris, 1953.

Benn, Gottfried. *Frühe Prosa und Reden*. Wiesbaden, 1950.

Bespaloff, Rachel. *Cheminements et carrefours*. Paris, 1938.

Blackmur, R. P. *Eleven Essays in the European Novel*. New York, 1964.

——. *A Primer of Ignorance* (ed. Joseph Frank). New York, 1967. Blackmur's splendid and virtually unobtainable *Anni Mirabiles, 1921–1925* is included in this collection.

Booth, Wayne C. *Rhetoric of Fiction*. Chicago, 1961.

Brée, Germaine and Guiton, Margaret. *An Age of Fiction*. New Brunswick, New Jersey, 1957.

Burke, Kenneth. *Attitudes Toward History.* 2 vols., New York; 1937.

Cooperman, Stanley. *World War I and the American Novel.* Baltimore, 1967.

Durzak, Manfred. *Hermann Broch: Der Dichter und seine Zeit.* Stuttgart, 1968.

Eoff, Sherman H. *The Modern Spanish Novel.* New York, 1961.

Frank, Joseph. *The Widening Gyre.* New Brunswick, New Jersey, 1966.

Fraser, G. S. *Vision and Rhetoric: Studies in Modern Poetry.* London, 1959.

Friedmann, Hermann, and Mann, Otto (eds.). *Deutsche Literatur im zwanzigsten Jahrhundert.* Heidelberg, 1955.

Frye, Northrop. *Anatomy of Criticism.* New York, 1967.

Gide, André. *Journal, 1889–1939.* Paris, 1948.

Goldmann, Lucien. *Pour une sociologie du roman.* Paris, 1964.

Hamburger, Michael. *From Prophecy to Exorcism.* London, 1966.

Hauser, Arnold. *Sozialgeschichte der Kunst und Literatur.* 2 vols., Munich, 1953.

Heiney, Donald. *America in Modern Italian Literature.* New Brunswick, New Jersey, 1964.

Hoffman, Frederick J. *The Twenties.* New York, 1955.

Hyman, Stanley Edgar. *Standards: A Chronicle of Books for Our Time.* New York, 1966.

Jens, Walter. *Statt einer Literaturgeschichte.* Pfullingen, 1957.

Kahler, Erich. *Die Philosophie von Hermann Broch.* Tübingen, 1962.

Kaiser, Ernst, and Wilkins, Eithne. *Robert Musil.* Stuttgart, 1962.

Kermonde, Frank. *The Sense of an Ending.* New York, 1967.

Lalou, René. *Histoire de la littérature française contemporaine.* 2 vols., Paris, 1947.

Lewis, R. W. B. *Trials of the Word.* New Haven, 1965.

McAlmon, Robert. *Being Geniuses Together.* London, 1938.

Magny, Claude-Edmonde. *L'Age du roman américain.* Paris, 1948.

——. *Histoire du roman français depuis 1918.* Paris, 1950.

Maurois, André. *De Gide à Sartre.* Paris, 1965.

Mohrmann, Hermann. *Kultur-und-Gesellschaftsprobleme des amerikanischen Romans der Nachkriegszeit.* Giessen, 1934.

Naughton, Helen Thomas. *Jacques Rivière: The Development of a Man and a Creed.* The Hague, 1966.

Ortega y Gasset, José. *La Rebelión de las masas.* Madrid, 1968. (first edition 1929).

——. *El Espectador.* Vols. vii–viii, Madrid, 1964 (first edition 1929, vol. vii; 1934, vol. viii).

Peyre, Henri. *Hommes et oeuvres du vingtième siècle.* Paris, 1938.

——. *Writers and Their Critics.* New York, 1944.

Plessner, Helmuth. *Die Einheit der Sinne.* Bonn, 1965 (first edition 1922).

Raymond, Marcel. *From Baudelaire to Surrealism.* Trans. "G.M." New York, 1950.

Ruland, Richard. *The Rediscovery of American Literature: Premises of Critical Taste, 1900–1940.* Cambridge, Mass., 1967.

Wellek, René. *Concepts of Criticism* (ed. Stephen G. Nichols, Jr.). New Haven, 1963.

Sobejano, Gonzalo. *Nietzsche en España*. Madrid, 1967.
Spender, Stephen. *The Destructive Element*. London, 1938.
——. *The Struggle of the Modern*. Berkeley, 1963.
Swinnerton, Frank. *Figures in the Foreground*. London, 1963.

Articles

Anonymous. "Lower Case Lover," *Times Literary Supplement*, no. 3483 (28 Nov. 1968), 1339–1340. Excellent on E. E. Cummings.
Basler, Adolphe. "Le Nouvel esthètisme," *Mercure de France*, vol. 210, no. 737, 322–339.
Beresford, J. D. "Le Declin de l'influence de la psychoanalyse sur le roman anglais," *Mercure de France*, vol. 190 (1926), 257–262.
Bertaux, Félix. "*Les Etats-unis et la guerre*, par Emile Hovelaque," *Nouvelle Revue Française*, XIII (1919), 469.
Bate, W. J. "The English Poet and the Burden of the Past," *Aspects of the Eighteenth Century* (Baltimore, 1965).
Blackmur, R. P. "T. S. Eliot," *Hound and Horn*, I (March, 1928), 187–213.
Booth, Wayne C. "The Rhetoric of Fiction and the Poetics of Fictions," *Novel: A Forum on Fiction*, I, no. 2 (Winter, 1968), 105–117.
Borenstein, Walter. "The Failure of Nerve: the Impact of Pío Baroja's Spain on John Dos Passos," *Nine Essays in Modern Literature*, ed. Donald E. Stanford. Baton Rouge, 1965.
Brooks, Cleanth. "Poetry since *The Waste Land*," *Southern Review*, I, no. 3 (new series, 1965), 487–500.
Cestre, Charles. "American Literature through French Eyes," *Yale Review*, X (October, 1920), 85–98.
Derleth, August. *Three Literary Men: A Memoir of Sinclair Lewis, Sherwood Anderson, and Edgar Lee Masters*. New York, 1963. (A monograph.)
Fergusson, Francis. "T. S. Eliot and his Impersonal Theory of Art," *The American Caravan* (New York, 1927), pp. 446–453.
Fonzi, Bruno. "The American Novel and Italian Fiction," *Confluence*, II, no. 1, 23–30.
Guy-Grand, Georges. "M. Bergson et la civilisation moderne," *Mercure de France*, vol. 236, no. 816 (1932), 513–531.
Kermode, Frank. "Novel, History, Type," *Novel: A Forum on Fiction*, I, no. 3 (Spring, 1968), 231–238.
Lalou, René. "*Gatsby le magnifique*," *NRF*, xxix (1927), 270.
Lenormand, J. P. "American Literature in France," *Saturday Review of Literature*, xi (Oct. 27, 1934), 244–245.
Levin, Harry. "Some European Views of Contemporary American Literature," *American Quarterly*, I (Fall, 1949), 264–279.

Levin, Harry. "France–Amérique: the Transatlantic Refraction," *Comparative Literature Studies*, I, no. 2 (1964), 87–92.

Lynes, Carlos. "André Gide and the Problem of Form in the Novel," *Southern Review*, vii (1941), 161–173.

O'Brien, Justin. "American Books and French Readers," *College English*, I (March, 1940), 480–487.

Praz, Mario. "Hemingway in Italy," *Partisan Review*, xv, no. 10 (Oct. 1948), 1086–1100.

Schinz, Albert. "Ce qu'on lit aux Etats-unis: experience d'un éditeur américain," *Mercure de France*, vol. 218, no. 760 (1929), 50–71.

Simon, Jean. "French Studies in American Literature and Civilization," *American Literature*, vi (May, 1934), 176–190.

Simon, J. "L'Amérique tel que l'ont vue les romanciers français (1919–1937)," *Etudes Anglais*, I (1937), 498–520.

Simons, H. "The Genre of Wallace Stevens," *Sewanee Review*, LIII, no. 4 (Autumn, 1945), 566–579.

Thibaudet, Albert. "Reflexions sur la littérature: Unanimisme," *NRF*, XVII (1921), 85–92.

Trilling, Lionel. "Contemporary American Literature in Its Relation to Ideas," *American Quarterly*, I (Fall, 1949), 195–208.

Warren, Robert Penn. "Faulkner: The South and the Negro," *Southern Review*, I, no. 3 (new series), 501–529.

Williams, William Carlos. "Federico García Lorca," *Kenyon Review*, I, no. 2 (Spring, 1939), 148–158.

Ziolkowski, Theodore. *Hermann Broch*. New York, London, 1964. (A monograph).

Index

Index